Biofictions

The starting point for this collection of essays is the observation that as a literary subject, fictionalized and dramatized "lives" in the form of fictional biographies/biographical fiction, bio-dramas, and bio-pics are very much in evidence on the contemporary scene. And it appears that the lives of the British Romantics and the myths surrounding them have a special appeal for contemporary writers. *Biofictions* sets out to explore this renewed interest in Romantic artist-figures in the context of the current renaissance of "life-writing." The essays collected here deal with Romantic "biofictions" by such authors as Peter Ackroyd, Adrian Mitchell, Ann Jellicoe, Liz Lochhead, Judith Chernaik, Amanda Prantera, Robert Nye, Tom Stoppard, Howard Brenton, Edward Bond, and others. Thomas Chatterton, William Blake, James Hogg, Sir Walter Scott, Percy Bysshe Shelley, Mary Shelley, John Polidori, John Clare, and — most prominently — Lord Byron feature as the "biographical subjects" in the works discussed.

Martin Middeke and Werner Huber teach in the Department of English at the University of Paderborn, Germany.

Studies in English and American Literature,
Linguistics, and Culture

General Editor
James Hardin
(*South Carolina*)

Series Editor
Reingard M. Nischik
(*Constance*)

Biofictions

The Rewriting of Romantic Lives in Contemporary Fiction and Drama

Edited by
Martin Middeke
and Werner Huber

CAMDEN HOUSE

First published 1999
by Camden House

Camden House is an imprint of Boydell & Brewer Inc.
PO Box 41026, Rochester, NY 14604–4126 USA
and of Boydell & Brewer Limited
PO Box 9, Woodbridge, Suffolk IP12 3DF, UK

ISBN: 1–57113–123-X

Library of Congress Cataloging-in-Publication Data

Biofictions: the rewriting of romantic lives in contemporary fiction
and drama / edited by Martin Middeke and Werner Huber.
     p.   cm. – (Studies in English and American literature,
linguistics, and culture)
    Includes bibliographical references (p.   ) and index.
    ISBN 1–57113–123-X (alk. paper)
    1. English literature—20th century—History and criticism.
2. Authors in literature. 3. Byron, George Gordon Byron, Baron,
1788–1824—In literature. 4. Biographical fiction, English—History
and criticism. 5. Historical drama, English—History and criticism.
6. Romanticism—Great Britain. 7. Authorship in literature.
8. Biography in literature. 9. Artists in literature. 10. Poets in
literature. I. Middeke, Martin, 1963– . II. Huber, Werner,
1952– . III. Series.
PR478.A87B56   1999
820.9'3528—dc21   98–52965
                                            CIP

This publication is printed on acid-free paper.
Printed in the United States of America

Contents

Acknowledgements

A COOPERATIVE EFFORT LIKE THE PRESENT VOLUME is fed by various sources of inspiration. The theme of biofictions was first explored in three graduate seminars entitled "The Rewriting of Romantic Lives" and "Biographical Literature" conducted by Professor Rolf Breuer at the University of Paderborn during the academic years of 1991 and 1992. The editors are much obliged to Rolf Breuer for this opportunity and for his long-standing support and his readiness to engage in critical debates. *Biofictions* would not have been possible without various grants from the University of Paderborn; the Center for Cultural Studies (Zentrum für Kulturwissenschaften), the Research Committee as well as the Department of Languages and Literatures (Fachbereich 3) have made substantial contributions towards the making of this book. Special thanks also go to our contributors for their spontaneous responses to, and patience with, editorial requests; to our series editor Reingard M. Nimhih and general editor James Hardin for their critical advice and understanding; and finally to Angelika Schlimmer and Alice Graf for their help with the editorial work.

Martin Middeke
Werner Huber
Paderborn, October 1998

MARTIN MIDDEKE

Introduction

Life-Writing, Historical
Consciousness, and Postmodernism

THE POSTMODERN ZEITGEIST, AS IS WELL KNOWN, approves of uncertainty, ambiguity, and fragmentation; it distrusts the ideas of
totality, synthesis, or binary oppositions. Instead, the collage is pre-
ferred to the unifying whole, the paradox to the logical, subjectivity to
objectivity, relativity to truth, difference to identity, duration to origin,
metonymies to metaphors, the signifier to the signified. These features
give evidence of the linguistic turn which the humanities and, especially, epistemology have taken in the twentieth century, and which has
evolved radical constructivism and the structuralist and poststructuralist
philosophies of Michel Foucault, Roland Barthes, and Jacques Derrida.
Derrida's notorious statement of "il n'y a pas de hors-texte" has become proverbial in the context of a theory in which all knowledge and
experience are considered as language-based, in which any perception
of the world is regarded as being always preceded by language. This
language-centered epistemology has entailed the deconstruction, the
demystification, and, ultimately, the death of any authority, be it god,
the author, or the canon. Such authorities have been replaced by concepts of intertextuality; the unity of signs has been displaced into differences; meaning, truth, and knowledge have been decentered by a
radically subversive language whose potential spin-offs may hover between the dead end of ideological radicalism and the avenue of a politics of difference. The emphasis of difference, then, may give expression
to off-center minorities and to the de-marginalization of those marginalized by the traditional, authorial, canonical forces of power.

Postmodernism sets out to challenge the occidental idea of enlightenment and, especially, the cognitive and epistemological values which
the concepts of a historical past, a cultural heritage, or tradition have

conveyed right into our present. Indeed, "whatever means are used to
make sense in postmodern times, history does not seem to be one of
them."[1] A post-historical impression is reinforced by a socio-cultural
condition which Jürgen Habermas called "die neue Unübersichtlichkeit": a cultural state of affairs which has sprung from the alienating experience of socio-economic pluralization and segmentation. The twentieth century has witnessed the reversal of those eschatological promises
made by the processes of nineteenth-century modernization, a *Frankenstein*-like turning of the monster against its creator. And in the face
of disillusionment, unemployment, amorphous bureaucracies and sophisticated technologies which render global self-destruction possible,
there are not a few who grieve over the loss of utopian belief in the future.[2] In the face of such an historical situation it would seem paradoxical that postmodernism (or any other philosophy) should forego the
orientation inherent in the historical mode of thinking, which relates
the potential of human action and identity to the encompassing correlation of past, present, and future.

According to Jörn Rüsen, three essential questions arise here which
concern the human understanding of reality and also, by extension, of
art: firstly, we may ask whether a historical identity which has become
precarious is able to initiate changes in our historical thought and in
our modes of interpretation. Secondly, we may question the traditions
which define identity and, in reaction to this, demand a new way of
historical thinking aiming at the renewal of the old structures. And
thirdly, we may want to know the extent to which a new mode of historical thought can incite radical innovation.[3]

It goes without saying that what is asserted here about the condition of history also applies to the *writing* of history and the writing of
the history of lives — biography. Thus, the burden of the "nightmare
of history" (Nietzsche), which lies at the heart of both the historiographical and fictional discourses of postmodernism, may easily be
projected onto biography. With reference to life-writing — no matter
whether of the authoritative or the fictional kind — we may suspect a
postmodern emphasis on the indeterminacy of biographical knowledge
and the laying bare of epistemological uncertainties and blanks within
the context of the representation of biographical facts. Especially, we
may gather that the biographer, like the historian, is likely to be mis-
trusted for his declaration of neutrality and the assertion of the objective nature of what he is recounting.[4] Indeed, as Hayden White puts it,

> most contemporary thinkers do not concur in the conventional histo-
> rian's assumption that art and science are essentially different ways of
> comprehending the world. It now seems fairly clear that the nine-

teenth-century belief in the radical dissimilarity of art to science was a consequence of a misunderstanding fostered by the romantic artist's fear of science and the positivistic scientist's ignorance of art.[5]

A new revisionist historical consciousness would therefore have to accentuate that fiction and historiographic/biographical discourse are not mutually exclusive.[6] That is to say, such a consciousness would have to be aware of the fact that fiction and biography/historiography have affinities which are based upon the narrative nature of both genres. Hence, taking into account the epistemological findings of the linguistic turn in philosophy, both the deconstructive and the heuristic potential of fiction would have to be acknowledged. Yet to acknowledge the fact that linguistic representations create reality and may even change it does not mean that, in turn, we have nothing but linguistic representations. And to assert that there are structural parallels between fiction and biography is not necessarily to say that they are the same, that fact and fiction are indistinguishable, or that they are characterized by the same functions.[7] In fact, readers and critics of biofictions will find themselves reminded of the distinction between fact and fiction every time they consult the factual biographies in order to trace fictional deviations from the factual accounts of the lives at issue, deviations which may be considered relevant, that is, symbolic. No matter whether readers or critics are trapped into pursuing red herrings or whether biofictions entangle them in a game with the historical material, the factual world may be suspended, but hardly done away with. For the writer of biofictions this means that a fictional or empathic/sympathetic approach to the subject may make use of the historical material, may play with it, may even invert it, if necessary, and still arrive at a heuristically impressive and plausible interpretation of that life. As a consequence, the artist may incorporate and reflect upon epistemological uncertainties caused by the aporias of time and language, *without* obliterating historical consciousness.[8]

This holds true of all the novels and plays discussed in this volume, fictional rewritings of the lives of British Romantic writers for which we suggest the generic term "biofictions." Their artist-protagonists constitute a poetological and self-reflexive *conditio sine qua non* in that they focus our attention on what it means to be an artist and on the attendant circumstances in the creation of art. Contemporary biofictions may vary individually in the degree to which the novels and plays either comment self-reflexively on the processes of writing, or metabiographically center on the epistemological problem of recounting a life. Biofictions cast doubt on "our beliefs in origins and ends, unity, and totalization, logic and reason, consciousness and human nature, progress and fate, representation and truth, not to mention the notions of causality and temporal homogeneity, linearity, and continuity,"[9] but they do not deny the respective historical foil on which they are written — indeed, how could they without missing their point?

All the novels and most of the plays discussed here in poetological terms belong to what Linda Hutcheon calls historiographic metafiction; they are characterized by their overt historical referents (Blake, Chatterton, the Shelley-Byron circle, etc.). Since the carrier of this reference is language, the reference of the signifier to the signified, the relationship between the subject of contemplation and its object is seen as problematic. Even so, the valid historical foil counteracts a postmodern "anything goes" and thus transcends a purely autoreflexive, hedonistically autonomous or narcissistically solipsistic concept of art which is self-sufficient. However, the hermeneutic emphasis on interpretation, which is the aim inasmuch as it determines the structural principle of postmodernist biofictions, keeps these works of art from being mere chains of factual information. As Andreas Höfele has convincingly argued, the situation is fairly paradoxical: the texts *de*construct and, at the same time, *re*construct historical knowledge, and

> the concept of history as a consistent, teleologically streamlined process has broken down under the onslaught of deconstructionist theory proclaiming an era of 'posthistoire,' and the notion of the self as a clearly defined ontological entity has dissolved under the dissecting lens of psychoanalysis and role-theory, yet we find a conspicuous flourishing of the historico-biographical element in contemporary English literature.[10]

One fairly obvious explanation for both the aesthetic paradox at work here and the prominence of life-writing is the assumption that the classical modernist dilemma between cut-up forms and the perception of a fragmented reality on the one hand and the hunger for the mythically objective and stable on the other is more archetypically essential to human beings than postmodernists and poststructuralists would have us believe.

In order to make this point clearer, the works of postmodernist biofictions discussed here clearly have to be set apart from the aesthetically dubious but sociologically and anthropologically highly interesting phenomenon of countless sequels to the novels of another Romantic writer: Jane Austen. These sequels testify to a prevalent sense of nostalgia and a retrogressive desire — "retro-fashions" as Jean Baudrillard sardonically called the trend[11] — on the part of their readers. Julia Barrett (a.k.a. Julia Braun Kessler and Gabriella Donelly) concludes her sequel to Jane Austen's *Sense and Sensibility* after two-hundred-and-forty pages of fake Austen characters, fake Austen landscape and fake Georgian architecture as follows:

> To sanction ideal attachment — to argue, in effect, for love, and love alone — may be ill-advised in this or any age. Yet when all is said, the inclinations of the heart *will* prevail, whatever the consequences. And, steadfast Reader, what association for Margaret Dashwood could have been as exquisite as that which she presently contemplated?[12]

Here, the juxtaposition of historical past and Barrett's present brings about a vulgar nostalgia for emotion in the face of alienation, a ludicrous, grossly idealized Arcadia lulling readers into a sense of existential belonging in the face of disintegration, striving towards continuity in the face of isolated fragments. Yet even without the embarrassing address to a "steadfast" reader this retrospect idyll is unintentionally ironical.

Leaving the desire for sequels apart, the immense popularity of biography must be attributed to a similar desire to get to know others in what have become anonymous social environments. As Ira B. Nadel indicates, biography as a "verifiable fiction" has become the heir of the nineteenth-century realist novel. Founded upon the Aristotelian pattern of a beginning, middle, and end, as well as on a straightforward development of character, biography provides links to individual stability: it has become "an essential element of modern survival. Through its account of the lives of others, it shows us how to live. The popularity of biography exists in direct proportion to our need to feel that life, in a world of disharmony, dishonor and strife, must have value."[13] With regard to an analysis of biofictions in contemporary English literature a related question may be asked: does not a desire for life, authenticity, originality paradoxically underlie all fictional efforts to deconstruct the same? And can we not speak of a biographical desire essential to all human beings, the manifestation of an ineradicable subjectivity especially in times when philosophy and the experience of the world around us suggest the death of the self? We will therefore have to specify how writers of biofictions react to historical relativism, epistemological uncertainty, and twentieth-century aesthetic experiments and, at the same time, satisfy their own as well as their readers' desire for historical and biographical background. We will also have to ask if this revised historical consciousness reintroduces chances for enlightenment in seemingly posthistorical times.

De-Romanticized? The Relevance
of Romanticism for a
Poetics of Contemporary Biofictions

The prominence of the biographical mode and the artist-protagonist within historiographical metafiction and contemporary drama has not remained unnoticed on the evidence of novels such as D. M. Thomas's *The White Hotel*, Julian Barnes's *Flaubert's Parrot*, Peter Ackroyd's *The Last Testament of Oscar Wilde*, and plays like Christopher Hampton's *Tales From Hollywood*, Peter Shaffer's *Amadeus*, Barry Kyle's *Sylvia Plath: A Dramatic Portrait*, Pam Gems's *Stanley*, and Tom Stoppard's *Travesties* or, most recently *The Invention of Love*, to name but a few representatives of the genre not dealt with in this volume.[14] The fact, however, that in many contemporary biofictions the historical referents are writers of the Romantic period has largely been neglected. This is astonishing insofar as both the common ground and the differences between the Romantics and the contemporary novelist or playwright are obvious and, indeed, form an interesting link to the understanding of contemporary poetics.

Turning back to the Romantics as the historical foil of contemporary biofictions is a far from arbitrary gesture. The reason why Romantic lives like those of Shelley and Byron have not lost their mythical fascination is, of course, that they were simply interesting, unpredictable, and often notorious lives. Moreover, the Romantics were probably the first artist-figures in the modern understanding of the word. Similar to what Hegel conceived of in *The Phenomenology of Spirit* [*Die Phänomenologie des Geistes*] as the "inner revolution," the Romantic artists fashioned themselves after the ideal of a non-conformist, independent consciousness that strives to arrive at absolute freedom and, thereby, became icons of the artist. David Morse points out that, when one thinks of Blake or Shelley, the Romantic artist becomes the visionary, yet also the outsider, as the vision and the real world hardly ever match:

> In his attempts to communicate his vision to the world the artist faces the problem that the vision, because hypothetical, lacks credibility; the artist has no credentials that can validate his claims to prophetic status; in the act of communication itself the vision becomes warped, fragmented and distorted, while there is equally the danger that the artist was mistaken and that his vision was nothing more than a delusion, and a dangerous one at that. The artist veers between megalomania in his intoxication with his own ideas and impotence and despair at his inability to maintain his own sense of the visionary and to bring it into

some kind of meaningful relationship with the everyday world. The Romantic protagonist, whether anachronistic hero, artist or hypocrite, becomes a law unto himself. Estranged from the world and at variance with it, he has no choice but to assume that he is right and that the world is wrong. He increasingly figures as a Superman — a man who moves beyond ordinary criteria of good and evil and enters the world of moral relativity in which he knows no law but that of his own will.[15]

The variety in the representations of Romantic artists' lives in contemporary biofictions testifies to the fact that there is no one definition of Romanticism. Such aspects as the power of the artistic imagination, the return to nature, the emphasis on wonder, strangeness, and beauty, as well as the Faustian yearning for the infinite still may best be summarized by the keyword "subjectivity." Romantic subjectivity relates to the various manifestations of individuality and especially to the historicization of human existence. Romantic thought envisaged a potentially changing universe as a continuum of past, present, and future, and Romanticism set this view of an organically changing world against the traditionally rigid concepts of neoclassicism. That is why the Romantic era constitutes the starting point of a mode of historical thought that is based upon dynamic instead of static categories, and in which relativistic conceptions of truth replaced absolute and timeless ones. The idea of reforming society and setting human beings free from the fetters of external influences or the belief in things as they are [Die Dinge an sich] was prevalent in philosophical discourse ranging from Kant's *Critique of Pure Reason* [*Kritik der reinen Vernunft*], Fichte's *Foundations of Transcendental Philosophy* [*Wissenschaftslehre*], Schiller's *On the Aesthetic Education of Man* [*Über die Ästhetische Erziehung des Menschen*], and Schelling's *Of the Ego as Principle of Philosophy* [*Vom Ich als Prinzip der Philosophie*] to Hazlitt's *The Spirit of the Age*, Hegel, and John Stuart Mill's *On Liberty*.[16] The Romantics therefore began a process which late twentieth-century postindustrialism can hardly claim to have brought to a close. Moreover, the epistemological problems of how to connect, interrelate, and unify subjective points of view with objective reality and thereby arrive at an autonomous existence were central issues of the idealism of Kant, Schelling, and Fichte, and were also a dominant subject matter of Romantic poetry and Romantic theories of art. To give but one example, Samuel Taylor Coleridge, who was influenced by (and at times thoroughly mistaken about) German idealism, thought that the subject can only know and understand the object of contemplation when subject and object merge, dissolve, become one. This, however, would presuppose that the subject can self-reflexively become one with itself and, besides, suspend and escape temporality. In his *Biographia Literaria*, Coleridge put the epistemological problem in a nutshell when he commented on the infinite regress at work here:

> We can never pass beyond the principle of self-consciousness. Should we attempt it, we must be driven back from ground to ground, each of which would cease to be a ground the moment we pressed on it. We must be whirled down the gulf of an infinite series.[17]

The position of the artist as an outsider and the epistemological difficulties involved in linguistic representation and, accordingly, in self-knowledge are obviously reflected in Romantic heroes such as Wordsworth's Marmaduke, Byron's Manfred and Don Juan, and, of course, Coleridge's ancient mariner. They are all marginalized outsiders, lonely wanderers on a quest for a vision, who at the same time know that this vision is out of reach and indeed lost forever. Thus, Morse is right when he emphasizes that "the Byronic hero is not cause but consequence: he is always encountered *after* — a perennial fifth-act Hamlet or Macbeth."[18] With reference to twentieth-century poetics Coleridge's epistemological and poetological insight into the infinite regress inherent to understanding foreshadows the extremes of Beckett's minimalism, and it shows that the Romantics might well be considered protodeconstructionists — albeit to a varying degree which would have to be analyzed.[19] However, Coleridge insisted on establishing art and the imagination as the *causa sui* in the processes of understanding in order to sidestep the infinite regress: compared with postmodernist biofictions, Romanticism, then, is radically different, since it sets out to bridge the gap between subject and object. Yet the emphasis on fiction as imaginative truth, the re-establishment of historical consciousness, and the symbolic relevance of the past for the present within postmodern biofictions can certainly not deny traces of Romanticism.[20] To give another example illustrating this: in the "Second Manifesto of Surrealism" André Breton points out that Romanticism constitutes an important part of the cultural heritage of contemporary art. Like those of the Romantics, the visions of the surrealists cannot at once be those of every man, or, in other words, a temporary outsider position of the artist paves the way before intellectual stances can broadly be taken for granted. Furthermore, like the Romantics, the surrealists denounce a "ridiculous illusion of happiness and understanding." However, in contradistinction to the Romantics' turning to the imagination as the *causa sui*, as an instrument of unifying subject and object, the surrealists — like the postmodernists — "appear in the midst of, and perhaps at the cost of, an uninterrupted succession of lapses and failures, of zigzags and defections which require a constant re-evaluation of its original premises [. . .]." Thus, for Breton, Romanticism represents the ultimate beginning of contemporary art, yet only in the sense of the "first cry of a newborn child."[21]

As regards another side of the Romantic view of the artist: Wordsworth defines "good" poetry as "the spontaneous overflow of powerful feelings"; poetry, he argues, "takes its origin from emotion recollected in tranquillity [. . .]."[22] Percy Bysshe Shelley sets poetry apart from reasoning: "A man cannot say, 'I will compose poetry.' The greatest poet even cannot say it: for the mind in creation is as a fading coal which some invisible influence, like an inconstant wind, awakens to transitory brightness [. . .]."[23] In much the same vein and drawing largely on Coleridge, John Keats characterizes the poetic imagination as a matter of instinct rather than of quantitative, intellectual reasoning. "O for a Life of Sensations rather than of Thoughts," he pleads. Whereas reasoning offers an outward view, the imagination sympathetically looks inward, focussing on hidden intentions and realities of life. Hence the poet who, according to Keats, identifies momentarily with the object of his contemplation may neither pursue an "irritable reaching after fact and reason" nor ever have preresolved upon his object. Uniquely merging with that object of contemplation, the "camelion [sic] Poet" is different from "the virtuous philosopher," the poet "has no identity he is certainly the most impractical of all God's creatures."[24] In their entirety these statements reflect the Romantic view of the artist-genius:

> A cardinal axiom of Romanticism was that of the uniqueness, singleness and particularity of everything in the universe, and such an assumption has pervaded modern literary criticism with consequences so catastrophic that they verge on deliberate mystification and anti-intellectualism. In this view every artist is an entirely original and unique genius who creates a wholly idiosyncratic perceptual field that we name Blake, or Wordsworth, or Lawrence, or James, and which we interpret as the construction of a personal identity.[25]

The Romantic belief in the originality of the artist-genius and the nature of art as divine creativity has been contradicted by the postmodernist insistence on narrative structure, writing, the conventionality of signification, and on the status of texts as intertexts. History and society are seen as being constantly read and interpreted, as Julia Kristeva emphasizes:

> Nous appellerons INTERTEXTUALITÉ cette inter-action textuelle qui se produit à l'intérieur d'un seul texte. Pour le sujet connaissant,

l'intertextualité est une notion qui sera l'indice de la façon dont un texte lit l'histoire et s'insère en elle.[26]

This implies that the text contains a productivity beyond that of its creator: of course, the more such productivity is ascribed to the text itself, to reading, and to intertextual play,[27] the more the linguistic concept of the sign loses its transcendental signified in the process of signification, the more the idea of the Romantic genius begins to vanish. Hence the crucial problem that emerges from the juxtaposition of Romantic and postmodernist concepts of the artist within biofictions is how to encounter infinite regress, the never-healing wound of the subject-object difference within the process of human understanding. As mentioned above, the Romantics took refuge in the realm of poesy and made imagination — at least temporarily — overcome that gap.[28]

> Romanticism is the attempt to heal the break in the universe, it is the painful awareness of dualism coupled with the urge to resolve it in organic monism, it is the confrontation with chaos followed by the will to reintegrate it into the order of the cosmos, it is the desire to reconcile a pair of opposites, to have synthesis follow antithesis.[29]

Not only do poststructuralism and deconstruction seek to devalue such Romantic logocentrism, they also relish the very differences the Romantics suffered from. Thus, insofar as the re-writings of Romantic artists' lives within postmodernist biofictions are highly self-conscious and intertextual writings, they imply an ironic deconstructive distancing between the past and the present. The artists are no longer unreachable heroes; rather they are debunked, ironicized, or dethroned to textual trickster figures, anti-heroes, or, more realistically, to human beings who have common desires — for instance, Mozart in Shaffer's *Amadeus* — and, as Howard Brenton's Mary Shelley puts it, "lungs of mucus and blood."[30] But as I have stated above, as long as a revisionist historical consciousness, that is, ultimately, reality-reference, re-enters works of art that Werner Wolf accordingly describes as "moderate experiments,"[31] there is no reason to declare the Romantic cause as lost.

"If Winter comes, can Spring be far behind?"[32] — Shelley's reservedly utopian vision in the "Ode to the West Wind" is a political statement that draws on the necessity of political change in the context of the French Revolution and England's conservatism. It also hints at the socio-political relevance of Romanticism for our "posthistorical" times. As M. H. Abrams has said, "we continue to live in an era of conflict, revolution, inordinate expectation, recreancy, and counterrevolutions that was inaugurated by the Romantic age of revolutions."[33] Blake's and, particularly, Godwin's and Shelley's vision of creating a New Jerusalem characterized by a free personality in a free society is very much likely to have had a political impact on the contemporary political British playwrights and their attempts to set up theater (e.g. the London fringe movement) as a counter-culture to middle-class establishment. Indeed, the political and social criticism inherent in Blake, the young Wordsworth, Burns, and Shelley in particular render these four also proto-socialists, paradigmatic angry young men — a characteristic feature that accentuates the parallels to contemporary political playwrights and their refusals to conform to the pressures urged on them by mass culture and commercialism.[34] As expressed in Shelley's *Alastor*, the self-referential introversion of the artist should not exclude caring for the human race,[35] art should not outrun reality, and, in poetological terms, proto-deconstructionist art should not surpass the proto-socialist utopian vision.

This tension is further evidenced by the observation that a representative number of the works discussed in this volume center on one literary figure who has traditionally lived in the shadow of the canonized "great" six: Mary Shelley. Contemporary women writers have paid much attention to her life and her novel *Frankenstein*, both have also been widely discussed within feminist literary criticism. In the context of an opposition between a radically aesthetic, deconstructive approach on the one hand and a radically political or realist approach on the other, Mary Shelley and feminist criticism would somehow have to take up a middle position. Feminist theory has paid attention to the results of a deconstructive analysis which lays bare the conventionality of power structures which have enabled a few and disabled many. At the same time, feminist criticism would be expected to be politically relevant; a theory which has justifiedly not tired in pointing to the fact that women have been denied historical agency cannot afford to surrender a utopian perspective to purely deconstructive pluralization, let alone give in to an impression of posthistorical resignation and nothingness. The discussion of Mary Shelley and *Frankenstein* within contemporary biofictions and feminist criticism focuses on such aspects as female sexuality, the opposition between public man and private woman, guilt, alienation, orphanhood, intellectual activity. Mary Shelley's life and intellectual background including the influences of her parents William Godwin and Mary Wollstonecraft, her husband Percy Bysshe Shelley, and Byron, as well as the mythical genesis of *Frankenstein* imply the problems of motherhood and child-bearing; they underline the relationship between birth and death, and the crucial tension between a dangerous solipsism and the humanistic responsibilities of science; and, most of all, Mary Shelley and *Frankenstein* embody the fact that the

Romantic universe, or, to be more precise, Percy Bysshe Shelley's and Victor Frankenstein's universe, was a highly gendered construction, too. As Anne K. Mellor has aptly remarked, by controlling the biological functions of human reproduction, "Frankenstein has eliminated the necessity to have females at all." Mellor points out that Mary Shelley's ideal was to look upon nature as a "sacred life-force in which human beings ought to participate in conscious harmony." Obviously, Frankenstein's patriarchal cult of the individual, his egotism and selfishness are rejected in favor of an ideal, a life led in harmony between men and women. This also touches upon questions of aesthetics, as Mary Shelley "purposefully identifies moral virtue, based on self-sacrifice, moderation, and domestic affection, with aesthetic beauty."[36] Clearly enough, *Frankenstein* is an overt rejection of the radically subjective and, consequently, egocentric aspects of Romanticism. And likewise, the monster's narrative account of his existence reinforces the necessity of individual rationality and agency.

> Delivered at the top of Mont Blanc — like the North Pole one of the Shelley family's metaphors for the indifferently powerful source of creation and destruction — it is the story of deformed Geraldine in "Christabel," the story of the dead-alive crew in "The Ancient Mariner," the story of Eve in *Paradise Lost,* and of her degraded double sin — all secondary or female characters to whom male authors have imperiously denied any chance of self-explanation. At the same time the monster's narrative is a philosophical meditation on what it means to be born without a 'soul' or a history, as well as an exploration of what it feels like to be a 'filthy mass that move[s] and talk[s],' a thing, an other, a creature of the second sex.[37]

In much the same way as doubts are cast on radical individualism and solipsism, the Romantic male concept of free love is questioned here. Mellor is right in asking whose interests free love serves at all, and she does not hesitate to say that although Percy Bysshe Shelley is widely looked upon as a feminist, neither he nor any other Romantic poet "ever imagined a utopia where women existed as independent, autonomous, different, but equally powerful and respected authors and legislators of the world."[38] Howard Brenton puts it bluntly when he has his Byron accuse Shelley of hypocrisy:

> Y'bloody hypocrite! Where is your legal wife? In England! The two women you are with, Mary y'call your wife, Claire y'friend — concubines, sir! Y'mistresses, sir! All your idealism, revolution in society, revolution in your personal life, all trumpery! The practice of it, sir, the practice doth make us dirty, doth make all naked and bleeding and

real! [. . .] Y'damn theorising! All you want to do is get your end away.[39]

In order to counteract male Romantic ideology Mellor suggests the term "feminine Romanticism" for discussions of women writers of the period. This feminine Romanticism is characterized by a moderate subjectivity that acknowledges its individual rights, but also subscribes to an "ethics of care." It does not delegate social reform and the utopian change of society to the actions and visions of a small number of megalomaniac men, but rather to "communal exercise of reason, moderation, tolerance and the domestic affections that can embrace even the alien Other."[40]

The Essays

Continuing with the experimental line of contemporary novel-writing, many of the novels discussed here draw on the proto-deconstructionist potential of Romanticism. The works treated in the essays by Ansgar Nünning, Martin Middeke, Annegret Maack, Jill Rubenstein, and Beate Neumeier self-consciously attend to the inescapable gap between a past life and its narrative recounting and elaborate on the poetological implications of this difference.

Ansgar Nünning describes the reader of Peter Ackroyd's *Chatterton* as engaged in an "intertextual quest for Thomas Chatterton." As Nünning's analysis proves, Ackroyd's novel is a remarkable example of the metabiographical tendencies within biofictions. The novel is characterized by parody, the blurring of genres, different levels of narrative, perspective, and time, as well as a high degree of intertextuality. This intertextuality functions as the narrative link between past and present, aiming at the deconstruction of the Romantic tenets of originality and creative genius. Chatterton himself, the master-forger, epitomizes the dissolution of fact and fiction, copy and original. The novel's metabiographical stance emerges as an intertextual game that underscores the view that biographical facts always hinge on individual, subjective selection and that experience and knowledge are likewise pre-constructed by narrative and literary means.

Martin Middeke demonstrates how Amanda Prantera's *Conversations with Lord Byron* ironically centers around a double of Lord Byron that is created by computer artificial intelligence technology and is expected to shed light on hitherto obscure incidents of Byron's biography. However, as the computer is programmed with text, its output can refer to nothing but text and, accordingly, to further echoes in the echo-chamber of intertextuality. Moreover, Middeke argues, the computer image self-reflexively yet ironically comments upon the analogous element inherent in language and art that resists digital and self-evident one-to-one assignments of meaning. Biographical truth within writing is thus presented as being dependent upon reader inference, Byron as the historical foil of Prantera's novel is deconstructed in Derridean terms as a trace, as a paradoxical presence/absence whose re-writing becomes the subject of play and of metabiographical parody. The prevailing poetological principle of the novel is *différance*, which operates on all textual layers ranging from the narrative structure to the single letter.

In her comparative essay on Paul West's *Lord Byron's Doctor* and Robert Nye's *The Memoirs of Lord Byron*, Annegret Maack carefully traces historical and documentary evidence which underlies both texts. Both novels emphasize the enigmatic, paradoxical, and contradictory characters of Lord Byron and Dr. Polidori, West by quoting extensively from letters, poetry, and other literary works, Nye by using "literary ventriloquy" and pastiche to re-write Byron's lost *Memoirs*. Both texts, however, accentuate that the search for the ultimate truth remains an illusion. Nye's Byron and West's Polidori are nothing but verbal constructs, fictional ghosts, as it were, that render both the vampire, the ghost, and intertextuality feasible metabiographical images.

Literary ventriloquism is further explored by Jill Rubenstein, who looks at what might be called "autobiofictions" of the lives of Sir Walter Scott and James Hogg. Here it is the choice of material that suggests perhaps more than elsewhere in this volume a double autobiographical perspective of chronological recollection combined with present reflection. Allan Massie's *The Ragged Lion* (1994) is a biofiction based upon Scott's autobiographical writings as well as Lockhart's *Life*, with an editor recovering a long-lost memoir in a manner reminiscent of Henry James and "The Aspern Papers." Kenneth R. Johnston's *The Love Adventures* (1991) is the dramatization of a story by James Hogg, one which Hogg claimed was autobiographical. The story's interest is clearly in ethnobiography, describing the customs and manners of the Borders, while the biographical dimension is restricted to the performance aspect. In Frederic Mohr's solo play *Hogg: The Shepherd Justified* (1985), the dimension of performance reinforces the double structure of retrospection and reflection, as Hogg addresses an unidentified visitor in 1833, offering his views on politics, Scott, Burns, and on his own past life. The autobiographical performance highlights the problematics of self-invention and myth-making that lie at the heart of biofictions.

The juxtaposition of truth and fiction is also the constitutive structural element of Judith Chernaik's *Mab's Daughters*. Beate Neumeier points to the fact that the novel, apart from its deconstructive intentions, incorporates both a realistic concern about subverting public images and a biographical investigation of gender relations within the Shelley circle. There is a notable political implication in the fact that Chernaik focuses exclusively on the perspective of four women. On the one hand, Neumeier argues, claims of authenticity are satisfied by the conventions of the journal entries and letters which the novel is composed of; on the other hand, journal and letter writing implies a high degree of subjectivity and unreliability. Furthermore, the multiperspectivity of the letters and journals of four different women keeps alive the tension between attainable truth and the conviction that the truth, after all, is beyond reach. Less radical in its deconstructive potential than Ackroyd's and Prantera's texts, Chernaik's novel is concerned with the interaction between private concerns and public obligations.

Christine Kenyon Jones begins her essay by identifying the proto-science fiction themes in Romantic writing and in the biographies of the leading figures in the Byron-Shelley circle: time-travel, catastrophism, myths of creation. She explores this link, the affinities between Romantic lives and science fiction, at a point where the two meet again late in the twentieth century. Departing from a possible common source, Brian Aldiss and his pioneering use of the Romantics in *Frankenstein Unbound*, Kenyon Jones distinguishes two important subgenres in which biofiction and science fiction converge. On the one hand, there are cyberculture novels like William Gibson and Bruce Stirling's *The Difference Engine*; on the other hand we find biofictional fantasies such as Tim Powers's *The Anubis Gates* and *The Stress of Her Regard*. Both are concerned with the organization and disorganization of self. The former are clearly out to deconstruct human individuality in an environment of technological fantasies, while the latter put Romantic biographies to the postmodern acid test of *bricolage* and imaginative reconstruction.

As Frances Wilson points out, the same doubts about factual information arise from the notorious ghost story contest at the Villa Diodati found at the heart of Derek Marlowe's *A Single Summer with L. B.* Wilson asserts that the major flaw of Marlowe's novel, which itself is but another literary result of the contest in the line of *Frankenstein*, Byron's fragment of a vampire story, and Polidori's *The Vampyre*, is that it sets out to present the elusive contest "as it really was." The more Marlowe insists on the factual truth of his novel the more such truth dissolves into the fictions of individual versions. Wilson sees these versions of different beginnings and origins of ghost stories as creating a *mise-en-abyme*, a Chinese-box structure motivated by a "playful desire of imitation," in which all the characters and Marlowe himself are involved. Since these imitative versions are necessarily altered in the process of being passed on over the centuries, Wilson concludes, they resemble ghost stories, which are changed as they are repeated and recited.

The metadramatic character of Tom Stoppard's *Arcadia* forms an interesting link between the experimental novel and contemporary drama. As Peter Paul Schnierer points out, Stoppard's Byron characteristically remains absent throughout the play. This physical absence on stage is the striking outer reflection of the characters' inability to complete and verify the fragments of Byron's life. Schnierer interprets the inevitable failure of the biographical project undertaken by the characters in *Arcadia* as a sign of the twentieth-century reaction against the pastoral mode. The pastoral mode, Schnierer argues, is fundamentally characterized by "evasion." Thus, the wish for wholeness in biography brought about by absence and evasion of the biographee is unmasked as belonging to pastoral thinking. It highlights Stoppard's belief in the twentieth-century non-existence of Arcadia, be it of the Romantic, biographical, or hermeneutic kind — however strong such a desire for Arcadia within life-writing and literary criticism may otherwise be.

The idea of absence as the highest form of presence is also isolated by Christopher Innes, who looks at two radically different engagements with the life of John Clare, the long-neglected "peasant poet" and Romantic epigone. Innes compares Edward Bond's play *The Fool* (1975) with John MacKenna's novel *Clare* (1993). Bond presents Clare as an icon for the politically committed artist who refuses to compromise in view of fundamental changes in British rural society such as the enclosure system, while, to MacKenna, Clare becomes the absolute poet, for whom everyday reality is nothing but a curb on his imagination. In both texts Clare is the missing poet — in the sense that in the play he remains aloof from the main action on stage, while in the novel he is only indirectly present, as a focal point for the narrative framework. Nevertheless, in both cases Clare functions as a mask for the writers' respective views on art, and Innes explains the discrepancies between the two reworkings of Clare's life as differences of generation and genre.

As the case of Bond and Clare suggests, the lives of Romantic poets (especially those with a reputation for radicalism and eccentricity) begin to assume a special paradigmatic function for the playwrights of the second generation of the New British Drama. One extreme variation of this phenomenon is Adrian Mitchell's *Tyger* (1971), subtitled *A Cele-*

bration Based on the Life and Work of William Blake. As Bernhard Reitz shows, the play, with its looseness of style and organization and disunity of action is more an expression of post-1968 theater aesthetics than a serious engagement with Blake, the archetypal revolutionary, and his ideas. The play's central interest is in its polemical energy directed against cultural politics and the culture industry. *Tyger* is more an appropriation of Blake's life for contemporary causes and pet hates of the anti-Establishment scene than a coherent re-working of his life story.

Percy Bysshe Shelley as a figurehead for a whole culture of dissent that stretches from the 1960s well into the Thatcher era is the subject of two plays that are concerned with Shelley's personality, his role of the poet as misfit, his radical idealism and political utopianism. Uwe Böker analyzes Ann Jellicoe's *Shelley, or The Idealist* and Howard Brenton's *Bloody Poetry*, paying special attention to intertextual relationships (allusions, quotations, borrowings) between the two bioplays and Shelley's original texts.

Liz Lochhead's *Blood and Ice* is the subject of Silvia Mergenthal's essay. Mergenthal demonstrates how in the play two periods in Mary Shelley's life — 1824 (after Byron's death) and 1816 (the ghost story competition and the origins of *Frankenstein*) — merge with a fictional third one, that is, *Frankenstein* as an autobiographical text, an image of sexuality and procreation. Contextualizing the play, Mergenthal points to Lochhead's preoccupation with cultural myths, Scottish identity and its affinities with representations of the divided self, the productive reception of *Frankenstein* dramatizations, and various contemporary critical approaches. The myth of female creativity emerges as the common theme reflected in these varied perspectives.

The important role Mary Shelley and *Frankenstein* play within the context of pop culture representations of the Romantics is also revealed in various film narratives, as Ramona Ralston and Sid Sondergard establish. Tracing the major inspiration of various filmmakers back to Mary Shelley's 1831 introduction to her novel, Ralston and Sondergard point out that directors and critics have attempted to represent Mary Shelley's life and her work as interrelated. Likewise, they have aimed at an aesthetic in which the construction of the character of Mary Shelley is embedded in a gender conflict between female authorship and the male hegemony over art and writing. The many examples cited by Ralston and Sondergard range from James Whale's *The Bride of Frankenstein* (1935) to Kenneth Branagh's *Mary Shelley's Frankenstein* (1994), and the diverse film representations portray Mary Shelley as either a passive reflector, a female overreacher, a threat to the Romantic family, or as an independent, thoroughly modern woman.

A Conclusion Against
"Necrophilic" Writing: Past and
Present in Contemporary Biofictions

In conclusion, we may now try to answer the questions raised at the beginning. As regards the new historical consciousness: no matter whether the impact of Romantic theory and Romantic artists' lives on contemporary novelists and playwrights is grounded in the proto-deconstructionist, proto-socialist, or proto-feminist aspects of Romanticism, the poetics of contemporary biofictions are not lined with a traditionally historiographical desire to explain the past. They are characterized by a revisionist historiographical consciousness that acknowledges parallels and points of reference and plays with the inevitable differences between the early nineteenth and the late twentieth century. Contemporary biofictions are therefore not characterized by a retrogressive but by a decisively progressive movement to explain and interpret the present. Romanticism, the historical foil of contemporary biofictions, constitutes an epistemologically and even hermeneutically valid point of departure. As time passes, however, the Romantic past can hardly be viewed as an alternative to present action. Reflecting the stance taken by Hayden White, these works of art see no reason "why we ought to study things under the aspect of their past-ness rather than under the aspect of their present-ness."[41] As White points out, echoing Nietzsche, the interest in the past must not be an end in itself. This means that the author of contemporary biofictions must be neither antiquarian enjoying the nostalgic escapism into a personal, idealized past, nor "a kind of cultural necrophile, that is, one who finds in the dead and dying a value he can never find in the living." Indeed, similar to the contemporary historian, the writer of contemporary biofictions seeks to provide "perspectives on the present that contribute to the problems peculiar to our own time."[42]

Works of contemporary biofiction are highly intertextual and "interauthorial"[43] writings; they refer back to texts and discourses of earlier periods and, at the same time, comment on the present reception of these works by making past authors and present authors and readers interact in the process of interpretation.[44] The fact that this is a highly self-conscious process shows that contemporary biofictions are concerned with the hermeneutical problem of juxtaposing, correlating, and, after all, understanding our own experience in relation to the received experience of the past. Critics have pointed to the aesthetic means that have evolved from this metafictional intention: a departure from coherence, the insight that all knowledge of the "other" is necessarily characterized by difference and affected by perspective and that former teleological, linear forms of representation stressing the hermeneutic determinacy of historical truth have been replaced by autoreflexive, allusive, collage-like, achronological discontinuities. Prevailing stylistic features include palimpsest, the paradox involved in repetition, travesty, parody, and pastiche. These challenge Romantic concepts of originality, framing the metaphorical contexts of the past with contemporary issues, questions, and interests, and thus necessarily highlighting the difference between past and present, subject and object. However, although a well-conceived pastiche may challenge the idea of originality and genius by accentuating the contextual factors in the production of a work of art, it cannot really throw all originality overboard. After all, it is highly original to write a good pastiche; and no matter how elaborate our means of technological reproduction and simulation may become in the future, it can nevertheless be said that Peter Ackroyd's pastiche of Oscar Wilde's writing, for instance, or Andy Warhol's prints of Marilyn Monroe are, after all, more skillfully done than most others — unless this (or any such) critical judgment has altogether become superfluous.

Contemporary biofictions deconstruct Romantic originality, a last trace of which, however, can hardly be set aside. These works question the past, but they do not reject it entirely. There is no question that the past existed; the question is how to gain knowledge of the past and make it valuable for the present.[45] Yet again, the historical referent involves the questioning and the laying bare of the epistemological problems inherent in human understanding and knowledge of the past; on the other hand, it entails the appeal not to surrender the search for such knowledge to the idea of an encompassing relativity and arbitrariness. Indeed, contemporary biofictions go beyond individual imagination as they imaginatively recount past experience. This transcending of experience illuminates inevitable differences, but it also emphasizes the desire for a capacity of understanding that supersedes minds limited to the actuality of an immediate present. Besides, the historical referents of the re-writings of the Romantic lives at issue are not arbitrarily replaceable: a fictional statement on the life and character of Byron remains an interpretation of the historical Byron — and the fact that this referential relationship is maintained indicates that a fictional statement on a historical life can be a convincing or, in other words, a poetically true one in the first place. Thus, the fact that contemporary biofictions ultimately consider poetic truth more valuable than factual accounts is an echo of the Romantic view of the imagination. "What the Imagination seizes as Beauty must be truth," says Keats, " — whether it existed before or not."[46] In the poetological discourses of both Romanticism and contemporary biofictions stress is laid on the commensurability of history and fiction, which takes care of the possibility that a fictional statement on a particular life may invariably look as committed to real life as an historical account. In other words, as long as we do not surrender the claim to poetic truth, it must remain a criterion in the critical analysis of contemporary biofictions. Setting past against present experience, contemporary biofictions Romantically re-authorize enlightenment in the face of posthistorical emptiness. Biofictions retain the Romantic tension between a deconstructive mind and a longing for story and history as they keep the hermeneutic process of interpreting and understanding present and past, subject and object, moving — often tongue in cheek, though, since they do *know* better.

Notes

[1] Rüdiger Kunow, "Making Sense of History: The Sense of the Past in Posthistoric Times," in *Making Sense: The Role of the Reader in Contemporary Fiction*, ed. Gerhard Hoffmann (Munich: Fink, 1989), 169.

[2] Jürgen Habermas, *Die Neue Unübersichtlichkeit* (Frankfurt am Main: Suhrkamp, 1985); see also Jörn Rüsen, *Zeit und Sinn: Strategien historischen Denkens* (Frankfurt am Main: Fischer, 1990); Christian Meier, "Vom 'fin de siècle' zum 'end of history'? Zur Lage der Geschichte," *Merkur* 44 (1990): 809–23.

[3] Jörn Rüsen, "Die Kraft der Erinnerung im Wandel der Kultur: Zur Innovations- und Erneuerungsfunktion der Geschichtsschreibung," in *Der Diskurs der Literatur- und Spachhistorie: Wissenschaftsgeschichte als Innovationsvorgabe*, ed. Bernard Cerquiglini and Hans Ulrich Gumbrecht (Frankfurt am Main: Suhrkamp, 1983), 29–46.

[4] Linda Hutcheon, *A Poetics of Postmodernism: History, Theory, Fiction* (London and New York: Routledge, 1988), 88.

[5] Hayden White, *Tropics of Discourse: Essays in Cultural Criticism* (Baltimore, MD: Johns Hopkins UP, 1992), 28.

[6] There can be no doubt that good biography must be more than a compilation of facts: Phyllis Rose is unequivocal about the fact that "biography — and I mean by that the highest reaches of biographic art, self-conscious, artful biography, composed and not compiled biography — aspires to the condition of the novel" ("Biography as Fiction," *Tri-Quarterly* 55 [1982]: 111);

Dennis W. Petrie comments upon the degree to which design plays a role within life-writing: "Although criticism should concern itself less with the historical authenticity of a biographer's facts *per se* and more with the manner in which the biographer has presented them, the two factors are — and should be — irrevocably entwined. And a biographer's purpose will surely affect the structure and style of his work. For example, hagiographers violate facts to achieve their adulatory aims: and directly because of this, their art becomes pattern-moulded and cliché-ridden. On the other extreme, Lytton Strachey manipulates literal truth to construct brilliantly formalized, compact portraits of subjects whom he loathes. Thus, the circumference of truth in biography is always design — design in function, form, and fashion. Ideally, the biographer can wrestle with the problems that these three elements encompass and manage to strike a fair and pleasing equilibrium." (*Ultimately Fiction: Design in Modern American Literary Biography* [West Lafayette, IN: Purdue UP, 1981], 16–17). See also Helmut Scheuer, "Kunst und Wissenschaft in der modernen literarischen Biographie," in *Literatur und Sprache im historischen Prozeß: Vorträge des Deutschen Germanistentages*, ed. Thomas Cramer (Tübingen: Niemeyer, 1983), Vol. 3, 287–300, and Malcolm Bradbury, "The Telling Life: Thoughts on Literary Biography," in *The Troubled Face of Biography*, ed. Eric Homberger and John Charmley (New York: St. Martin's Press, 1988), 131–40. A slightly ironical remark was made by Katherine Frank: "[. . .] in contemporary literary biography it seems that it requires two books by two authors to approach biographical completeness, and that we must reconcile ourselves to the fact that the narrative and analytic biographical impulses are very different impulses. There will continue to be biographers who want to tell us a life story, and others who will want to tell us what the story means, but few of them will attempt to do both" ("Writing Lives: Theory and Practice in Literary Biography," *Genre* 8 [1980]): 513).

[7] Ina Schabert is right in pointing to the "unavoidable relativity of factual biography." And Schabert has made an important distinction when she points to the fact that even though a factual biography may itself be "degraded from the normal standards of biographical writing, [. . .] grossly tendentious, simplistic, inventive," "such violations of the compositional rules of factual biography do not produce a work of the fictional genre." "Both fictional and factual biographies," Schabert continues, "are based on the facts of history and of an individual's life, and both, in the sense that they are constructs made up from the facts, are fictions. Yet the constructs are different in kind." These differences touch upon the degrees of self-referentiality in factual and fictional biography, the aim of the factual being "correspondence to the world of historical knowledge" rather than "aesthetic coherence." Furthermore, the differences are matters of essentiality: while the factual elements within biofiction gain metonymic status and thus, as Schabert asserts, make fictional biography resemble a sophisticated anecdote, selectivity within factual biography hints at thematic unity. Moreover, "no actually false statement may be introduced for the sake of essentiality; whereas in a novel this can lead

to something 'poetically true,' in a factual biography this is only bad, tendentious writing" ("Fictional Biography, Factual Biography, and Their Contaminations," *biography* 5.1 [1992]: 1–16; quotations: 10, 13, 5, 7). Franz K. Stanzel points to reception theory: he sees the difference between fictional and factual biography in the way the reader reacts to the appeal-function of the blanks in the text ("Historie, Historischer Roman, Historiographische Metafiktion," *Sprachkunst* 26.1 [1995]: 113–23).

[8] Cf. Marianne Dekoven, "History as Suppressed Referent in Modernist Fiction," *English Literary History* 51 (1984): 137–52.

[9] Hutcheon, *A Poetics of Postmodernism*, 87.

[10] Andreas Höfele, "The Writer on Stage: Some Contemporary British Plays about Authors," in *British Drama in the 1980s: New Perspectives*, ed. Bernhard Reitz and Hubert Zapf, *anglistik & englischunterricht* 41 (1990): 79–91.

[11] Jean Baudrillard, *Kool Killer oder der Aufstand der Zeichen* (Berlin: Merve Verlag, 1978), 49.

[12] Julia Barrett, *The Third Sister: A Continuation of "Sense and Sensibility"* (London: Michael O'Mara Books, 1996), 240. Rolf Breuer is currently preparing a list of all the completions, continuations, and adaptations of Jane Austen's novels, together with an essay on "The Poetics of the Sequel."

[13] Ira B. Nadel, "Narrative and the Popularity of Biography," *Mosaic* 20.4 (1987): 134, 136.

[14] See Ina Schabert, *In Quest of the Other Person: Fiction as Biography* (Tübingen: Francke, 1990); Annegret Maack has published two important essays on the subject: "Charakter als Echo: Zur Poetologie fiktiver Biographien," in *Klassiker-Renaissance: Modelle der Gegenwartsliteratur*, ed. Martin Brunkhorst, Gerd Rohmann, and Konrad Schoell (Tübingen: Stauffenburg, 1991), 247–58, and "Das Leben der toten Dichter: Fiktive Biographien," in *Radikalität und Mässigung: Der englische Roman seit 1960*, ed. Annegret Maack and Rüdiger Imhof (Darmstadt: Wissenschaftliche Buchgesellschaft, 1993), 169–188. See also Barbara Schaff, *Das zeitgenössische britische Künstlerdrama* (Passau: Stutz Verlag, 1992).

[15] David Morse, *Romanticism: A Structural Analysis* (Totowa, NJ: Barnes & Noble, 1982), 6–7.

[16] See M. H. Abrams, "Revolutionary Romanticism," *Bucknell Review* 36.1 (1992): 19–26.

[17] Samuel Taylor Coleridge, *Biographia Literaria*, in *Samuel Taylor Coleridge*, ed. J. Jackson (Oxford and New York: Oxford UP, 1985), 301. On the interdependence of language and consciousness, see also Harold Bloom, *Romanticism and Consciousness: Essays in Criticism* (New York: Norton, 1970).

[18] Morse, *Romanticism*, 289; on the irreconcilable subject-object difference highlighted by the Romantic/Byronic hero see especially 284–92.

[19] For a more detailed analysis of the correlation between Romanticism and deconstruction see J. Drummond Bone, "Historicism and Deconstruction: Two Contemporary Perspectives on Romanticism," in *Beyond the Suburbs of the Mind: Exploring English Romanticism: Papers Delivered at the Mannheim Symposium in Honour of Hermann Fischer*, ed. Michael Gassenmeier and Norbert H. Platz (Essen: Die Blaue Eule, 1987), 212–24, and Christoph Bode, "Romanticism and Deconstruction: Distant Relations and Elective Affinities," in *Romantic Continuities: Papers Delivered at the Symposium of the "Gesellschaft für Englische Romantik" held at the Catholic University Eichstätt*, ed. Michael Gassenmeier and Günther Blaicher (Essen: Die Blaue Eule, 1990), 131–59. Bode's important essay contains a rich bibliography on the issue. On the reception and popularity of Romanticism within deconstructive theory, see also Hubert Zapf, "Dekonstruktion als Herausforderung der Literaturwissenschaft: Das Beispiel der englischen Romantik," *Anglia* 106 (1988): 360–379.

[20] Coleridge pointed out that a symbol "is characterized by a translucence of the Special [the species] in the Individual or of the General [the genus] in the Especial or of the Universal in the General. Above all by the translucence of the Eternal through and in the Temporal. It always partakes of the Reality which it renders intelligible; and while it enunciates the whole, abides itself as a living part in that Unity of which it is the representative. The other [allegories] are but empty echoes which the fancy arbitrarily associates with apparitions of matter." Quoted in Aidan Day, *Romanticism* (London: Routledge, 1996), 110.

[21] André Breton, *Manifestoes of Surrealism*, trans. Richard Seaver and Helen R. Lane (Ann Arbor: U of Michigan P, 1972), 152, 152–53, 151, 153. On the relationship between Postmodernism and Surrealism, see also Elizabeth Deeds Ermarth, *Sequel to History: Postmodernism and the Crisis of Representational Time* (Princeton: Princeton UP, 1992).

[22] William Wordsworth, "Preface to *Lyrical Ballads*," *William Wordsworth*, ed. Stephen Gill (Oxford and New York: Oxford UP, 1986), 598, 611.

[23] Percy Bysshe Shelley, *Shelley's Poetry and Prose*, ed. Donald H. Reiman and Sharon B. Powers (New York and London: Norton, 1977), 503–04.

[24] John Keats, letters of November 22, 1817 [first quotation] and December 21, 1817 (to George and Thomas Keats) [second and third quotation], in Maurice Buxton Forman (ed.) *Letters of John Keats* (New York: Oxford UP, 1935), 227–28 and 72.

[25] Morse, *Romanticism*, 2.

[26] Julia Kristeva, "Narration et transformation," *Semeiotica* 1 (1969): 443.

[27] See Mikhail M. Bakhtin, *Rabelais and His World* (Bloomington: U of Indiana P, 1988); Roland Barthes, "From Work to Text," in *Image Music Text*, ed. and trans. Stephen Heath (London: Fontana Press, 1977); Jacques Der

rida, *Of Grammatology*, trans. Gayatri Chakravorty Spivak (Baltimore: Johns Hopkins UP, 1976), 50.

[28] John Keats's thoroughly deconstructive lines in the concluding stanza of his "Ode to a Nightingale," for instance, dismantle the merely temporary soothing the imagination is able to bring about: "Forlorn! the very word is like a bell / To toll me back from thee to my sole self! / Adieu! The fancy cannot cheat so well / As she is fam'd to do, deceiving elf." (*Poetical Works*, ed. H. W. Garrod [Oxford: Oxford UP, 1986], 209). Similarly to this, Keats called the capacity of human beings to endure half-knowledge — or, in other words, difference — "negative capability," an important philosophical as well as poetological principle for Keats's most mature work. See Walter Jackson Bate, *Negative Capability: The Intuitive Approach in Keats* (Cambridge, MA: Harvard UP, 1939).

[29] Henry H. H. Remak, "A Key to West European Romanticism?" *Colloquia Germanica* (1968): 44. I am grateful to Rolf Breuer for drawing my attention to Remak's essay. For a similar diagnosis, see also Catherine Belsey, "The Romantic Construction of the Unconscious," in *Literature, Politics and Theory: Papers from the Essex Conference 1976–1984*, ed. Francis Barker, Peter Hulme, Margaret Iveson, and Diana Loxley (London and New York: Methuen, 1986), 68–69. A concise overview of the debate is provided by Day, *Romanticism*, 107.

[30] Howard Brenton, *Bloody Poetry* (London: Methuen, 1989), 13. See also Höfele, "The Writer on Stage," 81, 85, and Dieter A. Berger, "Künstlerdethronisierung als Dramatisches Prinzip: Zur Ästhetik des Gegenwartstheaters in Großbritannien," in *Studien zur Ästhetik des Gegenwartstheaters*, ed. Christian W. Thomsen (Heidelberg: Winter, 1985), 209–24.

[31] Werner Wolf, "Radikalität und Mässigung: Tendenzen experimentellen Erzählens," in *Radikalität und Mässigung*, ed. Maack and Imhof, 34–53 (esp. 45–51).

[32] Percy Bysshe Shelley, "Ode to the West Wind," *Poetical Works*, ed. Thomas Hutchinson (Oxford and New York: Oxford UP, 1986), 579.

[33] Abrams, "Revolutionary Romanticism," 31.

[34] See Catherine Itzin, *Stages in the Revolution: Political Theatre in Britain Since 1968* (London: Methuen, 1980).

[35] See Day, *Romanticism*, 161–62.

[36] Anne K. Mellor, "Possessing Nature: The Female in *Frankenstein*," in *Romanticism and Feminism*, ed. Anne K. Mellor (Bloomington: Indiana UP, 1988), 220, 228, 229. See also Elisabeth Bronfen, *Over Her Dead Body: Death, Femininity and the Aesthetic* (Manchester: Manchester UP, 1992), 130–39.

[37] Sandra M. Gilbert and Susan Gubar, *The Madwoman in the Attic: The Woman Writer and the Nineteenth-Century Literary Imagination* (New Haven and London: Yale UP, 1979), 213–247 (esp. 234–235).

[38] Anne K. Mellor, *Romanticism and Gender* (New York and London: Routledge, 1993), 28.

[39] Brenton, *Bloody Poetry*, 43.

[40] Mellor, *Romanticism and Gender*, 209 10.

[41] White, *Tropics of Discourse*, 48.

[42] White, *Tropics of Discourse*, 41. See also Michel de Certeau, *L'écriture de l'histoire* (Paris: Gallimard, 1975); Paul Veyne, *Comment on écrit l'histoire* (Paris: Seuil, 1971), and Dominick LaCapra, *History & Criticism* (Ithaca and London: Cornell UP, 1985).

[43] The terms "interauthoriality" ["Interauktorialität"] and "interauthorial" ["interauktorial"] are Ina Schabert's; see her essay "Interauktorialität," *Deutsche Vierteljahrsschrift für Literaturwissenschaft und Geistesgeschichte* 57 (1983): 679–701.

[44] See Schabert, "Interauktorialität," 679.

[45] Hutcheon, *A Poetics of Postmodernism*, 93.

[46] Keats, letter of November 22, 1817, in Forman, ed., *Letters*, 227.

ANSGAR NÜNNING

An Intertextual Quest for Thomas Chatterton: The Deconstruction of the Romantic Cult of Originality and the Paradoxes of Life-Writing in Peter Ackroyd's Fictional Metabiography *Chatterton*

Alas, what with the Death of the Author and the Disappearance of the Subject, even an ordinary biography is bound to be a problem these days. Biographies are said to be fictions revealing more about the biographer than they do about their subjects, who of course do not exist anyway.

Malcolm Bradbury[1]

Historiography (that is, "history" and "writing") bears within its own name the paradox — almost an oxymoron — of a relation established between two antinomic terms, between the real and discourse. Its task is one of connecting them and, at the point where this link cannot be imagined, of working as if the two were being joined.

Michel de Certeau[2]

Chatterton and the Paradox of Life-Writing

THE OBSERVATION THAT WRITING "EVEN AN ORDINARY biography is bound to be a problem these days" has a peculiar relevance to the case of Peter Ackroyd's novel *Chatterton* (1987). Pinning down biographical data on Thomas Chatterton is itself no mean task, given the fact that the "marvellous boy" was not only a brilliant faker of medieval poetry but also a highly successful forerunner of those modern authors accomplished in "the fine arts of eluding the modern biographer."[3] It is hardly surprising therefore that Ackroyd's book, in which Chatterton's death and the mystery surrounding it figures as a prominent leitmotif,[4] is indeed anything but an ordinary biography, fictional or not. What

Ackroyd has done, instead of accumulating evidence and writing a conventional narrative biography, is to juxtapose several stories that lead the reader through a strange intertextual, or rather intermedial, biographical quest for Thomas Chatterton. *Chatterton* provides various fictional versions of Chatterton's life that indeed reveal more about the individual biographers than they do about their elusive subject. The book does not represent the life of a Romantic poet, but problematizes the issues of representation and life-writing.[5] *Chatterton* is thus not so much a fictional biography as an ingenious literary *meta*biography.[6]

The two epigraphs above, taken from Malcolm Bradbury's hilarious satire on deconstruction, *Mensonge*, and from Michel de Certeau's seminal *The Writing of History*, reflect some of the issues that are of crucial importance for anyone trying to come to terms with the intricate structure of Ackroyd's novel, the significance of its dense intertextual network, and its poetological and metabiographical implications. They show in miniature the problems attached to any biography in general, and to a faithful recording of Chatterton's life and death in particular. A great part of our interest in *Chatterton* arguably derives from the fact that its complex structure, its intertextual network, and its metabiographical self-consciousness foreground the paradoxical relation between life and writing which the somewhat oxymoronic term "biography" tries to conceal. In line with de Certeau's succinct observations on historiography, one can argue that the term biography also "bears within its own name the paradox — almost an oxymoron — of a relation established between two antinomic terms," between life and writing. Whereas the task of conventional biographies, factual and fictional alike, "is one of connecting them and, at the point where this link cannot be imagined, of working *as if* the two were being joined." A fictional metabiography like *Chatterton*, then, emphasizes that there is an ineluctable difference between a life and a book. Illustrating de Certeau's thesis that "the past is the fiction of the present,"[7] Ackroyd's novel can be read as an expression, in theme and form, of the constructivist view that writing a biography, just like historiography, is a subjective and constructive process which cannot reproduce the past but only construct or reconstruct it intellectually.

Ackroyd's *Chatterton* is a paradigmatic example of the rewriting of Romantic lives in contemporary literature. Firstly, Ackroyd's novel exemplifies the current renaissance of life-writing, that is, the recent trend in postmodern literature to treat the life of historical personages in fictional biographies. Secondly, the historical figure occupying centre-stage in this novel is an artist-figure of the Romantic period, an artist, moreover, whose short but eventful life provides plenty of spectacular material as a basis for a colourful and sensational plot. Thirdly, Ackroyd's novel is revisionist in at least two ways: it questions and revises the official biographical record of Chatterton's life and death, and it also expresses revisionist notions of biography and biographical fiction. Fourthly, and arguably most importantly, *Chatterton* provides a paradigm of both the postmodernist trend of crossing traditional genre boundaries and the shift of emphasis from the mere writing, or rewriting, of an historical individual's life to the epistemological problematization of life-writing itself.

Using this as a point of departure, the present article seeks to examine both postmodernist modes of representing the life of a Romantic artist in Ackroyd's *Chatterton* and how this novel expresses changing attitudes towards literature and biography. I will argue that Ackroyd's novel can be seen as a typical example of a new generic variant of the fictional biography that might be designated "fictional metabiography" in that it is a novel concerned with the recording of history and the problems of biography. The remarkable achievement of Ackroyd's ambitious novel can be found in the ways in which it conveys a sense of the complexity of the problems attached to any biographical enterprise. In addition to rewriting Chatterton's life, or rather to questioning the very possibility of truthfully representing a person's life, *Chatterton* is a self-conscious examination of a number of key poetological notions closely associated with the Romantic movement. Rather than providing "an imaginative recreation of the life and legend of one of the cult figures of the Romantic movement,"[8] however, *Chatterton* focuses on the problems of biographical reconstruction. Exemplifying the paradoxes of life-writing, Ackroyd's novel deconstructs both positivist notions of biography and the Romantic cult of originality.[9]

"An Imitation in a World of Imitations": On the Deconstruction of the Romantic Cult of Originality in *Chatterton*

When the fictionalized Chatterton's publisher asks him whether the work of Rowley, whom Chatterton invented, was in fact not so much a forgery as "an imitation in a world of Imitations" (91), he unwittingly raises a question that is arguably one of the key issues of Ackroyd's novel: the question of whether such distinctions as those between an original and a forgery, between authentic documents and imitations, or between reality and fiction have not become obsolete in a world in which it has become well-nigh impossible to determine "what is real and what is unreal" (35). In contrast to those novelists who merely thematize such issues explicitly in the form of metafictional comments about representation and fictionality, Ackroyd also incorporates poetological, epistemological, and metabiographical self-reflections into the structure of his novel. That is why a closer look at the semantization of the novel's formal features, especially of the intertextual quest for Thomas Chatterton, can shed light on Ackroyd's anti-Romantic poetics.

As has been shown, it is not the representation of Chatterton's life itself that provides the focus of the novel but rather the process of historical reconstruction, which takes the form of a biographical quest. The relationship of history to the present is an important factor behind the complex structure of *Chatterton*, and there are several formal features that serve to direct the reader's attention from the past to the present. Like many other fictional biographies,[10] *Chatterton* is a multilayered and multiperspective novel. It takes into account both Chatterton's conception of himself and several other versions and representations of his life and death. Set in three different centuries, it is narrated in different voices, representing different narrative situations and different accounts of Chatterton's life and death.

Juxtaposing three stories taking place on different time levels, Ackroyd in fact presents the reader, not with Chatterton's life, but with several incompatible versions of it, with almost everything deviating from, and calling into question, the official biographical record. Set in the eighteenth century, one of these stories of Chatterton's life and death is rendered as a first-person narration from the point of view of the protagonist. According to this version, the young poet did not commit suicide but accidentally killed himself in an inept attempt to cure himself of venereal disease by swallowing a lethal overdose of some inexpertly prepared self-medication. According to quite a different version, however, Chatterton did not die at the age of eighteen at all but merely faked his death in order to publish more forgeries under assumed names, writing "in the guise of Thomas Gray, William Blake, William Cowper and many others" (127).

This spectacular second version, which entails both a radical challenge to literary history and the need to rewrite it, seems at first to be confirmed by the main plot, which is set in contemporary London, when the writer Charles Wychwood buys a painting which he believes to represent the aged Chatterton. In the course of the novel, however, the authenticity of both the painting and the documents which seem to support this theory becomes more and more dubious. Ackroyd deals with the production of Henry Wallis's well-known painting of the death of Chatterton, for which the poet George Meredith posed as a model, in a nineteenth-century subplot that consists mainly of conversations between Wallis and Meredith. The conversations focus on aesthetic problems of pictorial representation and on the ways in which an artist creates, rather than just represents, an event like the death of Chatterton. Although Wallis produces nothing but another version of Chatterton's death, and a highly stylized one at that, Meredith is convinced that "this will always be remembered as the true death of Chatterton" (157). To make things even more complex, a descendant of Chatterton's publisher Samuel Joynson offers yet another version, which seems to confirm the official biographical record. He reveals that his son forged both Chatterton's memoirs and the painting that Charles has discovered, and maintains that the desperate poet did indeed commit suicide at the age of eighteen.

The fact that these incompatible versions exist side by side and that Chatterton's fictional diary is embedded in the biographical endeavours of present-day historians serves to focus the readers' attention on the biographical quest for Thomas Chatterton. What holds the three plotlines together is the characters' attempt to "resolve the secret of Chatterton's portrait" (45), which takes the form of a "pilgrimage" (49) or quest, as Charles acknowledges when he announces: "The quest begins on Saturday" (45). The fact that there are several references to "mystery" (17–18, 55, 208) and "secret" (45, 59–60, 97) serves to reinforce the close connection that exists in Ackroyd's novels between history and mystery, something which is also underlined by the analytical structure of both *Hawksmoor* and *Chatterton*. Resolving the secret of Chatterton's portrait and the mystery surrounding his death in fact amounts to a complex semiotic process: "And then we'll decode Chatterton" (57).

Although the process of decoding Chatterton turns out to be more difficult than the characters have anticipated, it provides a realistically motivated framework for linking the three time levels and for exemplifying key notions of Ackroyd's poetics. Searching for pertinent documents, Philip Slack, for instance, finds a collection of literary reminiscences, which contains, among other things, an illustration entitled "Chatterton's Monument in Bristol Churchyard" and a short text about George Meredith, "who, in the early months of 1856, in the utmost extremity, and with thoughts of self-murder after his wife's desertion, sat in the gloomy environs of St Mary Redcliffe in Bristol, lo, even in the shadow of Chatterton's Monument" (70). Similarly, when Charles and his son Edward visit the Tate Gallery and look at Henry

Wallis's painting of the death of Chatterton, the three time levels again seem to merge.

Moreover, Ackroyd's novel establishes a great number of thematic parallels between the different time levels, which do not only serve to link the past and the present but also to foreground its postmodern poetics. Among the themes that figure among the more prominent leitmotifs is the notion that the artist is immortalized through his art, that "poetry never dies" (148). Similarly, Charles is convinced that posterity will bestow due recognition on him in due course: "My genius will one day be recognised" (39). Other leitmotifs foregrounding central themes and reinforcing the novel's coherence are the repetition of such phrases as "poetry and poverty" (10), "despondency and madness" (3, 35, 233), "everlasting fame" (57–58) or "eternal fame" (69), and "seeing is believing" (116, 129). The repetition and variation of such motifs not only serves to link the three time levels, but also to illustrate structurally the notion that history, like literature, repeats itself, "the phenomenon of *déjà vu*" (69).

More than any other topic, perhaps, the theme of the death of the author permeates *Chatterton*, linking the three time levels in complex ways[11] and expressing another central poetological notion: the deconstruction of the Romantic idea that the author is an autonomous subject or the single source of a text. It is not, however, Roland Barthes's well-known notion of the death of the author alone that the novel openly toys with.[12] The subject of the death of the author in fact reappears in several ways in Ackroyd's novel, all of which are realistically motivated. First of all, there is, of course, the mystery surrounding Chatterton's death, with which the characters on the other two time levels are intensely preoccupied. Secondly, there is Charles Wychwood's death, which serves to underline the close connection between him and Chatterton that is established right from the beginning of the novel when Charles adopts the pose Meredith assumed when he acted as Wallis's model. Thirdly, the issue of the artistic representation of the death of the author features prominently. Not only does the production of the only existing portrait of Chatterton, Wallis's painting of his death, provide the nineteenth-century plot-line, the problem of pictorial representation — and not just of Chatterton's deathbed scene — is also the central topic in the conversations between Wallis and Meredith. In addition, Harriet's friend Sarah Tilt, an art critic, has been working on a study of the images of death in English painting for six years, a study to which she has provisionally given the ambiguous but telling title of *The Art of Death* (33).

Like the recurrent thematization of the subject of the death of the author, the high degree of intertextuality serves a twofold function: to provide links between the past and the present and to highlight one of the central poetological issues continuously brought to the fore in *Chatterton*, namely the deconstruction of the Romantic cult of originality and the creative genius and its replacement by the notion of literature as, and originating from, a discursive intertextual game. *Chatterton* epitomizes recent developments in postmodernist biofiction in that it displays all the kinds of pastiche and overtly parodistic intertextuality that have been identified as hallmarks of a new and self-conscious mode of historical fiction.[13] *Chatterton* abounds in different layers of intertextual references, many of which imitate or parody genre conventions, literary styles, and individual texts. They include almost every conceivable mode of intertextuality, from various forms of genre cross-references to innumerable allusions to and quotations from specific intertexts.

With respect to its themes, plot, and structure, *Chatterton*, like *Hawksmoor*, draws on and subverts the conventions of the detective novel. It also directly alludes to that paragon of a detective, Sherlock Holmes. When Philip asks who the figure depicted in the portrait is, Charles solemnly announces: "This is the mystery, Holmes. Once I've solved it, I'm a rich man!" (18). Ackroyd's novel thus bears out Wesseling's thesis that the self-reflexive innovation of historical fiction can be seen as "a cross-fertilization of two generic models, the historical novel and the detective novel."[14]

The allusions to specific intertexts range from marked and unmarked quotations from English canonical classics, for example from Shakespeare, Marvell, Blake, Wordsworth, Dickens, Wilde, T. S. Eliot, and various other authors, to self-quotations from Chatterton and Meredith. They even include references to Wittgenstein's well-known "Whereof we cannot speak, thereof we must be silent?" (36) and to Harold Bloom's notion of "the anxiety of influence" (100). What is more relevant in the present context than the mere identification of specific intertextual references, however, is the question of the degree to which Ackroyd's use of the device of intertextuality throws light on his poetics. Answering this entails identifying the functions that intertextual allusions have in Ackroyd's fiction, as one of the epigraphs of *English Music* (1992) suggests:

> The scholarly reader will soon realize that I have appropriated passages from Thomas Browne, Thomas Malory, William Hogarth, Thomas Morley, Lewis Carroll, Samuel Johnson, Daniel Defoe and many other English writers; the alert reader will understand why I have done so.[15]

In Ackroyd's novels, intertextuality is, first and foremost, an important means of thematizing and exemplifying the continuity of the past in the present. The wide range of intertextual references to be found in *Chatterton* presents the reader with the various ways in which the English past lingers on in the present. Ackroyd's postmodernist biofictions incorporate a great number of echoes that will be part of the background of every educated Englishman and Englishwoman. Through the numerous intertextual allusions that are woven into the settings, characters, dialogue, and incidents represented in *Chatterton*, Ackroyd formally foregrounds Englishness, England's cultural heritage. The persistent use of almost every conceivable mode of intertextuality keeps reminding the reader of how literature, works of art, and music have contributed in significant ways to defining an Englishman's sense of his cultural nationality. Like the metahistorical novels of Andrew Sinclair and Antonia S. Byatt, *Chatterton* is a highly self-conscious reflection upon the continuity of the English past in the present.

In addition to conveying an impression of an Englishman's cultural heritage, Ackroyd's novel illustrates the possibilities offered by postmodernist biographical fiction for demonstrating the impossibility of ever escaping the prison-house of literature and intertextuality. Exemplifying both Chatterton's literary method and his view of literature, according to which "we see in every Line an Echoe" (87), *Chatterton* may well be called an "echo-chamber" (to adopt Roland Barthes's felicitous term) of England's cultural history.[16] The characters in *Chatterton* are eminently conscious of the fact that their discourse is permeated by echoes from English literature. When Harriet is told that she has just been misquoting she curtly replies: "'Don't you think I know? I've been quoting all my life! [. . .] Of course I knew it was a quotation,' she added, 'I've given my life to English literature'" (35). Similarly, when Charles reminds Andrew Flint, who is writing a biography of George Meredith, that all the great English poets are actually present in the nation's collective memory — "Think of them all around us, watching us, Blake, Shelley, Coleridge [. . .] And Meredith. All of them influencing us" (77) — he is once again overtaken by the inescapable intertextual echo-chamber constituted by cultural history: "'The dream unfolds,' he said. 'The sleeper awakes, but still the dream goes on.' And he realised at once that these were not his words, but those of someone other" (78). And when Philip gives up his attempt to write a novel because he feels that it "had become a patchwork of other voices and other styles" (70), this insight can also be read as a self-conscious allusion to Ackroyd's poetics.

Through its complex network of literary allusions *Chatterton* not only foregrounds a literary past, England's cultural heritage, Ackroyd also impresses on the reader T. S. Eliot's notion that the whole of the literature of Europe has "a simultaneous existence and composes a simultaneous order."[17] By locating history in the here and now, Ackroyd's novel serves to illustrate T. S. Eliot's poetic evocation of a state in which past, present, and future are one. Both in the Tate Gallery (131) and in the echo-chamber of the library (69–78)[18] the three time levels of the novel and all the periods in the history of English literature merge into the timeless presence of an intertextual universe: "They [the books] seemed to expand as soon as they reached the shadows, creating some dark world where there was no beginning and no end, no story, no meaning. And, if you crossed the threshold into that world, you would be surrounded by words" (71).

Moreover, Ackroyd's use of intertextuality and a broad range of other postmodernist narrative techniques undermine the traditional assumption that the relationship between fiction and reality is based on mimesis and the notion that realism is more "natural" or less artificial than other literary conventions.[19] According to the poetological notions implied in *Chatterton*, it is most rewarding to conceptualize fiction as an active force in its own right. Words do not reproduce reality but constitute it, as both Chatterton and Meredith emphasize: "Without words, Chatterton thinks, there is nothing. There is no real world" (210). Meredith even goes so far as to argue that "there is nothing more real than words. They are reality" (157). According to Meredith, nothing demonstrates these notions quite so well as Chatterton's poetry, which after all constituted a whole world through language:

> 'I said that the words were real, Henry, I did not say that what they depicted was real. Our dear dead poet created the monk Rowley out of thin air, and yet he has more life in him than any medieval priest who actually existed. The invention is always more real. [. . .] But Chatterton did not create an individual simply. He invented an entire period and made its imagination his own: no one had properly understood the medieval world until Chatterton summoned it into existence. The poet does not merely recreate or describe the world. He actually creates it. And that is why he is feared.' (157)

What needs to be emphasized, however, is that *Chatterton*'s (as well as Chatterton's and Meredith's) rejection of a mimetic conception of art by no means results in an emphatic celebration of the role of the imagination or of the creative and autonomous genius. On the contrary, according to Chatterton, "original genius consists in forming new and happy combinations, rather than in searching after thoughts and ideas which had never occurred before" (58).[20] As Wesseling shrewdly observes, *Chatterton* in fact "dismantles the Romantic glorification of the autonomous, creative imagination."[21]

It is Chatterton's imitative poetry or literary forgery[22] more than anything else that provides the best illustration of the poetics exemplified in *Chatterton*. Forging both medieval poetry and "authentick Histories" (89), Chatterton calls himself "the great Parodist" (81), using an epithet that applies equally well to Ackroyd himself and to the protagonists of two of his other works, Oscar Wilde and T. S. Eliot. Both Chatterton's and Ackroyd's works represent hybrid intertextual genres, entailing a radical reconceptualization of such dichotomies as history versus fiction or the real versus the fictional. Chatterton's imitations are so authentic that his copies are taken for originals:

> I reproduc'd the Past and filled it with such Details that it was as if I were observing it in front of me: so the Language of ancient Dayes awoke the Reality itself for, tho' I knew that it was I who composed these Histories, I knew also that they were true ones. (85)

In Ackroyd's poetics it is by juxtaposing several voices and quotations from other works that a poet acquires his or her own unique voice.[23] As Ackroyd observes in his discussion of *The Waste Land*, "in their combination the words cease to be merely a collection of sources [. . .] they have become a new thing."[24] Just as Eliot "found his own voice by first reproducing that of others,"[25] Ackroyd himself developed his own literary style by borrowing, imitating, and parodying the voices of Dickens, Wilde, Eliot, and a host of other writers.

Far from being parasitic or minor imitative literary species, such intertextual modes as parody and pastiche are shown to play a creative role in transforming literary history and genre definitions. Both Chatterton and *Chatterton* demonstrate what Maack has aptly described as the generative and original effect of intertextuality.[26] Ackroyd himself has suggested that "writing does not emerge from speech, or from the individual, but only from other writing."[27] His observations on T. S. Eliot's "gift for dramatic impersonation and stylistic allusiveness" could just as well be read as an adequate summary of both Chatterton's methods as a writer and the poetics exemplified in *Chatterton*: "But if these passages veer close to parody or pastiche they are still not simple 'imitations' but rather the creative borrowing of another style and syntax which releases a plethora of 'voices' and perceptions."[28]

Demonstrating that every work of literature inevitably contains innumerable echoes of a host of pre-texts, *Chatterton* implicitly rejects the Romantic celebration of the creative imagination. One of the results of such a reconceptualization of intertextuality as the real origins of art and writing is the deconstruction of the Romantic cult of originality. Ackroyd's novels "deconstruct the author as single source of the text and thus dismiss the Romantic concept of originality."[29] *Chatterton* in fact "suggests that Chatterton, the forger of medieval poetry, exemplifies the account of the origination of literary works in the poststructuralist terms of intertextuality and not in the Romantic terms of creation *ex nihilo*."[30] The complex network of intertextual allusions serves to drive home the postmodernist idea that such intertextual modes as parody and pastiche have a generative force of their own, an idea which replaces the Romantic notion of originality: "Remembering and reinventing the past in the form of an intertextual fabric ought to rule out the notion of an origin or a primary text that can be discovered."[31] Moreover, as Finney observes, "Ackroyd's impersonation of an earlier writer reflects his belief in the disappearance of the subject in postmodern art."[32]

Presenting Chatterton as the prototype of the artist as a parodist in an intertextual universe, *Chatterton* self-consciously exemplifies a postmodernist poetics which is diametrically opposed to the Romantic ideas, or ideals, of originality and of the artist as an autonomous subject and creative genius. In a world in which it has become impossible to distinguish copies, imitations and forgeries from their originals, it makes perfect sense to argue, as Chatterton does, that "the truest Plagiarism is the truest Poetry" (87). With its radical rejection of the Romantic ideals of originality and of the artist as creative genius, Ackroyd's novel both thematizes and formally realizes the kind of aesthetics which prominent spokesmen of postmodernism have outlined, as the obvious similarity between the metafictional self-consciousness of *Chatterton* and Raymond Federman's well-known description of imagination demonstrates: "imagination does not invent the SOME-THING-NEW we often attribute to it, but rather [. . .] (consciously or unconsciously) it merely imitates, copies, repeats, proliferates — plagiarizes in other words — what has already been there."[33]

One might add in passing that what has been said above about the functions and poetological implications of intertextuality applies also to the many references to visual art. In *Chatterton*, the blurring of genres extends beyond texts to include references to other art forms and media, thereby turning the present-day historians' biographical endeavours into an intermedial quest for Thomas Chatterton. In addition to the painting that Charles discovers and to the nineteenth-century subplot there are a host of other references to art that serve to underline the novel's postmodernist aesthetics. It turns out, for instance, that Joseph

Seymour's paintings were in fact fakes, painted by his assistant Stewart Merk rather than by Seymour himself. When Merk asks what is in fact a rhetorical question — "But who is to say what is fake and what is real? You're sure you know the difference, yes?" (113) — he again raises one of the novel's central poetological issues, the question of how anyone can tell the difference between an original and forgeries, copies, and fakes. When it finally turns out that the alleged portrait of Chatterton is not only another fake but a palimpsest — "the painting contained the residue of several different images, painted at various times" (205) — any attempt at solving the mystery of the painting or of Chatterton's death, of identifying origins and originals, is shown to be in vain.[34]

"Who's to say what is real and what is unreal?": Epistemological and Metabiographical Implications of *Chatterton*

As the discussion of both the structure of the biographical quest and the intertextual network of Ackroyd's novel may already have indicated, the narrative strategies by which *Chatterton* depicts the life and death of the Romantic poet reflect a number of the major tendencies that historically conscious biofictions have been exhibiting for the last ten years or so. Foregrounding unresolved contradictions between different versions of Chatterton's life and death, the pattern of the intertextual quest serves to raise important metabiographical issues. In addition to revealing parallels between the lives of the characters on the three time levels, the structural features of Ackroyd's novel also serve to bring to the fore the constructivist insight that subjectivity and constructivity are not to be eliminated as features of historical knowledge and of biographical constructions.

Fictional metabiographies like *Chatterton* represent significant innovations in the treatment of biography as a literary theme because they highlight the process of biographical reconstruction and the protagonists' consciousness of the past rather than a historical world represented as such. Instead of focusing on and portraying the lives of real historical individuals on the diegetic level of the characters, fictional metabiographies are generally set in the present but concerned with the appropriation, reconstruction, and transmission of the biographee's life. Such novels typically explore how characters try to come to terms with the past. What is highlighted in *Chatterton* are the biographical endeavours of the protagonists living in the present rather than the past itself. Moreover, *Chatterton* does not portray the past as a self-contained and complete world, but as something liable to the distortions that subjective reconstructions and recollections entail. It is therefore profitable to explore the connections between the structural properties of Ackroyd's novel and its poetological, epistemological, and metabiographical implications.

Focusing on an intertextual quest, *Chatterton* draws the reader's attention to epistemological and methodological problems of life-writing. Ackroyd's novel is not only closely concerned with the ontological status of history and the epistemological and methodological problems of biography, but also displays the high degree of metafictional self-consciousness characteristic of historiographic and biographical metafiction in general. The central question implicitly raised by the complex quest structure and the dense intertextual network of *Chatterton* is formulated by Ackroyd's character Harriet Scrope when she asks, "who's to say what is real and what is unreal?" (35).

Chatterton can be read as a fictional metabiography that expresses the constructivity of experience, knowledge, and life-writing through literary means. By showing how biographers actively structure the information they encounter in their sources, Ackroyd's novel scrutinizes both "history in the making" and "historiography in the making."[35] Whereas Chatterton's journal sheds light on "history in the making," the other two time levels are primarily concerned with biography in the making, with the making of biographical images.

The polyphonic and fragmentary montage structure of *Chatterton* emphasizes the discrepancies between Chatterton's "real" life in the past and the remembered and textualized versions of his life, the insurmountable gap between a person's life and its written or artistic representations. The inability to grasp and narrate the complex processes that make up other persons' lives is implicitly expressed through the juxtaposition of heterogeneous versions of Chatterton's life and death, which remain enigmatic to the very end. The problems of the biographer are exacerbated by the questionable authenticity of sources and documents, most of which turn out to be fakes and forgeries: "'There has to be a copy,' he said to Philip [. . .]. 'How could we know that it was real without a copy? Everything is copied'" (93).

Concerning itself with the question of how much we can ever know about the past, *Chatterton* calls into doubt positivist notions of objectivity and truth and shows that any biographical representation is an intellectual construct. Both through its complex structural layering of historical reconstruction and its metabiographical self-consciousness, Ackroyd's novel shows that what is commonly regarded as a biographical fact inevitably depends on the selective bias of the individual biographer or artist. More specifically, the multiperspectival structure and the montage of texts from different genres draw attention to the distorting effects of the selection of sources, to the biographer's problem of having to rely on scanty evidence, to the partiality, contradictoriness, unreliability, and questionable authenticity of historical sources and documents, and to the close affinity between history and stories. The intertextual network of Ackroyd's novel and the metabiographical comments it contains serve to foreground the fact that subjectivity, relativity, selectivity, and constructivity are ineluctable features of biographical reconstructions. Ackroyd's novel thus exposes the aporias of a realist conception of biography and historiography, the goals of which include, as a character in Ackroyd's novel *First Light* observes, "total recovery, objective interpretation and comprehensive explanation."[36]

The impossibility of synthesizing the contradictory accounts of Chatterton's life and death serves to undermine the belief that biographical "facts" can ever be objectively known. The incompatible versions of Chatterton's life and death illustrate that human views of history do not mirror any particular aspects of a past reality. The structure of Ackroyd's novel thus shows that there is not one authentic representation of the past but a plethora of different versions. Highlighting the fact that biographers subjectively process the information they encounter in their sources, *Chatterton* lays bare the impossibility of producing an objective, totalized, and true account of either history or the life of an historical individual. Ackroyd's novel suggests that there is not one truth about Chatterton's life and death, only a series of versions which are dependent on, and constructed by, the observer rather than retrieved from the past: "The real world is just a succession of interpretations. Everything which is written down immediately becomes a kind of fiction" (40). This accords with Ackroyd's observation that there "is no 'truth' to be found, only a number of styles and interpretations — one laid upon the other in an endless and apparently meaningless process."[37]

Moreover, Ackroyd's novel shows that historians and biographers cannot check whether there are correspondences between their versions of history and the real events of the past because the latter are inaccessible except through textualized or visual representations, the authenticity of which is shown to be dubious at best. Fictional metabiographies like *Chatterton* thematize and blur the boundary between history and writing, because they draw attention to the "process of turning events into facts," "of turning the traces of the past [. . .] into historical representation."[38] The reader can compare the different versions of Chatterton's life and death delineated in the novel, but he or she cannot compare these versions with what they are supposed to depict, that is, the enigmatic, irretrievable events of the past.

The structure of both the biographical quest and the intertextual network also serves as a means of foregrounding the textual form through which history is mediated, of highlighting the fact that it is impossible to know the past by any other than textual means. If textual and artistic representations provide the only solid reason for believing that someone like Chatterton existed, or died, at all, then *Chatterton* demonstrates that there "is no such thing as an objective past, let alone a recoverable figure of Chatterton."[39] Moreover, what is shown to have shaped English cultural history is not the life of the historical artist as such but the ways in which this life is handed down by the media and in which it persists in the minds of present-day people.

By undermining the notion of historical truth, biofictions or fictional metabiographies like *Chatterton* call into question the ontological boundary between fact and fiction, the real and the imaginary. Both the complex structure of the novel and the metabiographical self-consciousness of the protagonists overtly bring to the fore the creative and interpretive role of the biographer, who constructs rather than reconstructs history.

Exploring, crossing, and undermining the border between fiction and (factual) biography, fictional metabiographies like *Chatterton* problematize the whole issue of representation. The fact that *Chatterton*, to use Linda Hutcheon's words, "is a novel self-consciously, even excessively *about* representation — its illusions and its powers, its possibilities and its politics" further confirms the thesis that it is a fictional *meta*biography rather than just a biography.[40] Like many other postmodernist historical novels and fictional metabiographies, *Chatterton* displays that "crisis in representation" which Hans Bertens has identified as the "common denominator to all these postmodernisms [. . .]: a deeply felt loss of faith in our ability to represent the real."[41] Ackroyd's novel illustrates that narrative, as the narrativist school of metahistorians has convincingly demonstrated, is not a transparent medium for representing historical reality but something that imposes a specific narrative shape on events.

Although *Chatterton* relies mainly on such indirect or structural modes of poetological self-reflection as intertextuality and the juxtaposition of different time levels and different versions of events, quite a number of the epistemological and methodological problems faced by biographers and historians are also explicitly thematized in the novel. There are, for example, some self-conscious references to the discrepancy between life and writing, between history as it is experienced and history as a written record of something that happened in the past. Like the unresolved tensions between different versions of Chatterton's life and death, such comments expose the epistemological problems faced by any biographer. After reading several historical representations of Chatterton's life, Charles finds it more and more difficult to write a preface for his edition of Chatterton's faked autobiography:

> He could not now remember whether all this information came from the documents themselves, or from the biographies which Philip had lent him. In any case he noticed that each biography described a quite different poet: even the simplest observation by one was contradicted by another, so that nothing seemed certain. He felt that he knew the biographers well, but that he still understood very little about Chatterton. At first Charles had been annoyed by these discrepancies but then he was exhilarated by them: for it meant that anything became possible. If there were no truths, everything was true. (127)

Both the subject and the overt scepticism of these reflections serve to underline that *Chatterton* is a fictional metabiography rather than just a fictionalized recreation of Chatterton. Despite the high degree of uncertainty and scepticism that Ackroyd's novels characteristically display,[42] however, it is not the factual existence of past events that the themes and structures of *Chatterton* call in question, but only man's ability to know or faithfully represent the true course of history: "Of course there *is* a reality — [. . .] But [. . .] it is not one that can be depicted. There are no words to stamp the indefinite thing" (133). Henry Wallis comes to a similar conclusion as far as the possibilities of artistic representation are concerned: "But if all this could not be painted — for what hope was there of capturing the general life of the world upon a canvas — how was he to depict the human form itself?" (163).

Like Julian Barnes's *Flaubert's Parrot*, *Chatterton* is particularly concerned with the incommensurability between an experience and any recording of it, either in writing or in painting, and with the concomitant contingencies of historiographical and biographical endeavours. Ackroyd's novel alerts the reader to the idea that our models of both another person's life and of literary history are as much an intellectual construction (albeit not necessarily a fiction, as Hayden White maintains) as the fictional world projected in the novel. The epistemological and metabiographical implications of Ackroyd's novel suggest that artistic, historiographic, and biographical representations may offer a mediated form of access to the past but that they can never provide a transparent reflection or a reliable account of the life of an historical individual. The actual and chaotic dynamics of other people's lives and historical events elude any attempt at delineating them comprehensively in writing or in any other medium. An insurmountable gap remains between the life of a person and any representation thereof:

> The historical person is not identical with the images which people have made themselves and continue to make of him. He is the mysterious source, the essence from which they derive, the final reality of which they constitute varying reflections and different views.[43]

"Biography is [. . .] a convenient fiction": The Constructivist View of Biography as Exemplified in *Chatterton*

It can be argued that *Chatterton* is a typical example of postmodernist biofiction in at least three respects. First, like other postmodernist British biofictions, *Chatterton* provides an impressive range of examples of the recent phenomenon of genre blurring and ample proof that nowadays it has indeed become more than problematic to tell "what the limits are between the novel and the short story collection [. . .], the novel and the long poem [. . .], the novel and autobiography [. . .], the novel and history [. . .], the novel and biography."[44] Secondly, *Chatterton* exemplifies those innovative kinds of biofictions which I have suggested might be designated fictional metabiographies. Rather than merely representing an artist's life, these novels focus on the complex processes and problems of biographical reconstruction.

Thirdly, and arguably most importantly, fictional metabiographies exemplify a constructivist view of biography in that they expose both the incommensurability between an experience and any recording of it, either in writing or in the visual arts, and the concomitant contingencies and constructivity of life-writing. By highlighting the distance between historical lives and events and written representations thereof, postmodernist biofictions like *Chatterton* testify to what de Certeau regards as the central paradox of historiography. The implication inherent in the term biography suggests that the biographer creates a nexus between a past life and writing. Postmodernist historical biofictions remind the reader that the gulf between the real past and discourse, between life as it is experienced and as it appears in the form of a biography, is, in the end, unbridgeable.

The analysis of *Chatterton* here has shown that the metafictional and self-reflexive questioning of the conventions of biography and the structural emphasis on subjectivity and constructivity reveal a constructivist view of biography. The juxtaposition of incompatible versions of

Chatterton's life and death and the persistent subversion of any attempt
at integrating the different versions and viewpoints in one coherent
story can be read as a literary reflection of the view that writing biography, just like historiography, is a subjective and constructive process
which does not reproduce the past but constitutes only an intellectual
and verbal construct.[45] From a constructivist point of view, the real
events of the life of historical individuals and the facts established in the
writing of a biographer are separated by an unbridgeable gulf which biography, as the word itself implies, unsuccessfully tries to overcome.
Since biographies do mirror historical individuals but are narratives
which are observer-dependent constructs, each version necessarily reflects the preoccupations and personal predilections of the individual
biographer. The same applies, as the nineteenth-century plot-line of
Chatterton amply illustrates, to artistic representations.

Being concerned with the question of how much we can ever know
about either the past or another individual, biofictions like *Chatterton*
can be understood as fictional metabiographies about the recording of
history. Affirming the reality of history but denying the possibility of
any objective knowledge of the past, such biofictions illustrate de
Certeau's thesis that "the past is the fiction of the present."[46] The fact
that many recent British biofictions abound with self-conscious remarks
about the problems faced by biographers underlines the sort of epistemological scepticism or constructivism that has become a hallmark of
historiographic metafiction. Emphasizing the central role that the human observer plays in all cognitive processes, these novels show that
facts are not the objective properties of an observer-independent world,
but are to be conceptualized as intellectual constructs that result from
an observer's cognitive processes. Since they are constituted by the biographer him/herself rather than simply given, they reveal at least as
much about him or her as about the biographee. This scepticism with
regard to (wo)man's ability to acquire objective knowledge of the past
or of the life of a biographee is reflected in many of the metabiographical observations which foreground the interpretive role of the biographer and historian: "The historian is an indissoluble part of his history,
as the poet is of his poem, as the shadowy biographer is of his subject's
life . . . "[47] Elisabeth Bronfen's shrewd observation on *Possession* thus
applies equally well to the epistemological and metabiographical scepticism underlying *Chatterton*:

> The act of reconstructing proves to be coterminous with refashioning
> a past life and a past poetic identity. For in their effort at retracing the
> movements of the dead poet [. . .], these scholars hope textually to
> resurrect him. In the course of this gesture of critical resuscitation,

discovery of the past always also bears traits of a new design, last but
not least because it is meant to satisfy the scholarly desires of those
undertaking the search.[48]

Both the structure and the metabiographical self-consciousness of
postmodernist biofictions like *Chatterton*, *Flaubert's Parrot*, and *Possession* reflect a deep-rooted scepticism about the objective nature of biographic constructions and, even more so, about the ability of historians
and biographers to know the past by any other than textualized means.
Foregrounding the textual form through which history is mediated,
Chatterton implicitly calls into question key concepts of positivist biography and historiography like objectivity, unity, truth, causality and linear teleology. In *Chatterton*, the metabiographical reflections lead to
the conclusion that biography, for better or worse, often has to rely
mainly on conjecture: "Why should historical research not also remain
incomplete, existing as a possibility and not fading into knowledge?"
(213).

Presenting "a world of Imitations" (91) and deconstructing the
conventional distinction between originals, copies, and forgeries, *Chatterton* ultimately raises the question of whether it is possible at all to
distinguish between fiction and biography or historiography. Ackroyd
himself has suggested that the distinction between factual and fictional
biographies is questionable at best. Not only does he admit that he
thinks of biographies "as other novels,"[49] but he also characterizes the
image of T. S. Eliot that his (non-fictional?) biography projects as follows: "So I wasn't concerned with the real Eliot at any point, I was
concerned with my recreation of *an* Eliot."[50] Or, to put it another way,
"the trouble with history," as Charles observes in one of the many unmarked quotations from Oscar Wilde, is that it is "the one thing we
have to make up for ourselves" (226). Ackroyd himself supplies what
might be, if not the last word on the status of (fictional) biographies, at
least an apt summary of both his theory and his poetics of the genre:
"Biography is in that sense a convenient fiction."[51]

Notes

I should like to thank Jon Erickson very much for reading and commenting
on an earlier draft of this article. I am very grateful to Silke Schloen and
Carola Surkamp for checking the quotations and for their careful proof
reading.

[1] Malcolm Bradbury, *Mensonge* (Harmondsworth: Penguin, 1993), 29.

[2] Michel de Certeau, *The Writing of History*, trans. Tom Conley (New York: Columbia UP, 1988), xxvl.

[3] Bradbury, *Mensonge*, 29.

[4] All page references to *Chatterton* will be to the following edition: Peter Ackroyd, *Chatterton* (London: Abacus, Sphere Books, 1988).

[5] Cf. Linda Hutcheon, *The Politics of Postmodernism* (London and New York: Routledge, 1989), 95.

[6] Cf. Ina Schabert, *In Quest of the Other Person: Fiction as Biography* (Tübingen: Francke, 1990), 44. Given the multifarious ways in which genre conventions are blurred in contemporary biofictions it does not make sense to subsume all such novels under one rubric, be it "historiographic metafiction" or "fictional biography." The great variety of biofictions dealt with in the present volume testifies to the need for a typology of the different variations of fictional biography and biographical drama. For a typology of metafiction, see Werner Wolf, *Ästhetische Illusion und Illusionsdurchbrechung in der Erzählkunst: Theorie und Geschichte mit Schwerpunkt auf englischem illusionsstörenden Erzählen* (Tübingen: Niemeyer, 1993), 230–59; for a typology and poetics of historiographic metafiction, see Ansgar Nünning, *Von historischer Fiktion zu historiographischer Metafiktion, Bd. 1: Theorie, Typologie und Poetik des historischen Romans* (Trier: WVT, 1995), 297–343.

[7] de Certeau, *The Writing of History*, 10.

[8] Hermann Josef Schnackertz, "Peter Ackroyd's Fictions and the Englishness of English Literature," in *Anglistentag 1993 Eichstätt*, ed. Günther Blaicher and Brigitte Glaser (Tübingen: Niemeyer, 1994), 493–502 (495); see also A. D. Harvey, "The Cult of Chatterton amongst English Poets c. 1770–1820," *Zeitschrift für Anglistik und Amerikanistik* 39 (1991): 124–33.

[9] For a more comprehensive analysis with a different focus, see my essay "'Die Kopie ist das Original der Wirklichkeit:' Struktur, Intertextualität und Metafiktion als Mittel poetologischer Selbstreflexion in Peter Ackroyd's *Chatterton*," *Orbis Litterarum* 49 (1994): 27–51. Cf. also Brian Finney, "Peter Ackroyd, Postmodernist Play and *Chatterton*," *Twentieth Century Literature* 38.2 (1992): 240–61, and Annegret Maack, "Der Roman als Echokammer: Peter Ackroyds Erzählstrategien," in *Tales and "their telling difference." Zur Theorie und Geschichte der Narrativik: Festschrift zum 70. Geburtstag von Franz K. Stanzel*, ed. Herbert Foltinek, Wolfgang Riehle, and Waldemar Zacharasiewicz (Heidelberg: Winter,1993), 319–35.

[10] Cf. Schabert, *In Quest of the Other Person*, 35–36.

[11] Another feature linking the past and present in *Chatterton*, which cannot be adequately explored here, is the semantization of space. Ackroyd's novels, more than anyone else's perhaps, show that settings can be more than just the physical locations of a novel's action by focusing attention on places that are resonant with innumerable echoes of England's past. Just as in other Ackroyd novels, from his *The Great Fire of London* (1982) to *Hawksmoor* and *The*

House of Doctor Dee (1993) to his recent *Dan Leno and the Limehouse Golem* (1994), traces of the past in *Chatterton* are reflected in houses, streets, sites associated with local legends, place names, and architectural art.

[12] Cf. Maack, "Der Roman als Echokammer," 319, 332–33.

[13] Cf. Linda Hutcheon, *A Poetics of Postmodernism: History, Theory, Fiction* (New York and London: Routledge, 1988), 124–40.

[14] Elisabeth Wesseling, *Writing History as a Prophet: Postmodernist Innovations of the Historical Novel* (Amsterdam and Philadelphia: John Benjamins, 1991), 94. For the affinity between *Chatterton* and the structure of the detective novel, see also Maack, "Der Roman als Echokammer," 327, and John Peck, "The Novels of Peter Ackroyd," *English Studies* 75.5 (1994): 442–452 (442, 444).

[15] Peter Ackroyd, *English Music* (Harmondsworth: Penguin, 1992), n.p.

[16] Witness the many references to "echoes" in Peter Ackroyd, *First Light* (London: Abacus, Sphere Books, 1990), 33–4, 99, 152, 173–74, 183, 194, 239, 298, and the structure and use of allusions in *English Music*; see also Annegret Maack, "Charakter als Echo: Zur Poetologie fiktiver Biographien," in *Klassiker-Renaissance: Modelle der Gegenwartsliteratur*, ed. Martin Brunkhorst, Gerd Rohmann and Konrad Schoell (Tübingen: Stauffenburg, 1991), 247–58; Maack, "Der Roman als Echokammer," 322, 335, and Schnackertz, "Peter Ackroyd's Fictions," 498.

[17] T. S. Eliot, *The Sacred Wood: Essays on Poetry and Criticism* [1920] (London: Faber, 1972), 49. More than in any other of Ackroyd's novels, the notion of simultaneity is emphasized in *First Light*, as the following quotation may illustrate: "Everything on the earth existed with him, shared his time with him in an ever-receding present moment; everything was connected, but this network of invisible relations was a network of simultaneity. Damian had to assume that there was such a thing as the past but any evidence for it was part of the present, too. All the world had ever known was a succession of present moments" (134).

[18] For the recurrent topos of the library as the place where all the ages merge into a timeless present, see also Peter Ackroyd, *The House of Doctor Dee* (London: Hamish Hamilton, 1993): "I find my refuge from bleating tongues here in my library where all the ages lie silently before me. [. . .] What I have kept and preserved here are the notable jewels which I have found scattered across the land, so that in this library lies something of the treasure of Britain's antiquity" (65–66).

[19] Cf. Meredith's rhetorical question: "So the greatest realism is also the greatest fakery?" (139). Charles also observes that "Realism is just as artificial as surrealism, after all" (40).

[20] Cf. also the epigraph from Sir Joshua Reynolds's second *Discourse* that Ackroyd quotes at the beginning of *English Music*: "Invention, strictly speaking, is little more than a new combination of those images which have been previ-

ously gathered and deposited in the memory; nothing can come of nothing" (n.p.).

[21] Wesseling, *Writing History as a Prophet*, 136.

[22] On the significance of literary forgeries in the eighteenth century, see Ian Haywood, "The Making of History: Historiography and Literary Forgery in the Eighteenth Century," *Literature and History* 9.2 (1983): 139–51, and Andreas Höfele, "Die Originalität der Fälschung: Zur Funktion des literarischen Betrugs in England 1750–1800," *Poetica* 18 (1986): 75–95.

[23] Maack, "Charakter als Echo," 256; see also Finney, "Peter Ackroyd," 250ff.

[24] Peter Ackroyd, *Notes for a New Culture* (London: Alkin, 1993), 56.

[25] Peter Ackroyd, *T. S. Eliot* (London: Cardinal, Sphere Books, 1988), 118.

[26] Maack, "Der Roman als Echokammer," 323.

[27] Ackroyd, *Notes for a New Culture*, 64.

[28] Ackroyd, *T. S. Eliot*, 117.

[29] Maack, "Der Roman als Echokammer," 319, 330; see also Finney, "Peter Ackroyd," 251, 255, and Schnackertz, "Peter Ackroyd's Fictions," 500.

[30] Wesseling, *Writing History as a Prophet*, 136.

[31] Schnackertz, "Peter Ackroyd's Fictions," 500.

[32] Finney, "Peter Ackroyd," 244.

[33] Raymond Federman, "Imagination as Plagiarism [an unfinished paper . . .]," *New Literary History* 7 (1975/76): 563–578 (565).

[34] Maack, "Charakter als Echo," 256.

[35] Cf. Wesseling, *Writing History as a Prophet*, who provides one of the most comprehensive and succinct accounts of the "metahistorical dissection of historiography" going on in postmodernist historical novels (135).

[36] Peter Ackroyd, *First Light* (London: Abacus, Sphere Books, 1990), 37.

[37] Ackroyd, *T. S. Eliot*, 119.

[38] Hutcheon, *The Politics of Postmodernism*, 57.

[39] Finney, "Peter Ackroyd," 250.

[40] Hutcheon, *The Politics of Postmodernism*, 96.

[41] Hans Bertens, *The Idea of the Postmodern: A History* (London and New York: Routledge, 1995), 11.

[42] Cf, for example, *First Light*, 187: "No one was certain of anything any more. Orthodox theories and even the most reasonable calculations seemed to decay or to dissolve in the face of these discoveries. And, as the expectations of the archaeologists wavered and changed, so did the evidence itself; the closer they came to the actual stones and relics, the more these objects retreated into a kind of unknowability."

[43] Schabert, *In Quest of the Other Person*, 184.

[44] Hutcheon, *A Poetics of Postmodernism*, 9.

[45] For a detailed account of the possibilities of applying radical constructivism to readings of fiction, see Ansgar Nünning, "'The Past is the Fiction of the Present': Constructivist Reflections on Susan Daitch's *L. C.* as a Novel about the Recording of History," in *Historiographic Metafiction in Modern American and Canadian Literature*, ed. Bernd Engler and Kurt Müller (Paderborn: Schöningh, 1994), 279–98, in which I suggest that constructivism can open up productive new perspectives on the relationship between literary texts and their ontological, epistemological, and metahistoriographic implications.

[46] de Certeau, *The Writing of History*, 10.

[47] Antonia S. Byatt, *Possession: A Romance* (London: Vintage, 1991), 385.

[48] Elizabeth Bronfen, "Romancing Difference, Courting Coherence: A. S. Byatt's *Possession* as Postmodern Moral Fiction," in *Why Literature Matters: Theories and Functions of Literature*, ed. Rüdiger Ahrens and Laurenz Volkmann (Heidelberg: Winter, 1996), 117–34 (122).

[49] Quoted from Finney, "Peter Ackroyd," 246; originally printed in Patrick McGrath, "Peter Ackroyd," *BOMB* 26 (1988/89): 44–47 (46).

[50] Quoted from Maack, "Der Roman als Echokammer," 333; originally printed in McGrath, "Peter Ackroyd," 47; also Finney, "Peter Ackroyd," 245. Cf. also the observation that the fictionalized Oscar Wilde makes in Ackroyd's novel *The Last Testament of Oscar Wilde* (London: Abacus, Sphere Books, 1984): "It was of no concern to me if the facts were accurate or inaccurate. I had discovered a truth which was larger than that of biography and history" (121).

[51] Ackroyd, *T. S. Eliot*, 239.

BERNHARD REITZ

Dangerous Enthusiasm: The Appropriation of William Blake in Adrian Mitchell's *Tyger*

A DRIAN MITCHELL'S *TYGER*, SUBTITLED *A Celebration Based on the Life and Work of William Blake*, is a poet's homage to a poet. However, it can be called an appropriation as well, serving purposes that reach beyond a reverential visualization of one who is certainly the most enigmatic of the Romantic poets. This article will discuss the scope of this appropriation and the artistic means employed in *Tyger*.

Breaking the Rules for the Theatre?

Adrian Mitchell, poetry editor of the *New Statesman & Society* since 1994, was already an acknowledged poet when he turned to playwriting. His first production, *The Ledge*, an opera with music by Richard Bennett, was performed in 1961 and became a moderate success. But it was to kindle a lifelong interest in musical theatre. Mitchell's gift for poetic speech in drama met wider recognition when he provided the verse adaptation of Geoffrey Skelton's translation of Peter Weiss's *Die Verfolgung und Ermordung Jean Paul Marats* (*The Persecution and Assassination of Marat as Performed by the Inmates of the Asylum of Charenton under the Direction of the Marquis de Sade*). During the London season of 1964, the response to Weiss's *Marat* was no less enthusiastic than it had been on the continent. In spite of the manifold conceptual differences between the two works, there is no doubt that *Marat* partly inspired Mitchell to try his hand at biographical drama. For, like Weiss had done with the protagonists of his play, Mitchell attempts to envisage the protagonists of *Tyger* in the context of revolutionary ideas.

Marat was a production of the Royal Shakespeare Company (RSC), directed by Peter Brook. Before he was to complete *Tyger*, Mitchell took part in another of this team's projects. In 1966, he contributed to *US*, the RSC's protest against the war in Vietnam, which was considered a theatrical scandal, not only because of the gratuitous burning of a butterfly during each performance. *US* was no less politically dedicated theatre than *Marat*, although in its use of techniques of montage and collage it pursued distinctively different aesthetic concepts. Both theatrical events though were devised as deliberate deviations from those established realistic conventions of political drama that Robert Bolt was to employ as late as 1977 in *State of Revolution* and which, for example, reduce Rolf Hochhuth's *Der Stellvertreter* (1962) to a sequence of politically controversial but dramatically wooden dialogues.

Mitchell has described his cooperation with Peter Brook as a formative experience.[1] His interest in theatrical experimentation is further evidenced by his work with Welfare State, which, according to Catherine Itzin, was "one of the most sophisticated 'performance arts' groups of the seventies."[2] Moreover, when the National Theatre — certainly not unimpressed by the public resonance of both *Marat* and *US* — decided to produce *Tyger* in the summer of 1971, the play was entrusted to Michael Blakemore and John Dexter, two directors of renown. And even though Mitchell was to match his successes of the sixties neither with *Tyger* nor with his later plays, he continued to work with important directors such as Peter Hall, for whose production of *The Magic Flute* he wrote a new verse adaptation of the libretto. However, on the basis of John L. DiGaetani's interview with Mitchell, the assumption that these distinguished directors might decisively have shaped Mitchell's notions of playwriting is revealed as unfounded. In key with his statement that he is as fond of *Oklahoma!* as he is of Brecht, Mitchell comments upon the "topic of postmodernist theatre" thus:

> It's a bit difficult to think of your own work in terms of a reaction against something. I myself love Beckett. I think his plays are absolutely supreme. I can't do that. I also don't think I'm reacting against Beckett, but unlike him I'm a populist I suppose. I greatly admire Willy Russell, who is currently writing for the theatre, and he's a populist in the best sense, like Dickens.[3]

Even for the seventies, when notions about postmodernism, and postmodernism in the theatre especially, were still somewhat vague, such a simplistic differentiation would have been inadequate.

For the nineties, Mitchell's argument is stunningly unfocused. But as evidenced by the interview, Mitchell is not prepared to respond to a probing for a theoretically more ambitious delineation of his poetics of drama. Instead of commenting upon the intertextual elements of *Tyger* or the play's possible conceptualization as a post-Wagnerian *Gesamt-kunstwerk*, he rather seeks to explain why he is so intrigued by Russell:

> I think Willy identifies with his audience, I don't think he ever writes
> down to them. I think he speaks to them like brothers, like the Beatles
> used to sing when they first used to perform. Russell's plays [. . .]
> have a wonderful kind of integrity. Russell's works sometimes break all
> sorts of rules for the theatre, but I find his work irresistibly moving.
> It's truthful. Andrew Lloyd Webber's work is about as truthful as the
> Stock Exchange.[4]

It is obvious that moral categories such as integrity and truthfulness supersede poetological considerations. Mitchell prefers Brendan Behan to Brecht because Behan is "less intellectual," and for the same reason he favours the kind of straightforward political argumentation which distinguished the productions of Joan Littlewood. Repeatedly, Mitchell asserts his predilection for a "kind of rough, British folk theatre," "a rough song and dance kind of play" which draws heavily upon the traditions of the British and Irish music-hall.[5] These preferences underscore that ambiguity of character and situation is not a prime concern to him. But whether such presuppositions are sufficient to deal with a character as complex as William Blake, as well as with the intricate referentiality of Blake's poetry and paintings, is open to debate. Mitchell's interview belatedly confirms what, in a not at all condescending review, Mary Holland had written about *Tyger* in 1971:

> To be honest, I think the National audience has every justification to
> feel embarrassed and often bored by *Tyger*, if only because its proper
> place is not the National Theatre nor the West End. Its natural home
> is the market or the closest we can get to it in our theatre now — pro-
> vincial companies with young audiences, community centres, the
> Roundhouse.[6]

By describing *Tyger* as "a play in poster colours with poster thoughts,"[7] Holland neatly summed up the reservations expressed by the leading London critics. Charles Marowitz, then still the dedicated champion of all that was experimental in theatre, rallied to Mitchell's side and denounced the critics as "a bunch of well-educated, rather articulate, not-very-demanding journalists who do their rounds." Marowitz defended *Tyger* as a breaking away from "30 years of arid playwriting" and as being "obscenely misunderstood and underestimated."[8] However, with the advantage of hindsight and without the pressure of having to take sides on the issue of British drama's future in the seventies, *Tyger* can be assessed more even-temperedly.

To those in the audience who had been won over to the National Theatre (NT) by Laurence Olivier and who were willing to accept such extensions of the well made play as *The Entertainer* had provided, but would not readily go further, *Tyger* was a challenge indeed. The governing principle of *Tyger* is discontinuity of time, place, and action. And even if the first act builds up to a proper climax, the division into two acts seems more a concession to the audience's right to a drink during an interval than a dramaturgical requirement. Apart from scant references to Blake's biography, linear chronology is not only neglected but deliberately upset. The play begins in the studio of Sir Joshua Rat, introducing Reynolds and the Academy School as Blake's artistic antagonists. But numerous references, such as, for example, to the BBC or the Arts Council as well as to latter-day protagonists make it clear from the very beginning that there will be no separation between past and present. The biographical approach as suggested by the subtitle is not based upon a coherent historical perspective, and the dissolution of historical time into simultaneousness reaches its peak in the second act. It is Blake's birthday. But the event is revealed to be an anniversary, with Blake commenting upon the "Blake industry" which has appropriated him while he has "been dead for more than a hundred years."[9] The audience is given no time though to ponder how far scholarship may have created a distorted image of Blake, and to what degree the play is about to set this right. For, beginning with Chaucer and ending with Allen Ginsberg, the great British and American poets do arrive to celebrate. This set-up includes the Romantic Revival Band,

> [. . .] the heaviest of all the super-groups — The Romantic Revival! Willy Wordsworth on drums. Percy Bysshe Shelley — bass guitar. Samuel Taylor Coleridge. John Keats. And the singer, you've guessed it, star of sex, screen and Missolonghi — Bad Lord Byron! (*Group appear as they are named*. KEATS *and* COLERIDGE *harmonize behind* BYRON's *vocal*). (62)

In their birthday song, the Romantics praise Blake as the "Tyger of Jerusalem and Lamb of London" (63), and he is credited with not only having dreamed of a new Jerusalem, but with actually having built it. However, the apotheosis of this anniversary out of time is more sinister. Mitchell lets the conviviality fade into a courtroom scene, whereafter, by order of mad King George III, Blake is literally shot to the moon, exiled as an intransigent and ever dangerous arch-revolutionary.

In *Tyger* the discontinuity of historical time provides the framework for the no less encompassing discontinuity of place and action. Mitchell's play moves fast, and in the virtuosity of the transitions be-

tween scenes at least, an influence of Peter Brook's reflections on the
possibilities of the empty space can be recognized. Changes of location
and scene are not realized by shoving about elaborate props. Although
Mitchell makes use of projections, including some of Blake's finest
drawings, these too are subservient to the predominantly verbal, imaginative creation of scenic change. The "heightened language" of poetry
is employed to enhance and to define characters and issues through the
contrastive use of verse and prose. Moreover, poetry creates the space
for bringing the full repertoire of non-realistic means of presentation
into play, foremost those which include music. However, vaudeville
and music-hall quotations, musical, song and dance are not only dis-
tinctive markers of scene changes. Within the scenes, their function is
to focus issues which the sheer pace of the play allows no time to be
developed in depth. The little song sung by Blake at the end of the bar-
room scene in Act One, a quotation from Blake's "Annotations," illustrates how both these functions can be combined:

> When Sir Joshua Reynolds died
> All Nature was degraded;
> The king drop'd a tear in the Queen's Ear,
> And all his pictures faded. (20)

Blake sings these verses from the orchestra, while on the stage the tran-
sition from the bar-room to the Home Office is taking place. In spite of
their apparent simplicity, within the play the verses are a neat summary
of the previous discussions as well as of Reynolds's public role. At the
same time, by linking Reynolds to the monarchy, they also establish
Blake as a clear-sighted rebel in both the artistic and the political
sphere, thus foreshadowing the role Mitchell has assigned to the poet.
This employment of verse and song as summary, commentary and foreshadowing bears a striking resemblance to John Arden's structuring of
Live Like Pigs (1958) by means of songs, and, given their shared interest in verse in the theatre, it can be assumed that Mitchell was acquainted with Arden's play.

   However, more often than not the possibilities of musical theatre as
understood by Mitchell are not made use of as convincingly. The performance of the Romantics as a pop group, entertaining as it may be, is
an example in point. It fails to establish a perspective that would help to
illuminate the relationship between Blake and the Romantics, and it is
not an implicit comment upon the Romantics as a group or a movement either. Their celebratory birthday song is complimentary, but
much too superficial and unfocused as a comment on Blake's lasting

significance. In the style of the music-hall it builds up to a gratuitous joke told by Coleridge as a dream about Dylan Thomas:

> So I [Coleridge] said: 'The trouble with England is, poets are treated like shit.' And Dylan looked up and shook his head and he grinned at me and he said: 'No. The trouble with England is, *most* people are treated like shit.' (64)

Tyger abounds with examples of Mitchell's readiness to suspend or even to sacrifice an argument for the effects of a joke or a gag. But while latter-day readers or viewers might welcome this bathos as a counterbalance to the play's pathos, contemporary reviewers were offended by what they felt to be a lack of direction and formal discipline. In hindsight though, it becomes more obvious that in its structural conceptualization *Tyger* is very much a play typical of the spirit of the seventies. It evidences a lingering exuberance that centuries of censorship had come to an end, an exuberance which, in terms of sexual and verbal provocation, the Traverse Theatre's production of *Lay By* was to voice much more explicitly in the same year. Even if the appearance of the "Three Randy Women," who advertise their manifold sexual preferences in song, as well as the ensuing dialogue between Blake and Kate about how to bring about a clitoral orgasm (30–34) had seemed as gratuitous and juvenile in 1971 as they do now, it should not be forgotten that *Oh Calcutta!* was once discussed as a serious theatrical experiment. Neither should it be forgotten that before 1968 no joke with a four-letter word in it, nor any spoof of political institutions such as the Home Office or MI5 would have passed the censor either.

However, beyond the innocently anarchic relish in saying and doing on stage what had been forbidden for so long, a more serious structural problem emerges. When asked about an aesthetic commitment possibly shared by the young political playwrights, David Hare as late as 1975 responded thus:

> [. . .] I don't think either Howard [Brenton] or myself were ever technically innovative writers. We can now command the standards we want, the style of presentation that we want, there's never any argument about how the plays are to be done, where five or six years ago there would have been.[10]

Tyger exemplifies the point that in the seventies the exuberance about free speech in the theatre was extended to the self-assured belief that with the demise of the well-made play all poetological demands on playwriting had been abandoned for good. By his unstructured inclusion of just about everything that had been excluded by realistic drama up to that point, Mitchell too professed that he could now command the standards he wanted. Therefore it would be wrong to say that *Tyger* deliberately broke the rules of theatre, whatever they may be thought to be. *Tyger* is an assertion that there were no rules any longer and that the playwright was now free to choose whatever style of presentation he wanted. And because of this, the discontinuity that distinguishes *Tyger* is more than just a formal device. At least in terms of the discussion of the seventies, the very structure of *Tyger* was meant to be a political, revolutionary statement, an assertion of the freedom believed to be newly won. However, the question remains whether this commitment to the denial of form is also convincingly linked to the presentation of Blake as well as to the issues he is shown to be involved in.

Empire against Art, Remember?

When George Devine stepped down as artistic director of the English Stage Company in 1965, he proudly declared, "we fought the commercial theatre and won."[11] As early as 1961 though John Osborne had warned, "the big danger of the 1960s is the formation of a new theatre Establishment."[12] In the seventies, the majority of those who were part of Britain's theatrical set-up, especially those playwrights who still had to make their way, were more inclined to agree with Osborne. The enthusiasm of the swinging sixties had waned. Neither the RSC nor the NT nor the Arts Council had met the often exaggerated hopes of the new playwrights, who felt their talents were being wasted in the fringe, and Britain's then progressive economic decline gave no reason to expect that the Arts Council would ever be enabled to increase its support. In politics, the government's reaction to the war in Vietnam, as well as the student revolt of 1968, had confirmed the belief that the establishment's sinister control of both the arts and politics was far from being broken. And although Bond's *Lear* and Pinter's *Old Times* also premièred in 1971, these were not the plays that provided the context for *Tyger*. Mitchell has to be seen against the background of the deliberate anti-establishment productions of the fringe of that year. There, Arden and D'Arcy's *Two Hundred Years of Labour History*, *My Old Man's a Tory*, and *Granny Welfare and the Wolf* as well as David Edgar's *Tedderella* and *The National Interest* and Charles Wood's *Welfare* all asserted that the gap between "them" and "us" was not closing but widening again.

In *Tyger*, Mitchell is not out to challenge notions of an archconspiracy of the establishment. He confirms the fringe perspective by introducing "Rat" Reynolds as an ultra-conservative in the realm of arts as well as the sycophantic protégé of the rich and mighty who have procured his services as portraitist. This latter aspect is foregrounded by Mitchell and explains why Reynolds is never a match for Blake. For while Blake is stolidly unperturbed in his belief in his art, Reynolds is shown constantly worrying that a change of taste in painting might put an end to his social climbing. In politics, Reynolds's counterpart is the Home Secretary, likewise worried about anything that might threaten the stability of the system he profits from. By admonishing his vile secret agent, "Don't underestimate culture, Crab. Empire against art, remember?" (21), the Home Secretary also defines the binary opposition in *Tyger*, an opposition which translates as the Establishment versus the arts.

Such an opposition could leave ample space for a discussion of the period's theories of art and their possible political implications. But it becomes apparent very soon that a discriminating inquiry into what was revolutionary in Blake's art is no concern of Mitchell's. The initial barroom discussion between Reynolds and Blake, focusing on whether or not art should express the passions, is not developed beyond a banter. It only leads up to a brawl during which Reynolds's followers try to beat up Blake for not being appreciative enough of both the President of the Royal Academy and of the Arts Council's support of artists. And although Mitchell very effectively makes use of Blake's drawings for the illumination of scenes, even recreates them as *tableaux vivantes*, a proper discussion of art theory or poetry is not resumed thereafter. When, in the second act, Johann Heinrich Füßli (Henry Fuseli) is introduced as a supportive friend of Blake's, there, too, the artistic relationship between these two painters, both progressive and provocative in their time, is passed over.

Even given the fact that Blake's intricate referentiality of verse and image, as well as his complex symbolism, cannot be unravelled easily within short and fast-moving scenes, their nearly total exclusion from the argument must be considered a serious deficiency as well as evidence of how the play's refutation of a sustained, structured argument can turn against itself. *Tyger* volubly commits itself to the cause of revolution in art, but at the same time the play gives no coherent idea of what this revolution might consist of. Instead, rather smugly, it relies on the audience's presupposed knowledge of Blake, pretending like Russell's disillusioned professor in *Educating Rita* that Blake is essentially "simple" and "uncomplicated."[13] However, an audience that would bring a knowledge of Blake to the play would of necessity also be an audience that expects a more discriminating approach. Moreover, it would also become wary of the professed support for what is new in art when for the gratification of popular prejudice, a piece of art is described as something "the Tate Gallery thought [to be] a fake Salvador Dali by Salvador Dali," as Mitchell does (47).

In *Tyger*, it becomes evident very soon that Mitchell's interest is not the poetological, theoretical state of the arts past or present, but the culture industry and particularly the Arts Council's involvement in it. Throughout the introductory scenes, it is stressed that established artists, intellectuals and political representatives are part of a network. Klopstock, introduced as a member of the "British Cultural Committee," admires Reynolds, and it does not come as a surprise that Reynolds himself is a committee member. The committee is chaired by Lord Nobodaddy and includes Lady Twat, "an amateur author and censor" (36). Predictably she takes offence with what she falsely assumes to be a sexual reference, while later on she turns out to be as randy as her name suggests.

Mitchell places Blake's application for a grant from the committee at the center of Act One. But before Blake is heard, another applicant, Evelyn Graze, a society lady and editor of a literary magazine, is allowed to plead her case. As it turns out, she does not need the money for her obviously only superficial literary endeavours, but to meet "the rent and rates in St James Place," and she concludes:

> Now I know that belles lettres mean a great deal to you,
> And seven thousand every year would see me through.
> So do it for culture,
> Do it for literature,
> Do it for — Mummy! (37)

Since Evelyn Graze is apparently prepared to reward Lord Nobodaddy's generosity, she gets three thousand more than she has asked for, and after their unanimous decision, the committee members "hurl themselves into a rapid-fire orgy of groping, thrusting, back-scratching, feeling and puffing" (39).

Having thus established that the Arts Council is guided in its decisions by incompetence, class prejudice, nepotism, and, above all, lust, what remains to be proved is that a true artist stands no chance with it. Having waited for "forty-five years," and having been denounced as a madman by Southey, who himself is introduced as a drug-addict (40), Blake is ushered in and allowed to plead his case by reading from Plate Twelve of *Jerusalem*. When Blake notices that the committee members do not pay any attention at all, he turns to the audience and concludes his visionary lines with the appeal, "go on, builders in hope" (42). It is at this point at the latest that it becomes apparent how Blake is instrumentalized by Mitchell for purposes that can be related to him in only the most general way. As far as Evelyn Graze's application is concerned, the committee scene is scarcely more than a spoof at the expense of the Arts Council. Blake's function within this context, though, is twofold. First of all, his blatant rejection by the committee is meant to elevate the spoof to the level of a serious accusation. His case is used to substantiate the conviction prevalent in the seventies' fringe that state support for the arts was in fact a conspiracy to destroy the truly relevant — that is politically relevant — arts. As late as 1980, in his lampooning of Mrs. Thatcher's first cabinet in *A Short Sharp Shock!*, Howard Brenton was still spreading this idea. Yet at the same time Blake, or more precisely his belated acknowledgement as a great artist, is supposed to assert that true art can be neither suppressed nor destroyed. The audience to which Blake directs his appeal is therefore not addressed as the more objective evaluators of his application, but is supposed to be moved and to agree to a political statement. This appropriation of Blake for both accusation and self-affirmation, within a context that relates neither to his historical situation nor his art, makes even more pertinent the question of whether Blake's delineation as a revolutionary is equally unspecific.

Dangerous Enthusiasm

In his author's note to *Marat* Peter Weiss writes that his interest in "the conflict between an individualism carried to extreme lengths and the idea of a political and social upheaval" gave the play its shape.[14] That Blake approached the revolutionary ideas of his time, whether they were American, French, or British, with an extreme individualism was established very early on by Blake scholarship. Moreover, in a more recent study, Jon Mee has convincingly argued that the radicalism of Blake's rhetoric in the 1790s is much more fundamental than those critics who have stressed Blake's idealism have asserted.[15] Central images of Blake's poetry such as the "Tree of Mystery" include a political referentiality upon which a dramatic visualization of the poet as political agitator could well be founded. Of course, *Tyger* cannot be measured by the yardstick of later Blake criticism. But, at least in the second half of this century, anyone genuinely interested in Blake's ideas about revolution can draw upon a wealth of sources.

However, although there is no evidence of what Mitchell read about Blake, his choice of quotations does not confirm a very detailed interest. With but few exceptions, such as the lines on Reynolds quoted above, Mitchell draws upon the *Songs of Innocence and Experience* and, even more encompassingly, on *Jerusalem*. Quite obviously, he prefers those texts that a British audience would readily associate with the poet. Moreover, Mitchell has deliberately selected those poems or stanzas which are seemingly easy to understand and which can also be received as a direct comment on the corresponding situation in the play. Thus, when he is sentenced by King George, Blake retorts by quoting from "A Divine Image,"

> Cruelty has a Human Heart,
> And Jealousy a Human Face;
> Terror the Human Form Divine,
> And secrecy the Human Dress. (81)

Within *Tyger* though, this is also Blake's harshest pronouncement on the darker sides of human nature. For although the Romantics celebrate him somewhat mystifyingly as "Tyger of Jerusalem and Lamb of London" (63), in contrast to the play's very title, Mitchell takes great pains to evoke on stage the lamb rather than the tiger. Of the "two contrary states of the human soul" that create the tension constitutive to the *Songs*, Mitchell's Blake betrays nothing. Nor is he shown as the religious visionary he was, struggling for a prophetic realignment of Christianity, philosophy, and cosmogony that could explain man's contradictory nature and without which Blake's conviction of the necessity and the inevitability of a revolution cannot be understood. In short, everything that is complex and difficult about Blake is deliberately left out in favour of what turns out to be a Sunday school adaptation for the less well-read sons and daughters of Albion.

In *Tyger*, Blake is depicted as a loving husband and father who explicitly appreciates that children are capable of understanding his work:

> [. . .] I am happy to find a great majority of fellow mortals who can elucidate my visions, and particularly they have been elucidated by children, who have taken a greater delight in my pictures than I ever hoped. Neither youth nor childhood is folly or incapacity. Some children are fools, and so are some old men. (24)

That Blake here does not speak of contemporary reactions to his art but rather entrusts his work to more appreciative future generations becomes apparent in Act Two. There Reynolds and the Mad King indulge in a colloquy on the merits of baby-bashing, but at the same time express their fears that those well-bashed children might grow up and hit back (73). In contrast to their savagery and that of the system, Mitchell enhances Blake's altruism in two consecutive episodes later in the play. The second of these is convincing, as it shows Blake accepting the commission to illustrate J. G. Stedman's *Narrative* as a means of protesting against slavery.[16] However, this can hardly be said of the first, where Schofield, in *Tyger* the military tool of the powers that be, teases Blake by deliberately beating up the mechanical creature described as a Salvatore Dali faked by Dali. Blake attempts to buy the creature so that it is spared further misery, but suddenly finds himself the object of an auction from which he is saved by Stedman. As a scene preparatory to the encounter with Stedman, Blake's attempt to save the mechanical creature is not badly contrived. But as confirmation of both Blake's altruism as well as the first act's repeated curtain line, "for every thing that lives is Holy," it is far-fetched and hardly convincing.[17]

Mitchell leaves no doubt that his Blake is essentially a lamb, but at times his Blake is also in doubt whether he should not be a tiger. This becomes most apparent in his protest at the auction: "Flesh is not property. I can breathe. You can't buy my breath. My thoughts go on. I am a lamb. It is impossible to own a lamb. I am a tiger — " (50).

Whenever Blake is confronted with a direct threat, as in the assault of the "three intellectuals," he is prepared to hit back. Nor, being somewhat astoundingly able to control the creatures of his visions, does he hesitate to scare away the agent Crab by summoning the "Ghost of a Flea" to his studio. He reacts in the same vein when he encounters Reynolds in the supermarket. Having shoved his opponent into a pile of collapsing cans in his own shopping cart, Blake comments in the spirit of '68, "if you can't beat 'em, fuck 'em" (45). It is quite obvious that Mitchell does not want his Blake to be misunderstood as a wilt.

This reductive interpretation of Blake as a predominantly altruistic man would — within limits — be acceptable if it were not the play's implicit justification of an even more reductive interpretation of *Jerusalem*. At the end of *Jerusalem*, "All Human Forms identified, even Tree, Metal, Earth & Stone,"[18] although it is doubtful whether Blake had mechanical creatures in mind as well. Plate Ninety-Nine suggests that in the new Jerusalem all contradictions might be resolved. But, as evidenced by the ninety-eight previous plates, they are not to be resolved easily. By leaving out these arguments, Mitchell's Blake advertises a significantly different message, which seems as if it could have been derived from *The Rocky Horror Picture Show*'s motto, "Don't dream it — be it!" Even in his exile on the moon, Mitchell's Blake is clearly confident that the building of the New Age is already under way: "Revolutionaries, *all with their own visions of the Revolution*, will bring it about" (85, my italics).

As a reading of Blake, Mitchell's interpretation of *Jerusalem* is blatantly superficial, a reduction to nothing but the proposition that revolution is inevitable and that it will be triumphant. Moreover, it reverses basic notions about Blake and his time. For far from showing

Blake bringing the Romantic imagination to bear upon encrusted concepts of eighteenth-century rationalism, Blake and his beloved Kate turn out to be the only rational people in a mad world. Marowitz has described Mitchell's Blake as "a kind of catch-all symbol for every maverick, every victim of social injustice."[19] In *Tyger*, Blake is indeed a triumphant maverick, albeit one who is so removed from the man whose name he bears that he could well bear another. For increasingly obvious reasons Mitchell turns Blake into an icon. He celebrates not Blake, but the idea of poets being an embodiment of revolutionary energy and the trustees of a better future. All this requires the removal of everything that is biographically or historically unique about Blake. If the exploitation of Blake is a feature of the Blake industry, then certainly *Tyger* is part of it.

To those in the seventies who felt that there had to be a revolution, Mitchell's re-cast Blake did give affirmation and consolation at the same time. He is meant to encourage the hope that not only the theatre, but also the system can be changed if only one continues to write against it long enough. However, when the revolution came, it bore the name of Mrs. Thatcher.

Notes

[1] Adrian Mitchell interviewed by John L. DiGaetani in John L. DiGaetani, *A Search for a Postmodern Theatre: Interviews with Contemporary Playwrights* (London: Greenwood Press, 1991), 232.

[2] Catherine Itzin, *Stages in the Revolution: Political Theatre in Britain Since 1968* (London: Eyre Methuen, 1980), 70.

[3] DiGaetani, *Postmodern Theatre*, 234.

[4] DiGaetani, *Postmodern Theatre*, 235.

[5] DiGaetani, *Postmodern Theatre*, 234.

[6] Mary Holland, "Tyger," *Plays and Players* 18.12 (September 1971): 31.

[7] Holland, "Tyger," 30.

[8] Charles Marowitz, "'Tyger' Roars, but No One Is Listening," *The New York Times Theatre Review 1971–1972*, Ag 8, II:3:7.

[9] Adrian Mitchell, *Tyger: A Celebration Based on the Life and Work of William Blake* (London: Jonathan Cape, 1971), 59. All subsequent page references in the text are to this edition.

[10] "Commanding the style of presentation — David Hare interviewed by Catherine Itzin," *New Theatre Voices of the Seventies*, ed. Simon Trussler (London: Eyre Methuen, 1981), 117.

[11] J. C. Trewin, *Drama in Britain: 1951–1964* (London: Longmans, 1965), 6.

[12] John Osborne, "That Awful Museum," *English Dramatic Theories IV: 20th Century*, ed. Paul Goetsch (Tübingen: Max Niemeyer, 1972), 104.

[13] Willy Russell, *Educating Rita* (London: Methuen, 1981), II, 3.

[14] Peter Weiss, *The Persecution and Assassination of Marat as performed by the Inmates of the Asylum of Charenton under the Direction of the Marquis de Sade* (London: Calder and Boyars, 1965), 113.

[15] Jon Mee, *Dangerous Enthusiasm: William Blake and the Culture of Radicalism in the 1790s* (Oxford: Clarendon, 1992).

[16] Blake produced most of these engravings in 1793. The work they illustrate was published in 1796, under the title of *A Narrative, of a five Year's expedition, against the Revolted Negroes of Surinam, in Guiana, on the Wild Coast of South America; from the years 1772 to 1777,* by Captain J. G. Stedman.

[17] It should be noted though that Mitchell's stage directions assign a more-than-personal meaning to the creature: "*When hit, it emits sounds of despair, which should not be the sounds of one identifiable animal, but a mixture of sounds of animals, humans, wood, water and metal under pressure*" (44).

[18] *The Complete Writings of William Blake,* ed. Geoffrey Keynes (London: Oxford UP, 1966), 747.

[19] Marowitz, "'Tiger' Roars."

JILL RUBENSTEIN

Auld Acquaintance:
New Lives of Scott and Hogg

THE READER OF FICTION COLLABORATES WITH THE author; together they confer identity upon a character in a shaped narrative which, because it *is* shaped, is inherently artificial. The analytical reader of autobiography, however, is more likely to regard the author sceptically as a highly suspect, self-appointed authority figure, at best a manipulator and at worst a liar. Like fiction, autobiography is shaped narrative and thus artificial; nevertheless, no matter how mendacious, all autobiography is inherently *true* because it is always performative. That is, writing the narrative with all its attempts to reveal or to conceal is itself an act revelatory of the writer. Any kind of self-inscription, therefore, is inevitably both reflexive and representational. In drama, character develops not through narrative but through a series of encounters and social relationships, one of which, the relationship with the audience, shares many of the qualities of narrative. When the play is autobiographical, or based on fiction which is autobiographical, it becomes doubly performative, both as drama and as self-representation.

In *The Ragged Lion* Allan Massie offers a work of fiction closely based upon Walter Scott's autobiographical writings, primarily his *Journal*, begun in 1825, as well as Scott's authorized biographer John Gibson Lockhart's *Memoirs of the Life of Walter Scott*.[1] The text is supposedly derived from a manuscript bequeathed in 1993 to the ostensible editor by an elderly Neapolitan contessa. He had first encountered it twenty-nine years earlier seated "at a rococo table in the library of her apartment in the family palazzo" (viii). The contessa identified it then as a copy of Scott's final memoir, written in the last two years of his life and inadvertently abandoned in the Casa Bernini, his lodgings in Rome, when Scott, ill and only intermittently in full possession of his faculties, departed for his final journey home. The original was then given to Charles Scott after his father's death as he returned through Rome to his post at the British Legation in Naples. The contessa, an unlikely but knowledgeable devotée of Scottish literature, discloses that "Charles Scott presented [this copy] to my great-great-grandmother" and hints coyly of a romantic liaison between them (xii). Charles supposedly turned over the original to Lockhart, who used and then destroyed it, thus accounting for the marked resemblance between the two. The tale recalls the mildewed grandeur of "The Aspern Papers," especially when Massie compares Lockhart's destruction of the original to "the burning of Byron's memoirs by those who believed they were caring for his reputation" (xiii).[2]

Although the editor believes those passages in the memoir of "deep distress and confusion of mind" (xiii) actually demonstrate Scott's finest qualities of nobility and courage, he speculates that Lockhart must have thought otherwise and chosen not to use them. Thus, Massie gives himself freedom to invent incidents found nowhere else while covering his tracks when he does purloin material directly from the *Life*. The editor concedes that the manuscript might be "a fabrication," but he professes to believe the contessa's story.

The introduction deliberately blurs actuality and fiction, referring at one point to the Edinburgh edition of the Waverley novels and at another to Massie's own visit to Hastie's Close where, alas, raucous rock music prevented him from sharing Scott's supernatural encounters. The acknowledgements first cite the fictional Contessa, and then proceed to hot decidedly real people. On one point the editor notes a remarkable similarity between the memoir and A. N. Wilson's *The Laird of Abbotsford* congratulating Wilson on his "remarkable percipience" (xv), since he could not possibly have seen the manuscript, thus permitting Massie to acknowledge a debt without violating the fiction.

The "Afterword by Charles Scott, Esq." is subscribed Naples, March 1833. Charles claims he is the only person who knows of the memoir's existence. Although unsure precisely when Scott wrote it, Charles believes it was "during the last year of his life, and mostly during his sojourn in Italy" even though he "contrived" to make it appear the work of five or six years (230). In addition, he notes, the unnumbered pages may have been jumbled out of sequence. Thus, Massie cleverly sows uncertainty so that his Scott need not be overly scrupulous about chronology.

Charles attributes Scott's apparent credulity in the supernatural episodes to his "disordered and sadly perplexed fancy" (230). He recalls the three sources of guilt on which his father dwelt toward the end of his life. Here Massie invokes familiar questions about Scott's obsession with Abbotsford and about his marriage. The third source of guilt, the young boy "Green-breeks, 'the perfect specimen of the young Goth,'" comes as a surprise to the reader, who has only briefly encountered him in Lockhart.[3] As Scott's alter ego, Green-breeks dances "with the girl who is the Temptress, the Enchantress, the Queen of Elfland" and appears to surrender himself "to the spirits of darkness" (235).

Charles concludes his afterword with a final polite swat at his brother-in-law in particular and authorized biography in general:

> I know Lockhart will disregard much here; but he may find some things of value to him. Then I suspect he will — out of a wish to protect my father's good name of which he is the very jealous guardian — a wish that, in my view, would be quite mistaken — destroy the copy I send him. (237)

The framing apparatus in which Massie embeds his narrative provides the liberty necessary for biofiction to work. In the best tradition of a Waverley novel, the paratext appeases scepticism while soliciting collaboration, leaving the writer free to forage from history what he needs and to invent what he chooses.

The Ragged Lion presents a haunted Scott, beset by the duality of his own nature. Although most of the words are Scott's own, either as written by himself or as rendered by Lockhart, Massie supplements them with fiction. He elaborates the story of Green-breeks and links him to Byron ("the same impetuosity, courage, and fire") and to Scott's musings on his friend Richard Heber's unfortunate sexual predilection for stableboys (15). Green-breeks appears again in the visits to Hastie's Close, an obscure Edinburgh location off the Cowgate, here haunted by three spectral figures. Scott compulsively returns there six times in the course of the novel. Although Hastie's Close brings "a consciousness of circumvallent evil" (22), it lures Scott with its beguiling call to the Elfland of Thomas the Rhymer, a realm of forbidden pleasure, rest, and escape from duplicity. Hastie's Close represents Scott at mid-life and his pained awareness of diminished possibilities. There he must resist a barefoot seductress leading him to "the bonnie road that winds about the fernie brae" and, presumably, to that part of himself that "had hitherto been confined and denied" (98). Hastie's Close turns out a "sad delusion" where "Dante's line formed itself in the misty air: 'Lasciate ogni speranza, voi ch' entrate'" (100). Appropriately, Scott last encounters its three apparitions at the Lake of Avernus, Virgil's point of entry to the Underworld.

In addition to outright invention, Massie invokes other fictionalizing techniques. An incident which actually took place only in an exchange of letters here becomes a personal encounter,[4] fully narrated with dialogue and setting, as Scott tells the story of Sir John Sinclair's unwelcome attempt to arrange a marriage for him with the Dowager Duchess of Roxburghe. Massie also interpolates snatches of verse throughout the novel, some from the *Minstrelsy of the Scottish Border* and some of his own, which in the voice of Charles Scott he unblushingly praises. Suffice it to say that Scott frequently expressed disappointment that neither of his sons manifested the slightest degree of literary sensibility.[5] The bits of ballads from the *Minstrelsy* reflect Scott's inner life and, perhaps, his longing for that remnant of an organic society he claims to have found in his ballad-hunting expeditions to Liddesdale.

Massie structures the novel in alternating chapters of chronological recollection and present reflection until they come together at the end. This arrangement releases the Scott persona from the constraints of chronology and allows Massie to devise a not always seamless mélange from multiple sources. Shaping the narrative this way helps to alleviate the inevitable discrepancy of biography between the life as sequentially experienced and the Life as retrospectively written, what John Worthen calls "making things fit together and seem inevitable."[6] This alternating structure of recollection and meditation, the coexistence at the moment of writing of the subject's present consciousness and his retrospection, avoids that awkward hindsight of the biographer, writing from the vantage point of a knowledge of the future which has already become the past. Structured by association rather than by strict chronology, biofiction in this instance offers an alternative model for life writing that privileges self-invention and identity-formation, that is, process rather than product, as the central experience of a life.

The form sanctions speculation and even invention, which are, of course, unavailable to the biographer committed to some standard of truth. In biofiction the descent to the unconscious in Hastie's Close carries the same truth-value as any other incident in Scott's recollection. Desmond McCarthy neatly defines the distinction: "Biographers may be artists under oath, but novelists are under no such oath. They are licensed liars, and writing a novel can have the same function as a wish-fulfilment dream, or a nightmare, taking elements out of real experience as so much raw material for the expansion of fantasy."[7] The liability of this "expansion of fantasy" is that Scott becomes a character in a book, repeatedly insisting upon the subordination of literature to life, but possessing little more claim to reality than Jonathan Oldbuck or Jedidiah Cleishbotham.[8]

The novelist's freedom to invent necessarily undermines whatever superior moral authority we may implicitly grant to the biographer. All of Massie's sources — the *Journal*, the *Ashiestiel Memoir*, letters, Lockhart's *Life*, and Hogg's *Anecdotes of Scott* — are forms of self-presentation and thus performative and inherently unreliable. The overly collaborative reader will find them accreting into that odd phenomenon in which "[. . .] biographical untruths are accepted by audiences if they have been said two or three times and fit in with expectations."[9]

Because the biographical novelist steals his subject's voice and presumes to speak for him, the fundamental ethical question concerns not simply an invasion of privacy but the expropriation of another life, an act that clearly violates that conventionally accepted balance of truth and invention we expect of the biographer.[10] Massie intensifies the feeling of expropriation by concentrating squarely upon himself in the introduction, blurring actualities of his own life with actual and invented aspects of Scott's, all within the discussion of the contessa's fictive manuscript. He seems aware of the unease this obfuscation may elicit in the reader and commences the narrative with an anecdote about George IV's fabrication of his personal heroism at Waterloo. Scott generously classifies the story as "a species of romance" (1) and concludes that "if His Majesty really believes that he led the charge of his Hussars at Waterloo, he is a better man for the desire his lie expresses" (6).

Unlike the scavenger-biographers of fiction, however, Massie seems genuinely to venerate his subject, which inevitably brings a credibility problem, one which is magnified by an accident of timing. John Sutherland's *Life of Walter Scott* appeared a year after the publication of *The Ragged Lion*. Neither book is based upon original research, and each imposes its own kind of distortion. Where Massie esteems and reveres, Sutherland debunks, demystifies, and discredits. For example, Massie accepts Scott's own view of his heroic ancestors, that "fit pedigree for either warrior or Border minstrel" (10), which for Sutherland, in an inspired phrase, constitutes simply as "so much thuggery glorified."[11] Where Sutherland represents Scott's father as "everything that the young Scott wanted *not* to be" (10), Massie makes Walter Sr. "a man of infinite kindness" and glosses over his narrowness of mind and shortcomings as a parent (11). On a more sinister note, although Massie's Scott acknowledges that his elder son Walter "is not a clever lad," he takes satisfaction in his "happy marriage to a sweet girl" (135), a match Sutherland equates to "mat[ing] his son and daughter-in-law like a bull and heifer on one of his farms" (277). Although Massie's Charles Scott "was a particular friend" of the contessa's great-grandmother, Sutherland's Charles was probably homosexual.

Massie's oddly anachronistic allusions add a jarring note. Byron's travels take him to "the ringing plains of windy Troy" (Tennyson's "Ulysses"), and at the end of the 1822 Royal Visit, Scott returns to Abbotsford "when the captains and the King had departed" (Kipling's "Recessional"). If biofiction makes its peace with deconstruction by conceding that both subject and selfhood are merely linguistic constructs, beyond extraneous constraints of truth, referentiality, and sequence, then perhaps these anachronistic quotations are one of its privileges. They do, however, bring a sense of incongruity.

A few socio-political comments by Massie's Scott heighten this incongruity. In Paris after Waterloo, he pontificates on the barbarism of battle but notes that, on being introduced to the Czar, "I was wearing the blue-and-red uniform of the Selkirkshire Lieutenancy" (190), that is, of the troop of leisured young men he had organized to play soldier-games on the sands of Portobello. Commending the novels of Maria Edgeworth for having "done more to completing the Union of the nations of the British Isles than any number of Acts of Parliament could contrive to do," Scott in 1831 seems as unconcerned with the injustice of the Anglo-Irish Ascendancy as is Massie with the historical irony in 1995 (109). Finally, there is Scott's approbation of the proletariat: "The good sense and dignity they displayed [. . .] fortified me in my impression that the members of the Scotch labouring classes are, in their natural state, among the best, most intelligent, and kind hearted of human beings" (303). Is it only this reader who is irresistibly reminded of Hogg's heartfelt praise of "that most docile and affectionate of all animals — the shepherd's dog"?[12]

Two very different plays, one a dramatization of a Hogg story by Kenneth R. Johnston and the other a solo play by Frederic Mohr in which Hogg reflects upon his life, exemplify two variants of biofiction on stage. Hogg published the first part of "The Love Adventures of George Cochrane" in 1810 in *The Spy*, the Edinburgh weekly paper which he edited and largely wrote. Its ribaldry offended some readers and may have contributed to the demise of *The Spy* after only a year. The complete two-part version appeared ten years later in *Winter Evening Tales*. In his *Memoir of the Author's Life* Hogg claimed that the story was autobiographical,[13] and a reviewer in *Blackwood's* recollected listening to Hogg tell strikingly similar stories about himself.[14]

In his dramatization of this one of Hogg's most engaging tales, Kenneth Johnston retains the ribaldry as well as the self-deflating irony.[15] The play compresses the story by eliminating the narrative frame, composed mostly of the reflections of the narrator, an "old bachelor," and the first escapade, which lacks the dramatic potential of the next two. It consists of two parts, the bedroom farce of "The Night-Courtship" and the more boisterous misadventure in amorous pursuit of "The Gypsy Wrestler." George briefly summarizes his "third great love"; a singularly tasteless anecdote, it is best told in this form or omitted altogether.

Hogg's protagonist recounts his own story, recalling his love adventures from the vantage point of one presumably past his prime in these matters. Johnston captures this narrative stance through changes in lighting and direct address to the audience. The opening stage direction describes the set, a farm house in the Scottish Lowlands:

> *This structure comes UP into LIGHTS whenever ACTION commences, and FADES when George Cochrane's NARRATION to the audience resumes. Throughout the play, Cochrane moves back and forth between the stage set as an actor and stage front as narrator of his own life story. As the CURTAIN rises, Cochrane saunters down stage front to address the audience conversationally, with a plaid cape folded under his arm.*
>
> (2)

Many of Cochrane's direct comments to the audience reveal his silliness, foppishness and want of self-knowledge. Nevertheless, Johnston's George Cochrane is a more engaging hero than Hogg's. By omitting, presumably for reasons of stagecraft, much of his self-justifying and hypocritical meditation, Johnston provides his audience with a dramatic protagonist unencumbered by the offensive smugness of the story's character. At the moment, for example, when George believes himself about to be discovered hiding in wait for his beloved by her father, Hogg allows him to indulge in a long passage of self-serving reflection. He rambles on for a quite a few paragraphs and finally decides to resume his account. Johnston complies with the imperatives of farce by deleting such passages in favor of broad physical comedy, unsubtle but very funny. While he compresses for dramatic effect and otherwise remains largely faithful to the original, however, Johnston does not hesitate to exaggerate when it serves his comedic purpose. In the story George admits to being "*over head and ears in love*": "I often caught myself, while repeating her name without intermission, an occupation which I perhaps had been following out with great assiduity for an hour or two — 'Jessy Armstrong! Jessy Armstrong! dear, dear, sweet, lovely Jessie Armstrong!'" (115). Aware that what might weary the reader on the page may well amuse the audience on the stage, Johnston prolongs George's lament and ends it on a wonderfully ridiculous dying fall: "Dear! Sweet! Jessy! Arm! Strong!" (89).

Johnston also embellishes Hogg's extensive physical comedy with a full range of body language and facial expressions. Secreted under

Mary's bed while she entertains another suitor, George shamelessly mugs the audience in accordance with stage directions: "*Sardonic disbelief from George; George nods in gloomy agreement; Outrage from George. He recommences reaching and squirming toward the bell pull; George crawls with renewed determination and a vengeful smile toward the bell pull*" (42–44). And it is physical comedy in its broadest form — a threatened kick from Mary's father which would likely terminate George Cochrane's love adventures forever — that reveals to the audience exactly who is in charge here: "*He pulls George's legs wide apart and begins to aim a kick with his heavy shoes at the exposed target, when Mary raises her hand with a command, which stops him immediately*" (51).

George never does get the play's running joke, that both daughters easily dominate their ostensibly fierce fathers. In the second part, the physical comedy becomes even more violent in a tale of barroom brawls, "warstlin" contests, and a father vicariously reliving his youth through his daughter's lovers. In this part, Johnston relies more on dialogue than on direct address to the audience to replace incidental narrative detail of the original story.

While the autobiographical component of the "Love Adventures" is largely subsumed into the lively stage business, the play, like the story, functions as a sort of ethno-biography. As his opening lines make clear, the title character observes the manners and customs of the Borders from the point of view of a bemused anthropologist.

> After completing my education in England and my grand tour of the Continent, I returned home to my father's estate in Scotland to prepare my inheritance. We agreed I should choose a wife suitable to my tastes who would also improve our capital, and I thought to improve the opportunity by observing the colorful customs of the natives with a nicely refined eye. (3)

To emphasize the distance, George speaks in standard English while the other characters use Scots, and Johnston takes full advantage of the comic potential of this distinction. Jessy lays down her one condition for courtship: "Ye maun lick Tommy Potts or gie up your hopes o' me." The dismayed George responds, "I maun? I mean, I must?" (109). Both parts of the play explore Border customs for the edification of outsiders. George explains to the audience the ritual of night-courting: "Perhaps you from Edinburgh will be startled at this agreement, but it is a fact that every young woman in this country must be courted at night, or else they will not be courted at all" (3). The polite but hapless George loses his first fight to Tommy Potts because he declines to hit his opponent when he is down and thereby learns the hard way that "the border laws require no such courtesy!" (87). Instructed by a pedlar "but gin ye let yoursel' be lickit, nouther the lass nor her father will ever look at ye or hear ye speak," George ingenuously confides to the audience, "I perceived that there was something in Border life, manners, and feeling quite abstract from any thing I ever witnessed before" (71–72).

Johnston employs the conventions and imperatives of the stage to accent this ethno-biographical component of "The Love Adventures." The division between the George who acts and the George who comments to the audience nicely reflects several of those dualities in his creator, inadequately summarized in the familiar binary split of the Ettrick Hogg, raucous Border farmer, and the Edinburgh Hogg, familiar of the literati.

Frederick Mohr's *Hogg: The Shepherd Justified* (1985)[16] is a solo play in which Hogg, at home at Altrive Lake in the summer of 1833, addresses an unidentified (and unseen) American visitor.[17] In the first part of the play, Hogg chats, seemingly at random, about his relationship with Scott, his strong sense of rootedness in Ettrick Forest, his unsuccessful farming ventures and difficulties with publishers, the fate of *The Spy*, his early poetry, and resentment of the *Blackwood's* group, particularly John Gibson Lockhart. He vividly relates his awe on first hearing Burns's poetry recited and his ensuing certainty that "Ah wis born tae replace Burns" (i, 10). This conviction becomes Hogg's personal version of predestination: "But it wis that knowledge, that I hid been pricked oot by fate, destined tae be a poet, of the Elect, that sustained me aa' thae years, o' struggle, laneliness an' neglect" (i, 11).

Hogg most likely invented the story about sharing Burns's birthday just as he fabricated so many other facets of his persona. For dramatic purposes, however, Mohr renders it as conviction rather than invention, thus enhancing the poignancy of the subsequent disillusionment. "The awfae chasm that the parish records cracked open engulfed me in the black horrors. There wis an end tae certainty!" (i,11). The imperatives of performance fully justify the biographical liberty.

In the second and shorter part of the play, as Hogg sips his way from mellow to tipsy, he expounds on politics, marriage and family, and his ambivalence to the Ettrick shepherd persona supposedly foisted unwillingly upon him. He vents increasingly bitter anger toward Lockhart and the distortions of the *Noctes Ambrosianae*. To keep the audience positively disposed toward his character, Mohr wisely shifts the focus from Hogg's grievances to his triumph, *The Private Memoirs and Confessions of a Justified Sinner*. What Hogg says about his choice of narrative form in the novel may apply just as well to the biodramatist's own choice of form: "But Ah wanted aa'body whae read it tae be enabled tae see the horror o' what wis gaun on in the whorls o' that puir sinner's mind" (i, 7). When successful, the single-actor play provides access to the labyrinth of its subject's mind with an immediacy that no conventional biographer may hope to emulate.

Mohr takes full advantage of the opportunities offered by his form. Speaking toward the end of his life, this is a retrospective Hogg who dislikes much about modernity and the changes it has brought. His monologue is, to a large extent, "an auld man's lament fur lost innocence" and for a world in which the cash nexus rules over all:

> Oh, it's the modern way. We no longer breed herds. We must sell oor brains fur cash on a coontin' house stuil in Calcutta or some sic-like place. [. . .] Noo ye read an' write in toons fur wages that ye must hae tae pay taxes because ye hev wages. Noo we hae a thing cae'd 'an economy,' a great monster which maun be fed cash. (i, 7)

His political views, explained here perhaps more tellingly than in any other account, similarly deplore the changes wrought by new money. "This new Toryism is nae whit Ah ken. The auld Tories were aa' heart, inspired, heroic, whae wanted tae right wrangs. The new men hae nae background, men whae hae never hid servants tae teach them hoo a Servant o' the State should behave" (ii, 8). Hogg's analysis of contemporary politics may be less than astute, and there is something inherently comic about his notion of *noblesse oblige*; but the comment signifies an engaging idealism behind the conservatism.

Mohr writes almost the entire play in dialect but attains a remarkable range of rhythm and diction aptly modulated to suit the subject. On the failure of Hogg's Highland farming venture, the tone is all business and the words standard English: "The complications o' clan law allowed that a tacksman had a claim on ma lease an' wis pleadin' his case in the Coort O' Session" (i, 13). The diction is equally unadorned in Hogg's recollection of his youthful exuberance, but the rhythms make a vast difference: "There are days on the hill when the blood is young when ye wadnae change yer state wi' kings. The unconstancy o' the landscape can fill yer oors wi' delight an make the heart sae fu' that sang bursts oot like a spring frae the ground" (i, 8). Recalling his wedding, Hogg borrows the rhythms and diction of Scripture:

> We dined in this hoose an' in the morning we had the solemn Kirkin' in Yarrae when Dr Russell took as his text, "Blessed is the man whom thou honourest an causest tae approach unto thee." The tears filled my een wishin' ma dear deid mither could hae been there, tae haud in

her airms the lass whae wis the cause o' that honour, an' the blessins
that hae never ceased. (i, 25)

Much, of course, depends on the skill of the actor; in the hands of an
accomplished performer, these subtle inflections of language can provide a dimension of insight and sympathy wholly unavailable on the
page.

Mohr's play presents an engaging character who dislikes others
mocking him but is quite willing to make fun of himself in recounting
the failure of his plays, his social difficulties in Edinburgh, and an ine-
briated leap over a "cuddy" after the Abbotsford Hunt dinner. His
good humour is pervasive; the comedy is occasionally nationalistic and
more frequently ribald. "The English," he informs his American listener, "are a simple fowk an' fond o' fun an' aye on the look oot fur
ony excuse tae run riot" (I, 4). Accounting for his physical resemblance
to Scott, he leeringly elucidates the local gene pool: "Ah cannae say Ah
see it masel' but Hoggs an' Harden Scotts have aye run thegither an'
it's no uncommon fur a bitch tae get ower the waa'. At lest no in Ettrick. Fur which Ah've been gratefae in ma day." (I, 12) While Mohr
permits Hogg ample allowance of self-justifying complaints, the
dramatist clearly understands that a character in a one-person play must
engage the audience's admiration as well as its sense of justice. Thus,
the emotional balance of *The Shepherd Justified* tips toward magnanim-
ity rather than reproach. "Ach we cannae complain. There's meat an'
meal, beer in the barrel an' guid Glenlivet in the glass. No mony men
can mak a name, an' live an' dee an', when they're taken, enrich the
very ground they sprang from" (ii, 9).

All three of these biofictions exemplify what Catherine Peters calls
"ventriloquist biography [. . .] in which the biographer seeks to annihilate the distance between self and his subject by taking on the subject's own voice."[18] Peters sees this ventriloquism as an unscrupulous
practice designed to disguise "inadequate or dubious evidence" (45).
Certainly, the tactic allows the biofictionist or biodramatist to evade
those nagging questions about selfhood and truth, authenticity and
narrative, form and discontinuity, which bedevil the more conventional
biographer. By appropriating the subject's voice, each of these works
sacrifices the bracing tension between story (the life) and representation
of story (the shaped narrative). The occasionally permeable border between the two, and the healthy discipline it imposes, both disappear.
However, none of these texts aspires to the truth-value of biography.
All three assume much of the performative quality of autobiography,
gaining in immediacy what they sacrifice in accuracy and balance.
Hogg's hearty contempt for authorized biography offers ample justifi-

cation for the endeavor of biofiction: "Mythmakers aa'! Hoo can a man's life be copyright for yin man tae decide whit'll be remembered an' whit laid awa'?"[19]

Notes

[1] Allan Massie, *The Ragged Lion* (London: Hutchinson, 1994). All subsequent page references in the text are to this edition.

[2] Mr. Massie writes, "In constructing the fictional frame I was imitating Scott, not James" (letter of 10 February 1997).

[3] John Gibson Lockhart, *Memoirs of the Life of Walter Scott, Bart.* (Edinburgh: Robert Cadell; London: John Murray, 1837), I, 99–102.

[4] *The Letters of Sir Walter Scott*, ed. H. J. Grierson, Volume 10: 1826–1828 (London: Constable, 1936), 103–04.

[5] An exception to Massie's rather middling poetry is his fine rendering into Scots of the Twenty-Third Psalm, which concludes the body of the novel.

[6] John Worthen, "The Necessary Ignorance of a Biographer," in *The Art of Literary Biography*, ed. John Batchelor (Oxford: Clarendon, 1995), 227–44 (233).

[7] Quoted in Victoria Glendinning, "Lies and Silences," in *The Troubled Face of Biography*, ed. Eric Homberger and John Charmley (New York: St. Martin's, 1988), 49–62 (49).

[8] Massie would disagree. He writes "Biography, even the best [. . .] always seems to me an unsatisfactory art-form, telling you about its subject, but never able to allow you to feel what it was like to be him (or her). The subject of a biography has a pallid and unconvincing existence compared to a character in a novel. Natasha Rostov is more alive than even Troyat's Tolstoy, Charlus than Painter's Proust" (letter of 10 February 1997).

[9] Norman White, "Pieties and Literary Biography," in *The Art of Literary Biography*, 213–225 (216).

[10] This sense of transgression and the figure of the biographer as predator is a recurring theme in fiction. See Jon Stallworthy, "A Life for a Life," in *The Art of Literary Biography*, 27–42. Stallworthy discusses "The Aspern Papers" by Henry James, *Possession* by A. S. Byatt, *The Paper Men* by William Golding, *Flaubert's Parrot* by Julian Barnes, and *The Truth About Lorin Jones* by Alison Lurie.

[11] John Sutherland, *The Life of Walter Scott* (Oxford and Cambridge, MA: Blackwell, 1995), 2. All subsequent page references in the text are to this edition.

[12] James Hogg, "Dogs," in *The Shepherd's Calendar*, ed. Douglas S. Mack (Edinburgh: Edinburgh UP, 1995), 65.

[13] James Hogg, "Memoir of the Author's Life," in *Memoir of the Author's Life and Familiar Anecdotes of Sir Walter Scott*, ed. Douglas S. Mack (Edinburgh and London: Scottish Academic Press, 1972), 3–81(54).

[14] David Groves, "Introduction," in James Hogg, *Tales of Love and Mystery* (Edinburgh: Canongate, 1985), 1–31(11).

[15] Kenneth R. Johnston, adapter, *The Love Adventures (of Mr. George Cochrane)* by James Hogg, unpublished typescript, 1991. Professor Johnston very generously loaned me a copy of the script. The play was performed in 1993 by the Rowan Tree Company, directed by Judy Steel. It played at several venues as part of the Border Festival and at the Netherbow Arts Centre in Edinburgh to consistently favorable reviews.

[16] Frederic Mohr, *Hogg: The Shepherd Justified*, unpublished typescript, 1985. Mr. Mohr (*nom de plume* of David McKail) has generously supplied a copy of the script. The play was commissioned by the Scottish Arts Council for the Borders Festival and performed on tour and in residence at the Traverse Theatre, Edinburgh, in 1985. It was revived the following year for the Edinburgh International Festival.

[17] In the *American Monthly Magazine* 3.2 (April 1834): 85–91 and 3.3 (May 1834): 177–84, an anonymous writer recounts his visit to Hogg the previous year.

[18] Catherine Peters, "Secondary Lives: Biography in Context," in *The Art of Literary Biography*, 43–56.

[19] Mohr, *Hogg*, i, 3.

UWE BÖKER

Ann Jellicoe's and
Howard Brenton's Shelley

S HELLEY, LATE IN HIS LIFE, TOLD HIS FRIEND Thomas Love Peacock
that he considered "poetry very subordinate to moral and political
science."[1] That this was the case at least during certain periods of his
life is clearly evident in Shelley's treatise *A Philosophical View of Reform*,
an essay that remained unknown to the public until its publication in
1920.

Nevertheless, some of Shelley's contemporaries and, after his death,
many Victorian writers and intellectuals were afraid of his radical ideas.
They dismissed him for his alleged eccentricity and immorality and
called him deranged, insane, or mad.[2] Thus, in the opinion of Matthew
Arnold he was a "beautiful and ineffectual angel, beating in the void his
luminous wings in vain," and "not entirely sane."[3] Even as late as 1930,
the critic J. R. Ullman, aware of this critical tradition, agreed that
"Shelley was mad" in a way, although this "strange and alien being, a
cross-scarping on the Rock of Ages" had to be, considering society as it
was, "a misfit, a trouble maker, and a menace to organized society."[4]

It should not be too surprising, then, that such a controversial figure as Shelley, the immoralist, the deranged poet, the political misfit,
should be made into a dramatic character, similar to other writers portrayed in contemporary drama. The two plays analyzed in detail in this
essay are dramatizations of Shelley's personality, of his idealism at war
with the realities of life, and of his political utopianism. Whereas, as G.
Kim Blank's survey has shown, "post-modernist criticism and theory" is
above all concerned with Shelley's use of and reflections on language,
considering him to be one of its "proto-deconstructionist champions,"[5]
dramatists such as Ann Jellicoe and Howard Brenton are more inclined
to look into his personality as the place where individual and society
meet, or to read his works in the light of debates within the political
Left.

Critics of Ann Jellicoe's *Shelley; or: The Idealist* (1966) and Howard Brenton's *Bloody Poetry* (1985) should, however, not only contextualize both plays, but also assess the intertextual relationships between the Romantic poet's verse and the texts under discussion. As is demonstrated in Elma Dangerfield's *Mad Shelley: A Dramatic Life in Five Acts* (1936), the basis and range of intertextual reference may be nothing more than critical and biographical discourse, without any marked or otherwise obvious quotation from the Romantic texts themselves.[6] Dangerfield's aim was to save the Romantic poet from accusations of insanity, and to reconstruct a picture of him that is "true" to his personality, that is, "a huge talent that has to overcome tremendous difficulties and is continually fighting against conservatism."[7]

It is necessary for the reader or the audience to be aware of the various intertextual references between the plays by Jellicoe and Brenton and Shelley's works. Both dramatists make extensive use of intertextual reference, allusion, and quotation in order to establish meaning. Brenton even goes so far as to alter Shelley's original texts, or invent poetic lines that sound Shelleyan. Critical interpretations of Brenton's work note his intertextual techniques without arriving at an adequate understanding of his play; Jellicoe's allusions and references, however, have never been studied before. Therefore, the purpose of this essay is to do justice to the intertextual richness of both plays.

Ann Jellicoe, born in 1927, became known to English theatre audiences through *The Sport of My Mad Mother* (1958) and *The Knack* (1961; filmed in 1965). She has come to be considered an experimental playwright, practising a "theatre of demonstration" in which action, movement, and sounds are more important than language in its communicative function, reflecting the influence of Antonin Artaud's theories on British theatre.[8] *The Sport of My Mad Mother* in this respect is "an anti-intellect play" based on the characters' "irrational forces and urges" and intended to "reach the audience directly through rhythm, noise and music."[9]

Shelley; or: The Idealist, first produced at the Royal Court Theatre in 1965, is in a way a departure from some of Jellicoe's earlier techniques. As she herself said, she "wanted to write a play that would have a strong narrative" and "to build a story which would proceed step by step, each action drawing upon itself inevitable social consequences which would dictate the next action."[10] The actions of the characters, according to this plan, carry them to a point where they are forced to make a moral decision and explore its consequences.

Jellicoe's interest in Shelley coincides with the postwar tendency to downgrade the Romantic poet who suffered "permanent damage" from earlier attacks by literary scholars.[11] Her opinions obviously differed from those of the New Critics, as she was "in awe of Shelley. [and] thought, you mustn't tamper with this extraordinary man."[12] In the preface to her play she unhesitatingly declares, "I finally agree with almost every word that Shelley says."[13] This, in fact, is not quite true, because at the time she wrote the play Jellicoe still had doubts about the conventional image of Shelley as "the rational, intellectual and intelligent man." She thought that "people are driven by their emotions, and by their fears and insecurities."[14] This is why Jellicoe's Shelley emerges as a character who is shown in the process of still searching to define his philosophical vision of moral goodness. His vision — based on rational arguments — comes more and more into conflict with the realities of life and of human nature. This is also why Shelley is portrayed at moments as "engagingly comical because he was inexperienced, enthusiastic and intense"; yet he remains, according to Jellicoe, "a great man destroyed by his own tragic flaw: his blindness to the frailty of human nature."[15]

Jellicoe's *Shelley* is a three-act play. The first act shows the protagonist at the age of eighteen, being dismissed from college, subsequently meeting Harriet Westbrook and making his marriage proposal at the end of the first act (1810–11). The action of Act Two begins two years later: Shelley, married to Harriet, meets Mary, Harriet commits suicide, and Shelley is deprived of his children (1813–17). The last act depicts the Shelleys in Italy together with the Williamses and Trelawny. In the play's final scene Trelawny recounts the circumstances of the protagonist's death and cremation (1822).

From the beginning Shelley is depicted as a human being inhabiting the world of the spirit as well as that of everyday reality and of compromise. As a student at Oxford he is already making plans to change the world according to his rational insights into the utopian order of things. He is constantly trying to convince other people by means of logical reasoning and experiment. In the end he is defeated as a rationalist, although he is able to keep his "heart" unharmed.

The opening action without words gives us an impression of the eighteen-year-old intellectual who is acutely aware of what is going on in the world around him. As he walks on stage he is reading a book and at the same time eating cherries out of his hat. Having already dropped a coin into a beggar's tin he returns to give him some cherries as well. A few moments later, in the course of the dialogue between Shelley and Hogg, we become aware of the semiotic value of these red cherries as objects of sensual desire as well as symbols of love. Shelley's giving freely to the beggar is shortly after related to the poet's ideas. We find

Shelley in 1811 already quoting from *Queen Mab* (probably written in 1812, but not printed until May 1813) and emphatically describing virtue as pursuing the "gradual paths of an aspiring change" and ultimately arriving at a state of "perfect happiness." The earth then is heralded as the "pure dwelling place" of the "purest spirits" that have succeeded in overcoming "care and sorrow, impotence and crime" as well as "languor, disease, and ignorance" (21–22).[16] The opening book-and-cherry episode should, however, be related to the play's last scene — Trelawny's narrative of the cremation of Shelley's body. Jellicoe obviously wanted to evoke a metonymic equation of book and brains ("the brains seethed") and cherries and heart ("the heart, though bedded in fire, would not burn" [111]), respectively. The play's sixteen scenes then are structured in such a way as to show the failure of Shelley's rationalist philosophy, whereas the truth of his emotional being survives.

In the opening scene we are already implicitly shown that, contrary to the Fairy's words in *Queen Mab*, the "reality of Heaven" never can be achieved on earth. Following Shelley's and Hogg's shouts of "O happy Earth, reality of Heaven," there is an explosion. It is the result of one of Shelley's experiments that has miscarried, chasing away the beggar as the epitome of unhappy mankind whose situation Shelley had meant to improve. Whereas the cherry-opening throws some light on Shelley's philosophical aims, the off-stage explosion anticipates the idealist's ultimate failure, for Shelley is originally of the opinion that "if you teach men to reason they will behave reasonably — you must educate people to see the truth" (23). However, all of his "experiments" carried out in the course of the first act are failures because human beings are, in Jellicoe's own words, less governed by reason than "driven by their emotions, and by their fears and insecurities."[17] Thus, the provocative pamphlet *The Necessity of Atheism* (1811) is conceived by Shelley as a means to sway the Bishop "by the unanswerable splendour of its logic" (24). It, too, is destined to miscarry. We are shown the reasons: the timid scholar's narrow-mindedness (Master of the College), the future bishop's career-oriented self-interest (Coplestone), and the tutor's adherence to traditional truths. Again and again, Shelley's belief in experimental "proof, [. . .] the evidence of your senses, [. . .] logic" (46) as a means to educate, persuade, and emancipate people who originally "cannot see beyond their own narrow interests" (23) is defeated by the realities of society and human nature. The most important fact is that instead of convincing Harriet of the truth of his arguments for atheism and against marriage, he is trapped into marriage "against [his] principles" (63) by her father, who wants to raise the family's social standing.

Interestingly enough, it is the actual situation of women that shows the weak points in Shelley's idealistic reasonings. Females are, in Jellicoe's understanding, those without any power at all in society. The action of Act One, Scene Three clearly demonstrates the shallowness of the traditional education for young girls. Shelley's insistence on women's obligation to "stand against injustice" (52) is shown to be a male point of view that does not take into account the mental subjugation of women. Thus, Shelley seems to be unaware of the real pressures put upon his sister Hellen:

SHELLEY: ... there's no justice or dignity in anything they do, they are utterly corrupt and you must stand against them or you, too, will be corrupted.

HELLEN: Yes, but you — you're big and important, it's the big world, you're a man.

SHELLEY: The school is your world, within the context of school the situation is exactly the same.

HELLEN: But you're a man.

SHELLEY: It's no different for women.

HELLEN: It is.

SHELLEY: It's degrading what women put up with.

HELLEN: Degrading?

SHELLEY: It degrades me as a man.

HELLEN: I don't understand what you mean. (52)

Similar arguments are repeated in Act One, Scene Seven. Shelley asks Harriet to fight her "tyrant" father who is putting pressure on her to ensnare the young heir of a baronet; if she refuses, she is to go back to school. Harriet is already convinced that she has to resist her father "because he's being cruel and unjust" (59) and that to conform to his demands would be "degrading" for her. But she does not know how to fight against him as a woman:

SHELLEY: How?

HARRIET: Yes.

SHELLEY: I stood against my father's injustice, you must do the same.

HARRIET: But I haven't any money. I've nothing to live on, how can I live?

SHELLEY: I live.

HARRIET: But you're a man.

SHELLEY: Man, women, it makes no difference.

HARRIET: It does.

SHELLEY: It doesn't.

HARRIET: It does. (59)

A few moments later she explains in more detail:

> HARRIET: I'm not even fit to be a governess. If I was to leave this house,
> it would indeed be that — or dying of cold and starvation.
> [. . .] I must stand up for the dignity of women, I see that. I
> must resist him. Well, if I resist him he will turn me out of the
> house. That means a choice between going on the streets
> or . . . suicide. (60)

Thus, Shelley is ultimately driven, against his principles, to be her
"protector" (61) by marrying her. Two years later (Act Two, Scene
One) Harriet is both looking after their child, Ianthe, and working for
Percy by copying the pamphlet *Declaration of the Rights of Man*
(1812). Yet Percy is telling her how to feed the child. There is an ex-
hilarating dispute over breast or bottle feeding: "This is cow's milk,
Ianthe's not a calf . . . . Why aren't I a woman? Give her to me! Ianthe!
Drink! Drink! Here! Oh . . . Oh . . . Oh . . . my God" (69). Harriet
seems to be unable to really understand her husband's idealistic philosophy. This is obviously why he is yearning for somebody who resembles him to a greater degree: "The power to reason, to understand,
that makes her free to act. Educated as a man, to think as clearly and
boldly as the best of men. With such a woman — with such a woman I
could go" (72). These words are obviously ambiguous. To be educated
as a man could either mean to receive the same formal education as
men or to accept male ideology and male ways of thinking. It is not
clear whether Jellicoe herself was aware of this ambiguity. Be that as it
may, the next scene shows Mary Godwin and Shelley together at the
grave of Mary Wollstonecraft Godwin, author of *A Vindication of the
Rights of Woman* (1792). The sixteen-year-old Mary always carries a
book with her as does Shelley. She discusses philosophy with him, extensively quoting certain passages from *Queen Mab* which deal with
questions of marriage, friendship, and free love.[18] Mary, though, is already aware of the grim fact that a man and a woman actually do not
have "an equal right" to make choices (76). She is obviously in love
with Percy, but she knows what it means for a woman to live with a
man without being married to him: "I understand, because it is a lot,
these days, it won't always be like this, but it is a lot now for a woman
to — to . . . come to a man without being married to him . . . So it
seems to me, that it is so much that it should be the woman who offers,

don't you think? I mean if she really, if she really . . . " (76). The ana-coluthic sentence structure reveals her emotional disturbance, and it clearly shows that, according to Jellicoe, men and women are really driven by their emotions. But it is just a young woman's uttering of her thoughts and giving expression to her emotions in this way that obvi-ously changes the rationalist Percy into a being who is to show, ac-cording to the stage directions, "*a miraculous gentleness and warmth. He kisses her very gently. A very long pause. He reels from her embrace al-most fainting*" (77). This silent action is followed by Shelley quoting from Act Four of *Prometheus Unbound*, which was written, one should bear in mind, several years later, in 1819. His quoting at this moment from the concluding dialogue between Earth and Moon (Act Four, lines 418–23) is a clear indication of Jellicoe's intention to stress the fact that the two lovers have attained some ideal state of mind. In addi-tion, the conclusion of Act Two, Scene Three is followed by one of the two total blackouts in the play, and thus seems to be an embodiment of "*a moment's intense spiritual communication*" that may be equated with "*a lifetime of physical love*" (101).

But man and woman are still part of a society that does not allow such an ideal state of communication to be realized. As we see in the next scene, Shelley is torn between his obligations to Harriet, his love for Mary and his financial problems (he has borrowed money against his inheritance in order to finance William Godwin). To demonstrate Shelley's emotional stress, Act Two, Scene Four is different from all the other scenes in this play so far. In Act Two, Scene Four we are con-fronted with a quick succession of short interlocking scenes, juxtaposed against each other. Various characters appear on stage, either convers-ing with Shelley or driving him around, worrying and harassing him: these are Mary, Harriet, two moneylenders, the Godwins, and a bailiff with a summons to be served upon Shelley. The last part of this scene consists of a heated dialogue between the Godwins, their daughter Mary, Claire Clairmont, and Shelley, who at one point threatens to kill himself and Mary by means of laudanum ("*he holds the laudanum bottle as he would a pistol*" [84]). In the end Shelley succeeds in eloping with Mary, not without having assured Godwin that he will help the egotis-tical philosopher in order to "serve philosophy" (86).

The elopement seems to result in the lover's victory: Act Two, Scene Five is entirely made up of quotations from Canto VI of Shelley's *The Revolt of Islam*. By implication, we are shown the parallels between the play's events and Shelley, who in this poem "devoted to the love of mankind" wanted to illustrate "the growth and progress of individual mind aspiring after excellence."[19] Laon, who had narrated the battle against the tyrant at the beginning of Canto VI, now tells the reader about the physical consummation of his and Cythna's love,[20] suggesting that of Shelley and Mary. This dramatic highlight is contrasted in Act Two, Scene Six with the pressure put on Harriet by her father and the silent action of her suicide in the Serpentine, followed by a second complete blackout which couples the two climactic moments of love and death. In Act Two, Scene Seven the Lord Chancellor accuses Shelley of immorality and denies him custody of his and Harriet's children (this happened in 1817). At the end of this scene Shelley is still unable to understand the reasons for Harriet's hopeless situation and her subsequent suicide. If Shelley's "highest [philosophical] principles" have been "put to the test" (83), his idealistic experiment has ultimately miscarried. But it is not his philosophy based on Godwinian rationalism but the intensity of his feelings that will live on, as is shown in the next two scenes of the much shorter third act.

The action of these two scenes takes place immediately before and after Shelley's death by drowning at sea. The dialogue between Edward Williams, Jane Williams, Mary Shelley, and Trelawny about household matters is interrupted by Shelley coming back "drunk with poetry" (96), reciting parts of his new love poems in the midst of the others' down-to-earth remarks: "To Jane: The Recollection," "The Pine Forest of the Cascine Near Pisa," and passages from "The Witch of Atlas."[21] Later on, Mary in turn quotes, in a "*very cool, light tone*" (100), from Shelley's poem "Lines Written in the Bay of Lerici," composed for Jane Williams.[22] Jellicoe refrains from conveying by means of language Shelley's innermost feelings of intense physical and spiritual love for Jane, warring with the demands of the world. She is outlining his thoughts that "*are not to be spoken*" (101), leaving it to the actor to render them in body language: "*You know my values, dear Mary, I have striven, I have striven passionately — yes, I know the world thinks physical love a wicked and guilty thing. This is so terrible that — but for your sake I respect the values of the world. Nevertheless, for me there is no dividing line between a moment's intense spiritual communication and a lifetime of physical love*" (101). In the course of their dialogue Mary reminds Shelley of his former platonic love affair with Emilia Viviani[23] and of Harriet's love for him. She even threatens to commit suicide for the same reasons as Harriet. In the end, there is no solution to the demands of being true to oneself, acting responsibly and loving without "coercion [or] threats." On the one hand, Mary is portrayed as being right in not giving up her love, but on the other hand, so is Shelley with his emphasis on the "moment of truth" that is "*the moment of experience. When two souls reach out to each other. As true, valuable and beautiful as a lifetime of living*" (105). If Mary and Percy "are paying now for Harriet's misery," as Mary maintains, the reason is Shelley's lack of understanding of the situation of women and of the pressure society puts on the individual female being.

It is only in the last scene that we finally learn what the values are that are uppermost in the author's mind. Trelawny remembers the internment and cremation of Shelley's body:

> The body was a long time consuming, the fierce fire kept up and the largest bones were reduced to white cinders and nothing perfectly distinguishable — but the heart, though bedded in fire, would not burn — and after waiting an hour, continually adding fuel, we gave over, all exclaiming it will not burn. There was a bright flame all around it caused by the moisture still flowing from it — and on removing the furnace nearer the sea to cool the iron I took the heart in my hand to examine it. I sprinkled it with water, but it was still so hot as to burn my hand badly, and a quantity of this oily liquid still flowed from it. (111)[24]

The heart refusing to be consumed by fire is obviously symbolic of Shelley's intensity of feeling that cannot be destroyed by the world. In this respect, Jellicoe's play is, in its emphasis on unrestrained, even subversive emotionalism and love, a critique of British middle-class morality that came under attack by other playwrights, too, during these years.

The remark by Jellicoe's Shelley that the English would "drive us off the face of the earth if they could . . . I can feel their hate even here" (103) is implicitly directed at contemporary theatre audiences of the 1960s. Howard Brenton's own provocations are, indeed, much more explicit. Even before the fate of oppositional theatre had been put into question by the Conservative government, Brenton, the author of such controversial plays as *Christie in Love* (1970), *The Churchill Play* (1974), and *The Romans in Britain* (1980) had already established himself as the *enfant terrible* of the political Left in the British theatre. *Bloody Poetry*, first produced in 1984, may well be, as critics have remarked, an expression of the author's disillusionment during the Thatcher decade as well as a critique of "all his fellow architects of the modern utopia" who seem to be "quite at a loss."[25]

Critics have tried to contextualize the play within Brenton's socialist utopian ideas and the failure of the British political Left during the eighties. They have also tried to make sense of the intertextual dimensions of Brenton's play. But they have neither looked deeply enough into the textual changes between the two versions of *Bloody Poetry*,[26] nor tried to identify the whole range, depth and distribution of the play's intertextuality.[27]

The action of *Bloody Poetry* takes place between the summers of 1816 and 1822; the places of action are Switzerland, England, and Italy. In the opening scene Shelley, his wife Mary, and Claire Clairmont are on their way to Lake Geneva to meet Byron.[28] This scene consists of a series of quotations from Shelley's poems, interrupted by references in prose to the grim situation of the "little band of atheistical perverts, free-lovers, [. . .] poeticals — leaving England" (11/239).[29] The interweaving of poetic and prose utterances produces a contrapuntal effect, and the quotations themselves indicate a movement from the sublime heights of icy Mont Blanc to the political realities of England as incorporated in Shelley's "Sonnet: England in 1819" and his "Song to the Men of England." This downward movement is reinforced by the poet's "sinking beneath the fierce control / Down through the lampless deep of song" (11/239; these lines are obviously Brenton's own). As Shelley drives along the shores of Lake Geneva there is a closing quotation from the early poem "On Death," celebrating the world as the "mother of all we know."[30] As we shall see, this leaving of the icy prospects of Mont Blanc, plunging into the watery depths but nevertheless returning to the earth is the metaphorical framework of the whole play.

The Shelleys and Byron meet for the first time with the help of Claire Clairmont in Act One, Scene Two. Byron is "a god" to Claire, the "Olympian god of English poetry" and "England's greatest living poet" (12/240, 13/241); he himself overbearingly calls Shakespeare a "grotesquely talented little shit in the pay of royalty" (19/248) and is no less arrogant in his opinion of Wordsworth (21/249). Although the Shelleys and Claire do not quite behave as arrogantly as Byron, they partake in his elitist idea of turning "[. . .] communist. We are upper class renegades, we can afford it. [. . .] Plans, plans, of changing the world, of ripping human nature apart [. . .]." (24/253) Thus, at the beginning of the play the Romantics are depicted as characters who separate themselves from common humanity: they scoff at Dr. Polidori, who more or less personifies bourgeois norms,[31] and at the same time they boast of being the "great experiment," saying "we will find out how to live and love, without fear" (14/242). It is Mary who from the beginning sees through their posturing as "gods and goddesses, moving in brilliant light on a beach by a lake, in dresses of white silk flowing about limbs" (15/243). She reminds them that "statues" of this kind "do not — *With a glance at* BYSSHE. — have lungs of mucus and blood, they do not — *She looks at* CLAIRE, *pauses.* — have women's wombs" (15/243). As this is the first time that the noun *blood* has been used, we become aware of the semantic oppositions underlying Brenton's play: gods, statues, Olympian beings, the icy heights of Mont Blanc versus the human condition of sickness, childbearing, and, in addition, the situation of writers who are subject to "avenging Powers." In his second version, Brenton further underlines the idea of being at the mercy of the mighty political powers in England, in front of whose "firing squad," according to Claire, Shelley is threatened with death. These are the obvious implications of her quotation from Shelley's *The Revolt of Islam*: "We tread / On fire! the avenging Power his hell on earth has spread!"[32] Thus, "bloody poetry" becomes a variety of poetry that, as hinted at in Act One, Scene One, has to do with the dire political conditions prevailing in England and the growing self-awareness of the play's characters that they are far from god-like.

The semantic opposition of gods/height and humans/depth is reinforced and deepened in Act Two, Scene Three. In the course of their discussion about Claire and Byron's child, Mary calls into question the trust her half-sister has in her affections. Mary's aside "He hath no affections" seems to refer to Byron, but then she clarifies that she is speaking about "writing the story of a monster [. . .] He lives up in the snow, in the mountains" (27/255). The ambiguity of the grammar suggests that she may even be referring to her husband. Frankenstein-like monstrousness is the topic of the following scene. It begins with Shelley quoting extensively from Wordsworth's "Ode: Intimations of Immortality," emphasizing the loss of youthful vision (28–29/256–58). This self-diagnosis is related to the question of poetic honesty that Mary and Shelley, in contrast to Byron, find realized in Wordsworth; there seems to be some lack of honesty, though, in Byron's philosophy of Liberalism, the basis of which is the supposition "that *everything* is true" (31/260). After a short reference to Shelley's former electrical experiments the audience witnesses another such "experiment." Dr. Polidori is put in front of a wall, his hands tied behind his back, while the others act out Plato's "Allegory of the Cave" from the *Republic*. Dr. Polidori is manhandled and tortured in the course of this episode, during which the Romantics' bodies are projected upon the wall as distorted shadows (monsters). Byron equates Polidori's suffering throughout the whole episode with the harm done to man by poetry and philosophy in general (37/265). According to Shelley, Plato's philosophy is a form of ideological self-imprisonment (38/267) that turns even Shelley himself into a monster (39/268). If, as Jennifer Wagner has written, the "exposure of the Romantic idealist's neglect of the role of sympathy and affection in human happiness," is at the bot-

tom of Mary Shelley's *Frankenstein*,[33] then Shelley's Promethean visionary dreams are criticized as well, as they take precedence over his
affections as husband and father.

The further dramatic development leads to a sort of self-awareness
on the part of Shelley. This self-awareness is a result of his seeing himself "haunted" by ghosts. After the dramatization of Plato's cave allegory there follows a subtle intertextual play of echoes that ultimately
lead to Shelley's seeing a ghost. Mary had been referring to the monster plot of her novel; Byron, in turn, quotes from Coleridge's *Christabel*. Shelley is suddenly seized by a fit. Polidori, in an aside, alludes to
the episode in which Shelley had seen a monstrous woman during a
former reading of *Christabel*, "with eyes in her nipples, her nipples as
eyes, staring at him" (41/270). This vision is re-enacted with another
woman standing in Mary's place. Thus, the episode can be seen as the
beginning of Shelley's growing self-awareness, the aim of which is to
"find out what we are, what we can be" (45/273).[34]

This nascent self-awareness is clearly to be seen in Act One, Scene
Five. Shelley's monologue is devoted to the topic of being "haunted"
by one's own self: "We haunt ourselves. With man-made tyranny.
[. . .] We haunt ourselves, with the ghosts of what we could be, if we
were truly free" (42/270). There is some indication of self-awareness,
too, at the end of Act One. Byron and Shelley are on board a sailboat;
they have to fight a storm, and Shelley has to admit that he is unable to
swim. At this point Shelley's exclamations, "Cannot! Sinking! Down!
Through the lampless deep! Of song!" (46/274), echo the fake quotation of the opening scene, thus indicating that Shelley has in fact abandoned the "icy heights" of Mont Blanc, that is to say the region of
monsters (Frankenstein's), would-be gods, or bloodless statues.

But it is only after Harriet's suicide (Act Two, Scene One), which
Shelley hears about four weeks later (Act Two, Scene Two), that the
poet is ready to recognize his faults. At the end of Act One, Scene
Two, Mary is quoting from *The Revolt of Islam* about the necessity of
breaking the outward slavery so that "free and equal, man and woman"
may "greet / Domestic peace" (57/285). Whereas in the first published version of the play this is followed by a scene in which Mary and
Claire speak about the Lord Chancellor's decision, this scene is left out
in the second version, so that immediately after Mary's quotation from
The Revolt of Islam Shelley appears on stage, followed now by the
"haunting" ghost of Harriet Westbrook. He even speaks with Harriet's
ghost, who later follows him to the place where they are reading out of
Plato's *Symposium* — Diotima's answer to Socrates dealing with the
nature of love (61/289). Harriet's ghost seems to be happy, it even

"laughs" as Shelley and Claire kiss. The ghost is not advocating indiscriminate promiscuity, but positively reacting to Claire's and Shelley's "Can a man love two women at once? [. . .] Can a woman love two men at once?" (63/291) — both questions hinting at some new, that is, neither monstrous nor bourgeois way of living out one's affections (in a way similar to Blake's "lineaments of gratified desire," quoted on 60/288). The ghost even tells Percy not to worry: "When you touch her, tonight, you can remember touching me, and you will, won't you, husband" (64/291–92). Thus, there is some significant contrast between the fear-inducing ghosts of the *Christabel*-variety and the more benign reaction and influence of Harriet's ghost (cf. Harriet's mood of forgiveness immediately before committing suicide). Harriet's ghost is significantly absent when Shelley, on behalf of Claire's wanting to see her child Allegra, meets the cynical Byron, whoring in his Palazzo Mocenigo. Shelley, who is angry at Byron's cynicism and despair, admonishes him: "The people of England — they may well have the right to despair. So would you — if you were a mill-hand in Manchester, or child down a mine, or a mother to a labourer's children in a filthy hovel — [. . .] But for a poet to despair? Obscene!" (69–70/297). Shelley reminds Byron, with words reminiscent of his *The Defence of Poetry* (written only in 1821): "The great instrument of moral good is the imagination. We must not let it become diseased! We must be optimists for human nature!" (70/297). After that Byron is temporarily changed into a madman.

The ghost reappears as Shelley is reading the news about the Peterloo Massacre (16 August 1819). As his daughter has died just some moments before, Mary accuses him of having caused the child's death; Shelley in turn decides to dedicate "The Mask of Anarchy" to Clara.[35] The altercation between Mary and Shelley is evidence of the insoluble contradictions between the private and the political spheres. These contradictions are ultimately the result of the political atmosphere of the times, but they are not, as some critics have maintained, the outcome of callous Romantic utopianism. And the presence of Harriet's ghost in a number of important scenes is a clear indication of Shelley's growing awareness of the conflict he finds himself in as a political writer and the human costs that seem inevitable.

Shelley is even justified anew as a political poet, because his poetical style changes to become more song-like. Curiously enough, the Shelleys had not only praised Wordsworth because of his honesty to himself, but also because of his "Feeling [and] Song" (30/258). In Brenton's play, the quotations at the end of the play in Scene Twelve (second version) are noteworthy for their song-like qualities, either on private or on public topics. On the dark stage only Shelley's face is to be seen, and although these are the moments shortly before his death, Brenton does not want to have any "*storm effects*" (79/307). Shelley recites from "The Mask of Anarchy,"[36] significantly enough beginning with "As I lay asleep in Italy" (hinting at his re-awakening out of the monstrousness of the first act); the quotation ends with the well-known lines "Rise like Lions after slumber / In unvanquishable number — / Shake your chains to earth like dew / Which in sleep had fallen on you — / Ye are many — they are few" (80/308). According to Mary, this is the "great revolutionary, English poem — unpublishable" (74/302). But, in fact, it is one of the few of Shelley's poems that present no problems of understanding for the reader. The poems that are quoted subsequently have a similar song-like quality: there are lines from "The Fugitives" (ll. 1–4, 11–14), from "Lines: When the Lamp is Shattered" (ll. 1–4) and again from "The Fugitives" (ll. 31–35). The most important quotation, however, is from the fourth act of *Prometheus Unbound*. It ends with well-known lines from Demogorgon's last speech about the power of love, forgiveness, and hope: "To defy power which seems omnipotent — / To love, and bear — to hope till Hope creates / From its own wreck the thing it contemplates" (81/309). This kind of hope is called "Good, great, and joyous, beautiful and free."[37]

This element of hope is stressed even more during the ultimate scene of the play. Shelley's body "*is furled in the sail upon the stage*" (82/309). Byron stands behind it, and is, for the first time, together with Harriet's Ghost. In the original version, Brenton has Byron say: "I love him. And in the name of all the mercies, look what the sea did to his flesh" (82/310). Byron's words in the second version remind the audience and Brenton's critics that he is far from condemning Shelley's Romantic failure: "Thus is another man gone, about whom the world was brutally mistaken" (82/309). Byron's last wish — "Burn us all! A great, big, bloody, beautiful fire!" — alludes to the cremation of Shelley's body on the beach (cf. Trelawny's account in Jellicoe's play). It also relates back to the opening of the play and the picture of a distant, icy Mont Blanc, emblem of the Romantic poets' playing "at gods and goddesses." They were, as we have seen, unable to escape from the human condition of "lungs of mucus and blood." They, as well as their poetry, have become bloody, red, and full of emotional fire. Thus, there is no indication in the last two scenes that the Romantics are really "monsters" or that they succumb to an alleged female discourse of domesticity. And there is, although the utopian experiment has failed, no spirit of hopelessness.[38] The same may also be learned from

Brenton's introduction to the Methuen Theatrescripts edition of *Greenland*: "Whether they really failed in their 'Utopian dreams' is not yet resolved."[39] To which he added one year later, in the introduction to *Plays: Two* (1989):

> [. . .] the quartet are determined to invent a new way of living, free of sexual repression. They make a terrible mess of it. Some found the 'morality' of the play bewildering. I was not concerned with saying whether these people were 'good' or 'bad,' I wanted to salute their Utopian aspirations for which, in different ways, they gave their lives. It is a celebration of a magnificent failure. (xiv)

Those who have interpreted these words as an indication of Brenton's condemnation of the "monstrous" Romantics have put too much stress on the word "failure." Brenton obviously wanted to emphasize the words "salute" and "celebration." If critics had read further on, they would have learned that Brenton, only four years later in his openly utopian play *Greenland* (1988), staged "a world in which Shelley, Byron, Mary and Claire would be happy to live . . . " (xiv).

Jellicoe gives her audience an intimate picture of a tragic hero from literary history. The biographical interest intersects, though, with wider concerns which are rooted in the 1960s and the beginnings of a more radical culture of dissent. With her insistence on the precarious situation of women in society, Jellicoe belongs to those writers who drew attention to the causes and effects of marginalization that entered public consciousness only three years later, in 1968. The end of the 1960s was also the period of the fringe theatre and saw the emergence of Howard Brenton among others.[40] His concerns were and still are not only the wider political issues, but also the "world within" without which no reformation or revolution of society will succeed. The biographical interest is thus always intimately related to interest in the "world without," as can be learned from one of Brenton's *Sonnets of Love and Opposition*:

> Shelley said to me, when
> I asked for a tip, 'Write first
> For a new world within —
> Always of
> Men, women, nature and society —
> Never forget
> The world is old
> But its great age has yet
> To be made
> Let alone told —

And declare you are a public enemy
Of kingly death, false beauty and decay'
Ta, Percy. I'm on my way.[41]

Notes

[1] Quoted in Roland A. Duerksen, *Shelleyan Ideas in Victorian Literature* (The Hague: Mouton, 1966), 11.

[2] See Karsten Klejs Engelberg, *The Making of the Shelley Myth: An Annotated Bibliography of Criticism of Percy Bysshe Shelley 1822–1860* (London: Mansell, 1988), 44–59; for further studies of the criticism and reception of Shelley's work, see Nancy Fogarty, *Shelley in the Twentieth Century: A Study of the Development of Shelley Criticism in England and America, 1916–1971* (Salzburg: Universität Salzburg, 1976); James E. Barcus, ed., *Percy Bysshe Shelley: The Critical Heritage* (London: Routledge, 1975, repr. 1995); Kim G. Blank, ed., *The New Shelley: Later Twentieth-Century Views* (New York: St. Martin's Press, 1991); Michael Gassenmeier *et al.*, eds., *The Literary Reception of British Romanticism on the European Continent* (Essen: verlag die blaue eule, 1996).

[3] Quoted in Duerksen, *Shelleyan Ideas*, 132.

[4] James Ramsey Ullman, *Mad Shelley* (1930; repr. New York: Gordian Press, 1975), 5–6.

[5] Cf. Blank, *The New Shelley*, 5–10 and 247.

[6] Thus, Kirsten Sarna's study of Elma Dangerfield's play is an analysis of ways in which Dangerfield reconstructed the Romantic poet's personality and life from a wide variety of biographical and critical sources. According to Sarna, Dangerfield's dramatization is a contribution to the discussion about Shelley's alleged derangement, a stereotype going back as far as Thomas Medwin's opinion about his cousin's "insanity." Kirsten Sarna, *"Mad Shelley: A Dramatic Life in Five Acts" by Elma Dangerfield, O.B.E.: Evolving the Perception of a Biographical Character in Dramatic Play Form* (Essen: verlag die blaue eule, 1995).

[7] Cf. Sarna, *"Mad Shelley,"* 91.

[8] Ann Jellicoe, *Some Unconscious Influences in the Theatre* (London: Cambridge UP, 1967); Ann Jellicoe, "Covering the Ground," in *Women and Theatre: Calling the Shots*, ed. Susan Todd (London: Faber, 1984), 82–96; and Jellicoe's own preface in *Shelley; or: The Idealist* (London: Faber, 1966), 13–20. All subsequent page references in the text are to this edition.

[9] Quoted in Page, "Jellicoe," 279.

[10] Jellicoe, "Preface," 17.

[11] Cf. Fogarty, *Shelley in the Twentieth Century*, 10.

[12] Cf. Jellicoe, "Covering," 89.

[13] Jellicoe, "Preface," 17–18; cf. "Covering," 89.

[14] Jellicoe in an interview, as quoted in Hilmar Sperber, "Ann Jellicoe: *The Knack*, 1961," in *Das zeitgenössische englische Drama*, ed. Klaus-Dieter Fehse and Norbert H. Platz (Frankfurt am Main: Athenäum, 1975), 164–178 (176).

[15] Jellicoe, "Preface," 18; she mentions here, too, that she started to work on the play by reading a biography of Shelley, but then she searched "into his life [. . .] entirely from original sources. [. . .] this play is not a work of scholarship. But I tried to extract the truth of his life while stressing the points I wanted to make; events are sometimes telescoped but they are true to their inner nature."

[16] Thomas Hutchinson, ed., *Shelley: Poetical Works* (London: Oxford UP, 1967), 762 70; quotations are from *Queen Mab*, IX, ll. 146–51, and ll. 1, 4, and 8–11.

[17] From an interview quoted in Sperber, "Ann Jellicoe," 176.

[18] *Queen Mab*, Bk. IX, ll. 89–90, 76–79, and 80–85.

[19] Shelley's preface to this poem in *Shelley: Poetical Works*, 32.

[20] Quotations in *Shelley: Poetical Works*, 88, are from *Revolt*, ll. 2623–31, 2634–38, and 2650–58.

[21] "To Jane," ll. 29–31; "The Pine Forest," ll. 57–61; "The Witch of Atlas," ll. 153–56, 161–64, 1969–72, 289, 313 14, 369 73, and 409, see *Shelley: Poetical Works*, 97–100.

[22] *Shelley: Poetical Works*, 100–01; ll. 9–11, 15–18.

[23] Cf. *Shelley: Poetical Works*, 104; "Epipsychidion" (1821).

[24] Cf. J. E. Morpurgo, ed., *The Last Days of Shelley and Byron: Being the Complete Text of Trelawney's Recollections edited, with Additions from Contemporary Sources* (Garden City, NY: Anchor Books, 1960), 102–07.

[25] *Bloody Poetry* has been interpreted as exploring the contrast and parallels between Romantic utopias on the one hand and 1980s socialism, feminism, and the Fringe movement on the other. See, for example, Werner Huber/Martin Middeke, "Biography in Contemporary Drama," in *Drama and Reality*, ed. Bernhard Reitz, CDE 3 (Trier: WVT, 1996), 133–43 (139); Richard Boon, "Retreating to the Future: Brenton in the Eighties," *Modern Drama* 33 (1990): 30–41; Sandra Tomc, "'Disentangled Doom': The Politics of Celebration in Howard Brenton's *Bloody Poetry*," in *Howard Brenton: A Casebook*, ed. Ann Wilson (New York: Garland, 1992), 127–44 (138); Jennifer A. Wagner, "'I am Cast as a Monster': Shelley's *Frankenstein* and the Haunting of Howard Brenton's *Bloody Poetry*," *Modern Drama* 37 (1994): 588–602.

[26] The first version has been published separately as *Bloody Poetry* (London: Methuen, 1985); the second version is printed in *Plays: Two* (London: Methuen, 1989). Changes will be discussed in the course of the essay.

[27] In order to identify quotations, F. S. Ellis, *A Lexical Concordance to the Poetical Works of Percy Bysshe Shelley* (London: Quaritch, 1892) was used; this concordance is based on H. B. Forman's edition of *The Poetical Works of P. B. Shelley*, 2 vols. (London: Reeves & Turner, 1882). As to the intertextuality of Brenton's play, Richard Holmes's *Shelley: The Pursuit* (London: Weidenfeld and Nicolson, 1974), should also be considered.

[28] *Bloody Poetry* is again a play about figures from history. On Brenton's fascination with such figures that illuminate the present, see Hersh Zeifman, "Making History: The Plays of Howard Brenton," in *British and Irish Drama since 1960*, ed. James Acheson (New York: St. Martin's Press, 1993), 130–45. Obviously, the many anachronisms in *Bloody Poetry* are calculated to evoke the parallels between Britain at the beginning of the nineteenth century and during the 1980s. There is only one other play by Brenton that features a writer: Gorky in *A Sky Blue Life* (1966, rev. 1971).

[29] The page numbers given parenthetically in the text are those of the first and the second version, respectively.

[30] "On Death," ll. 13–14; Brenton has changed the original "This world is the nurse of all we know" (line 13) into "The world is the mother of all we know."

[31] Tomc, "Disentangled Doom," 129. Polidori, according to Tomc's interpretation, is a personification, too, of conservative politics and modes of behaviour; he is the target of Shelley's and Byron's attacks although there is no interaction between him and the Romantics. The curious fact is that he often appears on stage narrating past events instead of enacting them. It may well be that Brenton meant Polidori to be nothing more than a biographer for whom the past is no longer a living present.

[32] Canto X/xxii, ll. 3989–90.

[33] Wagner, "Cast as a Monster," 590.

[34] It is important to realize that Shelley is in fact haunted by Harriet's ghost. Cf. the play's epigraph "Shelley's life seems more a haunting than a history" from Richard Holmes's *Shelley: The Pursuit*. Wagner has pointed out the importance of this topic, although she is actually speaking about the impact of Mary Shelley's *Frankenstein* on Brenton's play.

[35] Cf. Boon, (38), who comments on Mary's question "Is the price of a poem — the death of our child?" (74/302 = II,10/II,9) by referring to Byron's earlier remarks on the harm which may be caused by philosophy or poetry (37/265). However, Byron's question, ("do you not know ideas can kill?") does not put Shelley into doubt but is an answer to Polidori, who, in the cave-parable enactment, is willing to "argue philosophy," but does "not

wish to come to any harm." Shelley is well aware of the fact that poetry may under certain circumstances be "bloody."

[36] Stanzas 1, 2, 3, 15, 33, 34, 37 and 91.

[37] *Prometheus Unbound*, IV, lines 572–75, 577.

[38] Cf. Tomc, for whom *Bloody Poetry* "is almost vituperatively critical of the intellectual Left, and in particular of its inability to convince and win those who are 'the salt of the earth,' it is also curiously reluctant to endorse a historical scheme in which the Left *could* succeed. [. . .] what emerges from his play looks less like optimism than like resignation and self-punishing futility" (141).

[39] Howard Brenton, *Greenland*, The Royal Court Writers Series (London: Methuen, 1988), 3.

[40] Cf. Howard Brenton, "Petrol Bombs through the Proscenium Arch," in *New Theatre Voices of the Seventies: Sixteen Interview from Theatre Quarterly 1970–1980*, ed. Simon Trussler (London: Methuen, 1981), 96–97.

[41] Brenton, "Introduction," *Greenland*, 3.

SILVIA MERGENTHAL

The Dramatist as Reader:
Liz Lochhead's Play *Blood and Ice*

IN 1981, THE SCOTTISH POET LIZ LOCHHEAD wrote her first play, *Mary and the Monster*, which was premièred at Coventry. As Anne Varty points out in a recent article on Lochhead as a playwright,[1] *Mary and the Monster* extends the dramatic monologue form which Lochhead developed in her 1981 collection of poems, *The Grimm Sisters*. *Mary and the Monster* can be regarded as the first version of what we now know as *Blood and Ice*, which was staged at the 1982 Edinburgh Fringe Festival and published in the same year. In 1984, Lochhead revised the script of *Blood and Ice* for the Pepper's Ghost Theatre Company in London. Two years later, the play was again rewritten, this time for a touring production by Winged Horse; in the course of these revisions, the play acquired a new subtitle, "A Tale of the Creation of *Frankenstein*." In addition, there is a radio version broadcast by Radio Four in 1990 as well as a television version broadcast in 1992. The following discussion will draw mainly on the 1982 printed version.

In an interview published in 1990, Lochhead states that her initial interest was in Mary Wollstonecraft, Mary Shelley's mother:

> It kept fascinating me, how this intellectual, rational woman, with all these incredibly powerful, almost too rational, views of female education, had been so haunted by bogeymen in her own life, and had tried to drown herself. And then it interested me that her daughter should have grown up to write *Frankenstein*, a horror book as far as I was concerned. Once I had started, that fact kept haunting me, so that I became gradually more interested in Mary Shelley, the heir to reason.[2]

As a result, *Blood and Ice* focusses on the consciousness of the author of *Frankenstein*, Mary Shelley. This focus is, from the beginning, reflected in the structure of the play.

The play operates on three levels: the first level features Mary Shelley in 1824, shortly after the death of Byron. This level of the play is established in the first scene and resumed in the final section; it thus serves as a kind of narrative frame which reduplicates, to an extent, the various framing devices of Mary Shelley's novel. In Mary Shelley's mind, Byron's death and, of course, the death of Percy Shelley in 1822 are inextricably linked with the death of her mother, with that of her own first child — and with that of her "brainchild," Victor Frankenstein's monster: "The dead," she says, "are constantly reassembling themselves."[3]

Already, on this first level, Lochhead weaves a dense fabric of intertextual references, for example, to Percy Shelley's and Byron's poetry, to Mary Shelley's journal, and to Shakespeare's *The Tempest.*

The second level of the play takes its departure from Mary Shelley's preface to the 1831 edition of *Frankenstein*, in which she famously describes the novel as having originated in a competition between herself, her husband, Byron, and John Polidori during the summer of 1816, which they spent together in Switzerland. Mary Shelley writes,

> 'We will each write a ghost story,' said Lord Byron; and his proposition was acceded to. There were four of us. The noble author began a tale, a fragment of which he printed at the end of his poem of Mazeppa. Shelley, more apt to embody ideas and sentiments in the radiance of brilliant imagery, and in the music of the most melodious verse that adorns our language, than to invent the machinery of a story, commenced one founded upon the experiences of his early life. Poor Polidori had some terrible idea about a skull-headed lady, who was so punished for peeping through a key-hole — what to see I forget — something very shocking and wrong of course; but when she was reduced to a worse condition than the renowned Tom of Coventry, he did not know what to do with her, and was obliged to despatch her to the tomb of the Capulets, the only place for which she was fitted. The illustrious poets also, annoyed by the platitude of prose, speedily relinquished their uncongenial task. I busied myself *to think of a story* [. . .].[4]

In Act I, Scenes ii to vii of *Blood and Ice*, the rather sinister and emotionally fraught atmosphere of that summer is recreated in a series of conversations between the Shelleys, Mary's step-sister Claire Clairmont, and Byron, but there are also several flashbacks, for instance to Mary's childhood and her relationships with her father, the radical philosopher William Godwin, and with Claire. This second level of the play culminates, in Act I, Scene viii, in the literary creation of the monster — and in the famous sentence from *Frankenstein*: "It was on a dreary night in November [. . .]."[5]

In her re-creation,[6] Lochhead suggests that Percy Shelley is sexually attracted to Claire (an attraction which is reciprocated) and that his friendship with Byron has a strong homoerotic component. Consequently, in the play, Mary accuses her husband as follows, "You'd almost think you were in love with [Byron] yourself." And she adds, "Claire also wants to be with Byron because she's jealous of me with you" (8). Byron, in his turn, is not averse to sleeping with Claire (and indeed fathers her child), but also shows a sexual interest in Mary.

Byron, incidentally, functions as a kind of mouthpiece of the author: it is Byron who contributes most of the biographical information on Mary Shelley, and it is he who introduces most of the intertextual references, for example, to works by Mary's illustrious parents, especially to Wollstonecraft's *Vindication of the Rights of Woman* and to Godwin's *Political Justice*. Particularly intriguing is his use of Shakespeare's *The Tempest*.[7] While this play is first alluded to by Mary Shelley — in the opening scene she describes Shelley's death by drowning as a "sea-change," thus comparing him, implicitly, to Ferdinand and herself to Miranda — it is Byron who takes it upon himself to expound the lessons that the play seems to provide. He condones the Mary/Miranda parallel, but likens Shelley to Ariel, and himself to Caliban, with Mary/Miranda called upon to align herself with one or the other of the two: "Mary, you are getting good and sick, I know it, of Ariel's head-in-the-clouds hopefulness. Come on, come down to earth, where you belong, come and curl up with old Clubfooted Caliban!" (19).

In the second act of the play, the two biographical levels described so far are juxtaposed with what might be called the fictional level, namely, with scenes from *Frankenstein* itself. While, as we have seen, the first act closes with the creation of the monster on paper, the second opens with his creation on stage. Both creation scenes are linked by Mary's continued presence on stage, and carry strong sexual overtones. The stage directions accordingly read as follows: "Scene I, vii: *Sinister music and sexual breathing noises. MARY presses her hands to her head*" (20). "Scene II, i: *MARY writing. Thunder and lightning. Door flashes open, she shuts it, etc. Out of the cupboard comes FRANKENSTEIN and the MONSTER strapped to his bed*" (21).

The other key episodes of the novel that are taken up in the play are, not surprisingly, the murder of Victor Frankenstein's younger brother William and the subsequent trial, the confrontation between the monster and his creator in the French Alps, Frankenstein's decision not to provide the monster with a bride, the murder of Frankenstein's own bride Elizabeth on her wedding-day, and the chase across the Polar Ice.

However, even in the dramatization of these episodes, the play consistently explores the possibility of reading *Frankenstein* as an autobiographical text, a possibility to which I shall return later. In *Blood and Ice*, the borderline between "life" and "fiction" or between the biographical levels and the fictional level is blurred by the most characteristic dramatic technique of the play, namely, that of doubling: while Mary, as befits her position at the center of the play, remains Mary throughout, the same actors play, respectively, Percy Shelley and Frankenstein, Byron and the monster, Claire Clairmont and Elizabeth, Elise (the Shelleys' maid) and Justine (the Frankensteins' maid). For example, at the end of Act II, Scene v, we leave Elizabeth and Frankenstein passionately embracing, only to re-encounter them, as Claire Clairmont and Percy Shelley, at the beginning of Scene vi — still passionately embracing. Again, as with the framing devices and with the allusive texture of the play, this doubling can be traced back to the novel with its plenitude of *Doppelgänger*: Frankenstein and the monster, Frankenstein and Walton, Frankenstein and Clerval, Elizabeth and Frankenstein's mother, Elizabeth and Justine, or Elizabeth and the monster's unfinished bride.

There are four ways — complementary rather than mutually exclusive — in which Lochhead's play can be contextualized. The first context is that of her own work. Lochhead's poem "Dreaming Frankenstein," published in 1984,[8] begins with the lines "She said she / woke up with him in her head, in her bed," thus focussing, like the play, on the consciousness of the author of *Frankenstein*. Other poems in this collection, notably "What the Creature Said" and "Smirnoff for Karloff," also refer to Shelley's novel or, in the case of "Smirnoff for Karloff," to dramatizations of it. Besides *Dreaming Frankenstein*, there is the dramatic monologue "The Bride," published in 1985,[9] and there is a general preoccupation in Lochhead's texts with the re-working of cultural myths. This revisionist tendency is particularly evident in two other Lochhead plays, in her 1985 adaptation of Bram Stoker's *Dracula* and in *Mary Queen of Scots Got Her Head Chopped Off* (1987).

The latter play opens up the second of our four contexts, the context of Scottish literature. In a recent article entitled "The Voice of Revelation: Liz Lochhead and Monsters,"[10] S. J. Boyd argues that Scotland is, like Frankenstein's Monster, put together from "all sorts of bits and pieces,"[11] and that Scottish literature has, throughout its history, evinced a preference for representations of the divided self, representations which very often take the form of the monstrous.

The third context is provided by the long history of dramatizations of *Frankenstein*. This tradition begins with Richard Brinsley Peake's play *Presumption; or, the Fate of Frankenstein* (1823) and has just entered its latest phase with Kenneth Branagh's *Mary Shelley's Frankenstein* (1995). Two films in particular may have left traces in Lochhead's play: the *The Bride of Frankenstein* (1935), like *Blood and Ice*, foregrounds Mary Shelley and introduces the concept of doubling. In *The Bride of Frankenstein*, the monstrous bride as well as Mary Shelley is played by Elsa Lanchester — to whom, incidentally, the speaker in the dramatic monologue "The Bride" compares herself. The second film, Christopher Isherwood and Don Bachardy's *Frankenstein: The True Story* (1973), suggests, through the use of a prologue closely modelled on that of *The Bride of Frankenstein*, that Shelley's novel be read as a *roman à clef*, with Percy Shelley as Frankenstein and Byron as Henry Clerval, who lures Shelley/Frankenstein away from his wife Mary/Elizabeth to create a new man.[12]

The fourth context is the one to which the title of this paper alludes, namely, the context of literary criticism. I should like to indicate three areas of literary criticism — again complementary rather than mutually exclusive — which seem to me to be pertinent to Lochhead's play and to suggest that Lochhead's play is both informed by these critical approaches and in its own way contributes to them, and thus to a better understanding of the novel.

The first area is that of biographical criticism. As Liz Lochhead admits in the interview already quoted, it is first Mary Wollstonecraft's life and then the life of her daughter that conditioned her approach to the novel: "Why would Mary Shelley write about monsters?"[13] Janet Todd notes that, more than most novels, *Frankenstein* seems to demand some biographical interpretation, owing to the extraordinary situation of Mary Shelley when she wrote it.[14] Indeed, as Johanna M. Smith points out in a recent article on the critical history of *Frankenstein*, most commentators have concentrated on the author rather than on the novel, particularly on the author as Percy Shelley's wife: "One aspect of *Frankenstein*'s critical history, then, is this tendency not to examine the novel in its own right."[15]

Among the various factors informing Mary Shelley's situation, Manfred Markus, for example, mentions her difficult childhood, her stormy affair with Percy Shelley, her frequent pregnancies, and the suicides of her step-sister Fanny Imlay and of Shelley's first wife.[16] Hence, Mary Shelley is said to have produced what can be called, in Freudian terms, a family romance,[17] although critics differ as to whether this imaginative activity relates primarily to the family in which she herself grew up or to the family that she tried to create with Percy Shelley.[18] Accordingly, the figure of William Frankenstein (who is murdered by

the monster) has been variously identified as the elder William Godwin,
Mary's father, as his son by his second wife, also named William, and as
Mary's own first son, yet another William. In *Blood and Ice*, Byron, in
his role as a representative of the author — and as a reader of *Frankenstein* who, like Lochhead herself, is interested in biography — draws
attention to this conflation:

> I'm sure it is silly of me to read between the lines though, Oh if only
> the naughty reader would keep his glad-eyes on the text. No profit in
> noticing an author name a character after her beloved baba, blonde
> curls and all, and then strangle him to death on page sixty nine — oh
> not nay mamas, especially not busy fingered distracted mamas, who
> have not occasionally, en passant, wished to silence the little darling.
>
> (28)

The second area of literary criticism to which Lochhead's play relates is
the question of what, in *Frankenstein*, constitutes the monstrous. The
play, much like the history of *Frankenstein* criticism,[19] suggests various
answers to this question, ranging from the monstrous in ourselves —
"Oh yes Mary," says Byron, "there is something in us which is very
ugly. [. . .] We are put together all wrong [. . .]" — to the monstrous in the Shelleys' situation as social outcasts — "Shelley, we are
treated like monsters, cut off from all the world" (29) — to the monstrosity of women writers, particularly of women writers writing about
monsters:

> I do not want to write of horror, and fantasy, and sickly imaginings.
> My mother wrote 'A Vindication of the Rights of Woman.' My father
> wrote 'Political Justice.' And I am to pervert my imagination to writ-
> ing foul fairy stories which do not elevate the spirit or have anything
> anchoring them to Real Life. Monstrous idea! Foolishness. I don't
> think we should play with such dangerous elements. (14)

This establishes a convenient link to our third area of literary criticism,
to the issue of female creativity. *Frankenstein* is frequently read as a
novel about the anxieties of authorship, both in the sense of producing
a work of art and in the sense of giving birth to a child. As Anne K.
Mellor[20] rightly points out, these two processes have been compared to
one another ever since Plato suggested that men write books to gain
the immortality women achieve by having children, but the comparison
does have special reverberations for women authors. More specifically,
then, *Frankenstein* can be said, as Barbara Johnson has argued, to be
the story of the experience of creating *Frankenstein*.[21] The 1831 preface
to *Frankenstein*, to which I have already referred, shows quite clearly
that Mary Shelley is a reluctant author, not only of *Frankenstein*, but

also of her own story as the daughter — and later, the wife — of a famous author. In the novel itself, she systematically censors her own speech by building a series of screens around her authentic voice. It is probably the monster's account of his education that is closest to Mary Shelley's own experience of growing up in the Godwin household. This narrative, however, is enclosed within two other narratives, and all three of them are, of course, told by male narrators. In a more overt form of self-censorship, Mary Shelley gave the manuscript of the novel to her husband, who suggested a number of revisions, all of which she incorporated in her text.

How does Lochhead's play address this question of authorship? As we have already seen, *Blood and Ice* focusses throughout on the consciousness of Mary Shelley. This aspect of the play is foregrounded by numerous direct comments, often provided by Byron, on the burden of Mary's illustrious parentage and on her need to distance herself from her parents in order to develop her own literary talents: "And how about you, Miranda-Mary? Won't you write a revolution — like your papa, Mary — Godwin was ever one for writing up a storm of Brave New Worlds, wasn't he?" (9).

In addition, as McDonald and Harvie argue in their article "Putting New Twists to Old Stories: Feminism and Lochhead's Drama,"[22] there are several scenes which can be regarded as self-referential, thus increasing audience awareness of the ways in which meaning is textually produced and controlled. McDonald and Harvie here single out the various mirror scenes in the play. The role of Byron as mouthpiece of the author can be regarded as yet another self-referential strategy. Finally, the metaphoric pairing of fire and ice, which, as Andrew Griffin has shown in detail, informs Shelley's novel,[23] is in Lochhead's play replaced by the pairing of its title, blood and ice. The last lines of the play read as follows, "I dreamed Shelley walked naked into the room bloodstained, skin in tatters, seaweed tangled in his hair crying out 'The sea is Invading The House! The Ice is invading the house. This house? A blood bath. A bath of ice. Will the Ice save me?'" (34).

On one level, this refers to an incident in Mary Shelley's life to which the play has already alluded in the penultimate scene. Mary, in one of her many pregnancies, had a haemorrhage and was saved by her husband, who plunged her into a bath of ice, thus stopping the flow. However, while blood in this context and in the lines just quoted is clearly associated with death as opposed to the life-saving qualities of ice, it is linked to authorship, specifically to female authorship, in another scene of the play. In a flashback to Mary's childhood and adolescence, Mary is shown menstruating for the first time: "MARY: (*Coldly fascinated*) Great . . . gouts and spatters . . . crimson trickle . . . a thin dark red line running . . . *scribbling as if a quill was dipped in blood and scribbled"* (12; italics mine).

Lochhead herself has argued in an interview quoted by Anne Varty that "a lot of women poets write as if ink were blood. But it's not. Ink is ink — and I would like to celebrate it for itself."[24] Can we then assume that blood and ice, in the context of the play, represent two forms of literary creativity, forms that can be described, respectively, as "bloody" autobiographical writing and as "icy" non-autobiographical writing? The first of these two forms can also be associated with emotion, the second with reason. As we have already seen, it was this dichotomy which initially attracted Lochhead to the Wollstonecraft/ Mary Shelley/*Frankenstein* material.

The fact that Lochhead, in her various revisions of the play, pays particular attention to the imagery of blood and ice certainly seems to point in that direction. If this is the case, then Mary Shelley's belief in the life-saving qualities of ice, however tentatively expressed, would suggest that, according to Lochhead, Mary Shelley did manage, in writing her novel, to deconstruct the mythologies she had inherited, including those of her illustrious parents; in other words, she did escape from the constraints of her biography. While Lochhead's intertextual and metatextual strategies would seem to support this reading of the play even in the 1982 version of *Blood and Ice*, the dramatic technique of doubling militates against it. It does not come as a surprise, then, that Lochhead, in later versions of the play, discards this overt roleplaying. By 1984, as Varty shows, the play has ceased to offer adequate explanations as to how the experience of Mary Shelley's life could give rise to the novel. Consequently, in the poem "Dreaming Frankenstein," the protagonist sits down to "quill and ink / and *icy* paper."

Notes

[1] Anne Varty, "Scripts and Performances," in *Liz Lochhead's Voices*, ed. Robert Crawford and Anne Varty (Edinburgh: Edinburgh UP, 1993), 148–69.

[2] Gillean Somerville-Arjat and Rebecca E. Wilson, eds., *Sleeping with Monsters: Conversations with Scottish and Irish Women Poets* (Edinburgh: Polygon, 1990), 13.

[3] Liz Lochhead, *Blood and Ice* (Edinburgh: Salamander, 1982), 34 All subsequent page references in the text are to this edition.

[4] Mary Shelley, *Frankenstein: Complete, Authoritative Text with Biographical and Historical Contexts, Critical History, and Essays from Five Contemporary*

Critical Perspectives, ed. Johanna M. Smith (Boston: St. Martin's Press, 1992), 21.

[5] Shelley, *Frankenstein*, 57.

[6] Here, as elsewhere, Lochhead is particularly indebted to Christopher Small's *Ariel Like a Harpy: Shelley, Mary and Frankenstein* (London: Gollancz, 1973).

[7] See Small, *Ariel Like a Harpy*, chapter 6 ("Ariel and Caliban").

[8] Liz Lochhead, *Dreaming Frankenstein and Collected Poems* (Edinburgh: Polygon, 1984).

[9] Liz Lochhead, "The Bride" (1985); repr. in Somerville-Arjat/Wilson, eds., *Sleeping with Monsters*, 14–16.

[10] S. J. Boyd, "The Voice of Revelation: Liz Lochhead and Monsters," in *Lochhead's Voices*, 38–56.

[11] Boyd, "The Voice of Revelation," 41.

[12] For a history of the dramatizations of *Frankenstein*, see Albert J. Lavalley, "The Stage and Film Children of *Frankenstein*: A Survey," in *The Endurance of Frankenstein: Essays on Mary Shelley's Novel*, ed. George Levine and U. C. Knoepflmacher (Berkeley and Los Angeles: U of California P, 1979), 243–89.

[13] Somerville-Arjat/Wilson, eds., *Sleeping with Monsters*, 13.

[14] Janet M. Todd, "Frankenstein's Daughter: Mary Shelley and Mary Wollstonecraft," *Women and Literature* 4 (1976): 18–27, see in particular 25–26.

[15] Shelley, *Frankenstein*, 189.

[16] Manfred Markus, "Mary Shelleys *Frankenstein* aus biographischer Sicht," in *Mary Shelleys "Frankenstein": Text, Kontext, Wirkung: Vorträge des Frankenstein-Symposiums in Ingolstadt (Juni 1993)*, ed. Günther Blaicher (Essen: verlag die blaue eule, 1994), 47–65.

[17] See Elisabeth Bronfen, "Rewriting the Family: Mary Shelley's *Frankenstein* in its Biographical/Textual Context," in *Frankenstein: Creation and Monstrosity*, ed. Stephen Bann (London: Reaktion Books, 1994), 16–38.

[18] On the former, see U. C. Knoepflmacher, "Thoughts on the Aggression of Daughters"; on the latter, see Ellen Moers, "Female Gothic." Both essays can be found in *The Endurance of Frankenstein*, 88–119 and 77–87, respectively.

[19] On the issue of monstrosity, see Fred Botting, *Making Monstrous: Frankenstein, Criticism, Theory* (Manchester: Manchester UP, 1991).

[20] Anne K. Mellor, *Mary Shelley: Her Life, Her Fiction, Her Monsters* (New York and London: Routledge, 1988), 52.

[21] Barbara Johnson, "My Monster/My Self," *Diacritics* 12 (1982): 2–10.

[22] Jan McDonald and Jennifer Harvie, "Putting New Twists to Old Stories: Feminism and Lochhead's Drama," in *Lochhead's Voices*, 124–47.

[23] Andrew Griffin, "Fire and Ice in *Frankenstein*," in *The Endurance of Frankenstein*, 49–73.

[24] Varty, "Scripts and Performances," 152.

BEATE NEUMEIER

The Truth of Fiction — The Fiction of Truth: Judith Chernaik's *Mab's Daughters*

> So this is how we live in two ages at once: the age of the author stud-
> ied, pursued, celebrated and hyped, and the age of the author denied
> and eliminated, airbrushed from the world of writing with a theoreti-
> cal efficiency that would be the envy of any totalitarian regime trying
> to remove its discredited past leaders from the record of history. The
> situation appears peculiar. For, seen from the common-sense point of
> view, there is no doubt that authors do exist, in quite considerable
> numbers. [. . .] They have lives and wives and lovers and mistresses,
> and from time to time they go to jail, or go to France, or win a fa-
> mous prize or a state accolade. [. . .] From all they say or do it seems
> evident that it was they, and not writing in general, that conceived and
> developed and produced their books, that the images and preoccupa-
> tions derived in some fashion from their own experience, that the hu-
> man figures they represent may even at times have something or other
> to do with their friends or their enemies.
>
> Malcolm Bradbury[1]

MALCOLM BRADBURY'S COMMENT POLEMICALLY pinpoints the present paradoxical gap between the postmodern prisonhouse of fiction with the concomitant view of the author as mere crossing-point
within an endless web of cultural intertextualities, on the one hand,[2]
and the equally strong contemporary interest in life-writing with the
implicit claim of truth about the relation between art and the individual
personality of the author, on the other. Despite the seeming incom-
patibility of self-conscious fictionality and the belief in fact, contemporary novelists seem to have become obsessed with the biographical or
autobiographical mode. Of course, this tendency can be explained as
part of the postmodern deconstruction of conventional modes of writing. But at the same time this obsession with the past bespeaks an in-

defatigable yearning for originality and truth. The claim that the "turn towards autobiography [. . .] is symptomatic of a continued obsession with the problem of identity"[3] equally applies to similar developments in the genre of biography in which historical figures appear as fictional autobiographers.[4]

Consequently, since the 1980s, an increasing number of novelists — many of whom are also critics and thus experts in current poststructuralist theory — have turned to using fictional biography and autobiography in order to express their dissatisfaction with the familiar postmodern relativism. Instead of refuting truth claims many of these authors use their critical knowledge of poststructuralist theory as a basis for an attempt to reclaim some form of truth via life-writing. Douwe Fokkema has explained this change of postmodernism in the context of the anti-relativism of movements with a political aim as epitomized in feminist, postcolonial, autobiographical, or historiographic writing.[5]

In keeping with Fokkema's description, Judith Chernaik's 1991 novel *Mab's Daughters: Shelley's Wives and Lovers: Their Own Story*[6] takes up — at least implicitly — issues of feminism, autobiography, and historiography. *Mab's Daughters* constructs and reconstructs a decisive period in the personal histories of the members of the "Shelley circle," beginning with the famous ghost-story writing competition at the Villa Diodati on Lake Geneva in 1816 and ending with the preparations of the Shelley family to leave England for Italy approximately one year later. This reconstruction is built around the perspectives of the four women intricately involved: Percy Shelley's first wife Harriet, his second wife Mary, her step-sister Clare and her half-sister Fanny. The facts of the story told in these women's journals and letters are well-known. They include the births of two children to Mary and Clare, the suicides of Fanny and Harriet, and the creation of two famous works of art, Mary's *Frankenstein* and Percy's *Laon and Cythna or The Revolt of Islam*.

Chernaik's novel evokes a number of expectations, as she takes up the lives of the most famous and notorious literary figures representing the Romantic period's desire for transgression not only in a philosophical and aesthetic, but also in a very personal sense. Since their lifetimes, Percy Shelley and Lord Byron in particular have inspired the imagination as well as the voyeuristic curiosity of literary scholars, fellow writers, and the general public alike. In addition to these archetypal rebels epitomizing the inextricability of life and art, the reader of the journals and letters in Chernaik's novel encounters images of quite a number of men of letters, namely William Godwin, Thomas Peacock, James Hogg, and Leigh Hunt. As assumptions are made about the relation between their work and the bio-historical events depicted, the reader is invited to verify this literary-historical game by reading or re-reading these authors' works.[7] This detective work also pertains to the women's literary achievements, foremost to Mary's, but also to her mother Mary Wollstonecraft's.[8]

Chernaik's novel plays upon popular speculations about "the postulated connection between sexual deviance and achievement."[9] The reader thus expects the revelation of the "true story" from the female perspective: what did the transgression of boundaries — the moral boundaries of marriage in particular — entail for the women surrounding Shelley (and Byron)? Did they embrace the concept of free love wholeheartedly, or were they prone to feelings of jealousy, rage, hatred or depression? How did they experience the consequences of this lifestyle, such as pregnancy and illegitimate childbirth? This is particularly interesting, as three of the women, Mary, Fanny, and Clare, are the daughters or step-daughters of the famous anarchist-feminist couple William Godwin and Mary Wollstonecraft.

❧

> Women have served all these centuries as looking-glasses possessing the magic and delicious power of reflecting the figure of man at twice its natural size. [. . .] if she begins to tell the truth, the figure in the looking-glass shrinks; his fitness for life is diminished.
>
> Virginia Woolf[10]

By choosing the point of view of four women in Percy Shelley's life, Chernaik partakes in the current interest fostered by feminist critics and women writers alike in seeking to recover and reclaim the past on behalf of those who have been silenced and marginalized by inequality and historiography.[11] This rebellion against the exclusion of women from historical discourse has led to a successful rediscovery of neglected women writers and consequently to a decisive rewriting of the literary canon. The concomitant interest particularly of contemporary women writers in their literary predecessors and in women overshadowed by famous men has been explained by Annegret Maack with specific reference to Mary Shelley as aiming at a subversion of the public image and at a deconstruction of the dominant male figures through the female perspective.[12]

Chernaik's book seems to exemplify both aspects pointed out by Maack. The subtitle of her novel, *Shelley's Wives and Lovers: Their Own Story*, takes up the notion of the derivative secondary nature of all the women surrounding the male poet as the center of their existence.

Thus, not only does Chernaik give a voice to the writer Mary Shelley, but also to those women of the "Shelley circle" who did not leave a literary legacy behind (although Clare and Hunt's wife are presented as harbouring artistic aspirations as well).[13] Moreover, Mary Shelley's name was in fact for a long time neglected and eclipsed by the fame of her husband and that of her parents. Her creations, Frankenstein and the monster, had taken on a separate existence as cultural myth long before the value of their fictional origin and its author were rediscovered. Meanwhile, however, Mary Shelley has been successfully reclaimed as an imaginative early nineteenth-century writer and figures prominently in the literary canon. In the light of the contemporary interest in nineteenth-century women writers, it is not an exaggeration to speak of a veritable Mary Shelley renaissance, including novels (from Brian Aldiss's *Frankenstein Unbound* to Fay Weldon's *The Lives and Loves of a She-Devil*), plays (for example, Liz Lochhead's *Blood and Ice*), and films (from the silent movie versions to Ken Russell's *Gothic* and Kenneth Branagh's *Mary Shelley's Frankenstein*) about her life and her fiction. Finally, an astounding amount of criticism has been written on her work, much of it centering on the relationship between life and art and attempting to explain *Frankenstein* through Mary's biography.[14]

As a literary scholar who has written a highly acclaimed book on Percy Shelley's poetry, Chernaik plays upon the reader's knowledge of criticism. Thus, the title of her novel, *Mab's Daughters*, echoes Gilbert and Gubar's epoch-making analysis of Mary Shelley's novel *Frankenstein* as a re-writing of *Paradise Lost*, where the author is presented as Milton's literary daughter, caught between obedience and rebellion. Chernaik playfully applies this intertextual reference to the literary *and* personal "affiliations" of *Mab's Daughters*.[15] But Chernaik's novel does not aim at just another psychoanalytical rendering of the creation of *Frankenstein*, or simply at a deconstruction of Percy Shelley through the female perspective. Instead, Chernaik is interested in investigating how the intricate relations of life and art are linked to the gender relations within the Shelley circle.

❧

Thus provided, thus confident and inquiring, I set out in the pursuit of truth.

Virginia Woolf[16]

Chernaik's promise to reveal the stories of the four women — their *own* stories that is — alludes to claims of authenticity as well as subjectivity of the journal and letter forms. The reader, familiar with some of the historical events and their relation to the artistic creations referred to in Chernaik's novel, thus hopes for the revelation of the ultimate "true story" beyond all assumptions and interpretations, while at the same time being aware of the partial and provisional character of all truth.[17]

Consequently, even before the story proper begins, the simulation of authenticity is both emphasized and undercut by the familiar double framing of the story. The author presents herself in the preface as the publisher of hitherto forgotten documents left to the Library of East India House by Thomas Peacock shortly before his death. This is followed by a note to the reader written forty-four years after the events of 1816–17 by the fictional Peacock, who explains his possession of these "uncensored records," which he intends to leave "to the judgment of posterity" (ix).

Thus, Peacock presents himself as a neutral keeper of those intimate letters and journals, which he ostensibly — as he all too eagerly claims — did not even peruse. Despite these protestations of non-interference, he at the same time claims to have withheld those papers from Mary Shelley at the time of Percy's death in order to spare her additional grief and guilt. Peacock's note thus undermines his own claim of neutrality, disclosing his interpretative partiality. At the same time this partiality is needed to evoke the reader's suspense that "the pages that follow may help to elucidate the most puzzling mysteries in the tangled relations of the Shelley circle" (ix). These expectations are further nourished by references to the fatefulness of that last year in England, and to Peacock's own important role in the matter: "I often think that if I had been able to persuade Shelley and Mary to remain in Marlow, they might have achieved the happiness that was the theme of our daily intercourse" (vii).

The illusion of "uncensored records" is further undermined by the division of the chronologically structured book into six parts — reminiscent of Shelley's experiment with epic structure, but also of dramatic three-part structure — registering changes in exterior as well as interior conditions: in locale, seasons, and moods. Thus, the reader follows a movement from the emotional and creative summer turbulences at Lake Geneva to an autumnal season in Bath and London ending in the suicides of Fanny and Harriet. This narrows the focus onto the increasingly antagonistic perspectives of the remaining two journal keepers, Mary and Clare, and their spring hopes for renewal and happiness in their new home in Marlow, including the birth of Clare's child by Byron and Mary's new pregnancy coinciding with the completion of her novel. The personal and sociopolitical clouds overshadowing this idyll, however, gradually thicken, climaxing in the disclosure of a summer liaison between Clare and Percy Shelley. Accordingly, the precarious emotional balance within the Shelley household ends — despite the birth of Mary's daughter, the publication of her novel, and the completion of Percy's *Laon and Cythna* — on a note of autumnal melancholia and a vague hope for renewed happiness in Italy.

The subtext of the "intimate chronicle" of the four women suggests as reasons for the Shelley family's move to Italy not the dampness of the house in Marlow or the legal hassles about Percy's children, but the entanglements between the people living together and their possible consequences. Italy, therefore, seems to offer an escape from open confrontation with each other and with their own hidden feelings through a turn to new surroundings in the hope of establishing new life patterns — or returning to older ones.

❦

[. . .] fiction is like a spider's web, attached ever so lightly perhaps, but still attached to life at all four corners. Often the attachment is scarcely perceptible [. . .]. But when the web is pulled askew, hooked up at the edge, torn in the middle, one remembers that these webs are not spun in mid-air by incorporeal creatures, but are the work of suffering human beings, and are attached to grossly material things, like health and money and the houses we live in.

Virginia Woolf[18]

Chernaik's use of the traditionally female forms of writing, the journal and the letter, raises the reader's expectations about confessions of the writer's most secret emotions.[19] This very intimacy, however, implies simultaneously a high degree of subjectivity and of unreliability, suggesting that there may be only subjective truths. At the same time, Chernaik's use of journal and letter counteracts the prejudice that women's journals and letters are restricted to a description of private, personal feelings. It demonstrates the complex interaction of the individual private and general public concerns of the women involved. It reveals the interrelations between theoretical beliefs and private feelings with regard to love and with regard to the political situation (for instance in their discussion of poverty in rural Marlow). Moreover, the contemporary reader is explicitly reminded of the public character of journal-writing in the nineteenth century, when Mary discusses the publication of her travel diaries. In addition, the self-consciousness about the journals being read by others is already emphasized in Chernaik's preface: "It was at this time [1814, after the elopement with Percy Shelley] that Mary and Clare first realized that the journals they had kept since childhood might have an interest beyond the merely personal" (vi). The basic tension between seemingly objective truth and subjective unreliability is further emphasized by the tension between the simulated objectivity of the dialogue parts, reminiscent of tape recordings, and the pointedly conscious and subconscious personal editing and censoring that is evident in the letters and journals.

Thus, Clare's affair with Percy Shelley is spelled out only in an additional hidden page of her journal. Harriet's secret about the origin of her pregnancy is veiled as a dream account, clouding her own memory. And Mary's knowledge of Percy's affair with Clare is acknowledged only briefly in her journal. Her feelings of jealousy and rage and later her desire for revenge are only hinted at. This may serve as an implicit reflection on the power of the writing process, on the belief that spelling things out on the page changes their reality status. In contrast to their suppression in the seemingly factual journal form, these feelings — as the reader surmises — are acted out in the fictional transformation of the events in *Frankenstein*.

Finally, the tension between a belief in the attainability of truth and a conviction of its inapproachability is played out in the very multiperspectivism of the letters and journals of the four women. The different viewpoints shed contrasting lights on the events, illuminating, contradicting, or complementing each other. Different truths appear, even for those involved, out of an intricate web of confessions, lies, delusions and self-delusions. Of course, this procedure echoes the interlocking of narrative perspectives in Mary Shelley's *Frankenstein*, where the three male perspectives of Frankenstein, his creation, and Walton as chronicler are also used to complement and correct each other, denying the reader the consolation of a single truth. Throughout the history of the novel's reception, however, readers — out of a desire for an ultimate truth — have attempted to attach "the truth" to one of these perspectives, turning alternately Frankenstein and his creation into the mould of the "real" monster. Thus, to a certain extent at least, the reader turns creator, whereas the autobiographer is revealed as "verbal construct."[20]

Chernaik's novel takes this up in the antagonism of the perspectives of Clare and Mary and in the ambivalence about their reliability. As in Mary Shelley's novel this aspect of a plurality of truths, however, is not extended so far as to suggest the constructedness of reality through the writing process. Taken together, the different subjective truths in the journals and letters do make a coherent picture. Thus, the "true story" seems approachable to a certain extent, although the "whole truth" eventually remains unattainable for the external reader as well as for those involved. The tension between fact and fiction, truth and lies, clairvoyance and delusion is kept throughout.

ॐ

> I treated art as the supreme reality and life as a mere mode of fiction.
>
> Oscar Wilde[21]

In Chernaik's rendering of the Shelley circle's fateful last year in England, these ambivalences and contradictions between theory and practice, ideal and reality surface also with regard to the concept of free love as experienced in the gender relations within the Shelley circle. They emerge as discrepancies between desire and guilt, freedom and duty, rebellion and constraint, egocentrism and altruism, issues of gender and love, which are also central concerns of Percy Shelley's *Revolt of Islam* and Mary Shelley's *Frankenstein*. In this process both the gap between theory and practice as concerns the equality of the sexes and the consequences of this gap become evident.

In Chernaik's novel the basis of the belief in the concept of free love, which is shared by all members of the Shelley circle at some point, is traced back from Percy Shelley to William Godwin and Mary Wollstonecraft. Thus — significantly — the biographical reference points for this belief function at the same time as parent and lover figures. William Godwin and Mary Wollstonecraft's marriage epitomized the tension between reality and the theoretical claims of anarchy and feminism.[22] The journals of Mary, Clare, and Fanny reveal their suffering from these tensions as the result of the conflict between Godwin's theoretical claims of liberty and equality and their experience of him as a distant patriarchal figure, who does not interfere in his second wife's conventional educational aims. While Clare radically opposes and criticizes Godwin (and her mother) for their hypocritical attitude, characterizing her father as "timid, conventional, vain, pompous" (140), Fanny breaks under the pressure of these tensions when she realizes her double loss of inheritance. Having been denied access to her mother's writing by Godwin during her adolescence, she realizes, after she is finally able to read it, the impossibility of living her mother's theory without having developed sufficient self-esteem and self-interest (25, 83). In addition, Godwin's disclosure of her illegitimate origin in conjunction with her enforced departure from the family home renders her an emotional outcast. When — as the journals reveal — even her sisters Mary and Clare as well as Percy Shelley fail to support her, she successfully commits the suicide her mother had only attempted. The contradiction between theory and practice, ideal and reality also proves fatal for Harriet, Shelley's first wife. After having met Shelley she claims Godwin's work as her Bible,[23] but her attempts at living the doctrine of free love only lead to disaster. If her elopement with Shelley and her new pregnancy after their separation stand for her belief in the concept of free love, her marriage to him and her wish for his return are evidence of her need for conventional safety. Like Fanny, she ends the intolerability of these tensions by taking her own life.

Unlike her sisters Fanny and Clare, Mary re-enacts her parents' dilemma, first living their belief in free love with Shelley but later marrying him (after the Christian rite). Unlike Clare, she condones her father's hypocrisies, such as his financial interests in Shelley or his hushing up of Fanny's suicide. She even dedicates her novel *Frankenstein* to Godwin, attesting to her "masculine mind." Mary also remains loyal to Shelley's ideals, particularly to his theory of ideal love as a search "for our 'other half,' the lost, irreplaceable twin" (75). In contradistinction to the "despotism of marriage"[24] Shelley evokes the Platonic ideal of the union of two halves, which he links to the brother-sister incest described in *Laon and Cythna*, the original version of the *Revolt of Islam*.[25] In her journal Mary professes her having received personal and literary inspiration from it:

> When I first saw my love, before we exchanged a word, I knew that he was my fate, he recognised me in the same flesh. [. . .] What is its source — that true affinity of soul? This I know: that it is the most precious single thing that we have, Shelley and I. If we were to lose it, to destroy it — but no, 'let me not think on't.' (75)

This remark, which in her journal is followed by the description of quarrels with her rival Clare, is at once proof of her theoretical adherence to Shelley's ideal and of her concomitant jealousy and real-life fear of losing him to someone else. Consequently, Mary's fears about a love affair between Percy and Clare are not allowed to surface openly. This becomes evident in her record of a seemingly theoretical, but obviously deeply personal "disturbing conversation" on the question of "whether love suffers or gains from being shared" (175). In this context Percy Shelley's repeated attempts to create love triangles involving his friend Hogg and his respective wives mark the potential turning point where a theory of freedom becomes tyrannical practice, with women as prostituted and silent victims of male bondage. Thus, ironically, like Harriet, Mary hopes that her husband will distinguish between his theories about free love and his practice of them, and she recoils at their convergence.

But in contrast to Harriet, Mary does not openly admit this contradiction, hiding her disappointment at "the male ego, its vanity and exaggerated self-esteem" (180) when she discovers evidence of Percy's affair with Clare. Through Mary's description and Clare's secret diary entry on this encounter, the reader is invited to recognize the inspiration for the passionate incestuous union in Percy's *Laon and Cythna*[26] in his sexual union with Clare, as it takes place on the very boat described by the historical Mary Shelley as the location of the conception of the poem. Moreover, the reader is tempted to suspect that it is only in Mary's novel *Frankenstein* that her emotional turmoil can surface and that it is indeed here that Percy's theory of the desire for the lost half attains a truly monstrous realization.

Of all four women Clare seems the only one who wholeheartedly lives the principle of free love. The diary, however, implicitly reveals her envy of Mary as Shelley's adored wife and as emerging novelist. Her secret satisfaction at betraying Mary turns out to be an ulterior motive for her affair with Shelley, which enables her to entertain delusions of having power over Mary and of her own potential as novelist. Clare's relation to Byron appears equally ambivalent; his shadowy, highly subjective picture in the novel is almost exclusively drawn by her. Clare's journal reveals an oscillation between a lucid description of her sadomasochistic bondage to Byron (13) and delusions about his real love for her and a conventional happy ending (14). Byron's life may seem to be the most consistent with regard to his theoretical ideas; but he remains too shadowy and aloof a figure in the women's journals to be assessed properly. Moreover, in the preface by the fictional Peacock, we are reminded that Byron put his daughter by Clare in a Catholic convent to be educated, where she eventually died. Even in his case the clash between life and a theoretical revolt against norms and conventions becomes all too obvious.

❦

We are never more true to ourselves than when we are inconsistent.

Oscar Wilde[27]

The images of the men and women of the Shelley circle change in the course of the reading of these intimate journals, but remain ambivalent to the very end. This is particularly evident with regard to Mary and Clare. Mary seems to lose her initial grip on life as her feelings of jealousy and rage emerge despite all efforts to hide them. But this is counteracted by the implicit insistence on her ability to transform those feelings creatively into her fiction *Frankenstein*, thereby gaining inde-

pendent strength as a novelist. Her rival Clare also gains strength to a
certain extent because of her sharp analysis of their family relations and
her own relation to Byron. But this is counteracted by recurring delusions about her own status as lover of Byron and Shelley and about her
own creative abilities. Moreover, the reader's views of both women
change because of Fanny and Harriet, who appear as the victims of the
others, raising questions of egotism and guilt. The deaths of these two
women exemplify — particularly for the women involved — the extremity of the conflict evolving from the tensions between theoretical
demands of liberty and the reality of their lives.

The theoretical paradigms of liberty and the ways in which they can
be realized seem to be a male prerogative set down for the lives of the
four women by Godwin, Percy Shelley, and Byron. This is epitomized
in Percy Shelley's wish for love triangles involving his wives and his
male friends. However, as has been shown, all of the men involved are
equally caught up in the tensions between theoretical ideality and prac-
ticed reality. This is most openly criticized in the journal's depiction of
Godwin's separation of theory and practice in the education of his
daughters. Contrary to the father figure of Godwin, Percy Shelley as his
intellectual disciple is not explicitly criticized in the journals and letters
of the four women, who unanimously adore his genius. Implicitly,
however, he is shown to disappoint all of them: leaving Harriet, who
blames Mary; letting down Fanny, who blames herself; betraying Mary,
who hides her disappointment and blames Clare; and finally, after their
brief affair, telling off Clare, who blames Mary. In contrast to Godwin's
seemingly successful separation of theory and practice with regard to
his daughters, Shelley, whom Peacock in the novel calls a revolutionary
in theory, but an aristocrat in life (171), remains caught up in the tensions between his principles and their realization. Though married
twice, he remains an advocate of free love, continuing to live his ideals
as put down in *Queen Mab* to the very end of his life, as the informed
reader knows.

The functioning of gender relations within the Shelley circle seems
to depend on the careful covering up of those tensions. Thus, the move
to Italy seems imperative in order to keep the precarious balance in the
relations of the people involved. But, as the reader knows, this hope
proves an illusion. Peacock's note to the reader summarizes the book as
"an intimate chronicle of the Geneva summer and that last fateful year
in England, its joy and heartbreak, its triumph and failure" (ix), referring to the abyss that opened up between the ideal and the real, between theory and practice during this time, when the fictions of truth

in the lives of the Shelley circle could only be endured by setting them off against the truth of fictions.

Notes

[1] Malcolm Bradbury, "The Telling Life: Some Thoughts on Literary Biography," in *The Troubled Face of Biography*, ed. Eric Homberger and John Charmley (London: Macmillan, 1988), 134–35.

[2] Cf. the once liberating well-known keywords of "the literature of exhaustion" (John Barth, 1967), the "literature of pla(y)giarism" (Raymond Federman, 1976), of the literary work as "chambre d'échos" (Roland Barthes, 1975) or cabinet of mirrors, and the many pronouncements of the "death of the author" (Roland Barthes, 1968), or even the death of the text (Harold Bloom, 1975).

[3] Alfred Hornung, "The Autobiographical Mode in Contemporary American Fiction," *Prose Studies* 8.3 (1985): 69–83. See also his articles "Reading One/Self: Samuel Beckett, Thomas Bernhard, Peter Handke, John Barth, Alain Robbe-Grillet," in *Exploring Postmodernism*, ed. Matei Calinescu and Douwe Fokkema (Amsterdam and Philadelphia: John Benjamins, 1987), 175–98, and "Autobiography," in *International Postmodernism: Theory and Literary Practice*, ed. Hans Bertens and Douwe Fokkema (Amsterdam and Philadelphia: John Benjamins, 1997), 221–34.

[4] Cf. Annegret Maack's distinction between "the historical figure as auto biographer," "the perspective of the biographer," and "memographiction" as contemporary forms of writing the life of dead poets ("Das Leben der toten Dichter: Fiktive Biographien," in *Radikalität und Mässigung: Der englische Roman seit 1960*, ed. Annegret Maack and Rüdiger Imhof [Darmstadt: Wissenschaftliche Buchgesellschaft, 1993], 169–88). See also Ina Schabert, *In Quest of the Other Person: Fiction as Biography* (Tübingen: Francke, 1990), and Daniel Aaron, ed., *Studies in Biography* (Cambridge, MA: Harvard UP, 1978).

[5] Douwe Fokkema, "The Semiotics of Literary Postmodernism," *International Postmodernism*, 15–42.

[6] Judith Chernaik, *Mab's Daughters: Shelley's Wives and Lovers: Their Own Story* (1991; London: Pan Books, 1992). All subsequent page references in the text are to this edition.

[7] This seems particularly important in the case of Peacock, whose novel *Melincourt* (1817) with its allusions to Mary, Shelley, and Byron is referred to in Clare's journal. Moreover, Peacock's *Nightmare Abbey* (1818) contains a love triangle resembling that between Shelley, Mary, and Clare. The picture drawn of the melancholy romantic hero, Scythrop Glowry, his wife-to-be, Stella Toobad, and her rival, Marionetta Celestina O'Carroll, gains an additional dimension on account of Peacock's amorous feelings for Clare and his

disappointment over her "betrayal" with Shelley as depicted in Clare's journal. Similarly, the journal entries on Hogg's sexual advances towards Harriet
and Mary, encouraged by his friend Shelley, seem to shed a new light on his
Life of Shelley (1858) as well as on its revisions by Peacock in his *Memorials of
Shelley* (1858). Finally, the family relations of the *Examiner*'s editor Leigh
Hunt with his wife and her sister, who were staying with the Shelleys at Marlow during the summer of 1818, are hinted at as a mirror image of their own
ménage with Percy in the journals of Clare (147) and Mary (156).

[8] This is particularly interesting because of Mary Wollstonecraft's firm theoretical stance in *A Vindication of the Rights of Woman* (1792) as opposed to
the ambivalence in *Mary, a Fiction* (1788) and the fragmentary piece *Maria;
or, The Wrongs of Woman* (1797), where feminist issues are in uneasy conjunction with the sentimental and gothic genres taken up twenty years later
by her daughter Mary in *Frankenstein* (1818).

[9] Robert Skidelsky, "Only Connect: Biography and Truth," *The Troubled
Face of Biography*, 1–16 (11).

[10] Virginia Woolf, *A Room of One's Own* (1928; Harmondsworth: Penguin
Books, 1970), 37.

[11] Ansgar Nünning, "Grenzüberschreitungen: Neue Tendenzen im historischen Roman," *Radikalität und Mässigung*, 54–73.

[12] Maack, "Das Leben der toten Dichter," 170–71.

[13] Hunt's wife is occupied with drawings and with restoring the statues of
Apollo and Venus as parting gifts for the Shelleys, while her sister is writing a
manual of gardening. Clare at the same time attempts to compose an autobiographical novel involving a Byronic hero, a jealous heroine, the authoress,
and her friend and brother, "a gentle poet, a dreamer and visionary [. . .]
who is happiest when he is drifting in his boat along the river [. . .]" (174).

[14] For criticism on Mary Shelley's *Frankenstein*, see Elisabeth Bronfen, *Over
Her Dead Body: Death, Femininity and the Aesthetic* (New York: Routledge,
1992), 130–40; Ellen Moers, *Literary Women* (New York: Doubleday,
1977); Mary Poovey, "My Hideous Progeny: Mary Shelley and the Femini-
zation of Romanticism," *PMLA* 95 (1980): 332–47; Margaret Homans,
*Bearing the World: Language and Female Experience in Nineteenth-Century
Women's Writing* (Chicago: Chicago UP, 1986); U. C. Knoepflmacher and
George Levine, eds., *The Endurance of Frankenstein* (Berkeley: U of California P, 1979).

[15] *The Madwoman in the Attic: The Woman Writer and the Nineteenth-
Century Literary Imagination* (New Haven: Yale UP, 1979). See the chapter
entitled "Horror's Twin: Mary Shelley's Monstrous Eve," 213–47.

[16] Virginia Woolf, *A Room of One's Own*, 27.

[17] Cf. such playful postmodern writers as John Fowles or Julian Barnes who
demonstrate the unattainability of truth. In contradistinction, politically en-

gaged postmodern, postcolonial writers like Salman Rushdie deconstruct the official truth in order to center the margin.

[18] Virginia Woolf, *A Room of One's Own*, 43.

[19] For a discussion of the journal and the letter as female forms of writing, see the special issue of the journal *a/b: Auto/Biography*, 2.2 (1986), on "Diaries," ed. Rebecca Hogan, as well as two collections of essays: Shari Benstock, ed. *The Private Self: Theory and Practice of Women's Autobiographical Writing* (Chapel Hill, NC: U of North Carolina P, 1988), and Domna C. Stanton, ed. *The Female Autograph: Theory and Practice of Autobiography from the Tenth to the Twentieth Century* (Chicago: U of Chicago P, 1987).

[20] Christine Brook-Rose, *Stories, Theories and Things* (Cambridge: Cambridge UP, 1991), 176.

[21] Oscar Wilde, *De Profundis* (1905; London: Methuen, 1908), 46.

[22] In her preface, Chernaik comments on Godwin's and Wollstonecraft's behavior: "But upon discovering that Mary was pregnant they set aside their principles and married quietly [. . .]" (vi).

[23] "It is all because of Mr. Godwin's book *Political Justice*, which though it was my Bible too for a time is full of pernicious ideas attacking marriage and preaching free love" (37).

[24] *Queen Mab* (1813), quoted from *The Complete Works of Percy Bysshe Shelley*, ed. Roger Ingpen and Walter E. Peck (London: Ernest Benn; New York: Gordian Press, 1965), 10 vols., Vol. I: *Poems*, 65–176; 142. Cf. Shelley's further elaborations on this subject, vol. I: 141–42.

[25] Jean Hagstrum describes Shelley as the embodiment of the Romantic sentiment "that as the bodies join, the souls mingle, and that love is the most beautiful which attaches itself to similars and ultimately attains the One" (*Eros and Vision: The Restoration to Romanticism* [Evanston, IL: Northwestern UP, 1989], 83–84.).

[26] *The Complete Works of Percy Bysshe Shelley*, I: 239–412.

[27] Oscar Wilde, "The Critic as Artist," *Intentions and the Soul of Man*, 191–92.

MARTIN MIDDEKE

The Triumph of Analogous Text over Digital Truth: Biography, *Différance*, and Deconstructive Play in Amanda Prantera's *Conversations with Lord Byron on Perversion, 163 Years after his Lordship's Death*

[. . .] the wise
Have a far deeper madness, and the glance
Of melancholy is a fearful gift;
What is it but the telescope of truth?
Which strips the distance of its fantasies,
And brings life near in utter nakedness,
Making the cold reality too real!

George Gordon, Lord Byron[1]

[. . .] if reading must not be content with doubling the text, it cannot legitimately transgress the text towards something other than it,
toward the referent (a reality that is metaphysical, historical, psycho-
biographical, etc.) or toward a signified outside the text whose content could take place, could have taken place outside of language, that
is to say, in the sense that we give here to the word, outside of writing
in general. [. . .] *There is nothing outside of the text.*

Jacques Derrida[2]

Towards a Poetics of *Différance*

BOTH OF THE TWO EPIGRAPHS ABOVE FOCUS UPON desire: the passage from Byron's "The Dream" points to the poet's frustrated
(because unrequited) feelings of love for Mary Chaworth; Jacques Derrida's famous description of the relationship between signifier, signified,
and text relates to the desire for meaning inherent in language, a dy-

namic which Derrida describes as never ending and, thus, equally frus-
trating for those who attempt to appoint an absolute signified or an essential origin of the signifier. The difference between the two passages,
however, lies in their overtones: the first is characterized by a melancholy gap between wish and wish-fulfilment and a painful cry for continuity, while the second pertains to much more hedonistic
surroundings. Indeed, the question how to cope with the gulf between
desire and its denied satisfaction leads to the heart of the postmodernist
debate, as Alan Wilde points out:

> Acceptance is the key word here. Modernist irony, absolute and
> equivocal, expresses a resolute consciousness of different and equal
> possibilities so ranged as to defy solution. Postmodern irony [. . .] is
> suspensive: an indecision about the meanings or relations of things is
> matched by a willingness to love with uncertainty, to tolerate and, in
> some cases, to welcome a world seen as random and multiple, even, at
> times absurd [. . .].[3]

Lord Byron's "dual personality" incorporates such melancholy, "ineffa-
ble longings and his ironic recognition of the unideal nature of the
world and himself." Lady Marguerite Blessington once complained —
although halfway charmed and fascinated — that "the day after he has
awakened the deepest interest his manner of scoffing at himself and
others destroys it and one feels as if one had been duped into a sympathy, only to be laughed at."[4] She recalls him saying that

> people take for gospel all I say, and go away continually with false im-
> pressions . . . Now, if I know myself, I should say, that I have no char-
> acter at all . . . But, joking apart, what I think of myself is, that I am so
> changeable, being everything by turns and nothing long, — I am such
> a strange *mélange* of good and evil, that it would be difficult to de-
> scribe me.[5]

Having "no character at all" to be pin-pointed, let alone pigeonholed
and "being so changeable," Byron could hardly be considered the ideal
object of a positivist biography that seeks coherence, identity, causality,
and the documentation of a character's development in a chronological, linear teleology. Yet Byron's enigmatic, elusive character forms the
ideal playground for postmodernist biofiction, which re-enacts the reality of the life at issue by making use of the potential of fiction in order
to comprehend it. But postmodernist biofiction also goes beyond such
re-enactment by applying life-writing and, especially, its *cul-de-sacs* to
addressing and interrogating critical, poetological, epistemological,
historical and philosophical issues.[6]

Amanda Prantera's 1987 novel *Conversations with Lord Byron*[7] transports the desire to revive, illuminate, and make at least partial sense of the Byron myth into a late twentieth-century research laboratory, where a professor and two of his assistants have designed the computer artificial intelligence program "LB" to represent a double of Lord Byron.

> The LB program [. . .] was a variation of what is nowadays called an 'expert system,' the variation being that it was — as most of us are supposed to be in our more boring ways — an expert about itself. Into it had been fed, in codified form, every detail and every snippet of information that was available about the poet's life and works: where Byron was on March the whatsit in the year x, what he ate for dinner on that day (assuming that he or anyone else recorded it), what he was feeling like, who he met, who he wrote to and what he wrote; what Byron thought of Shelley; what he thought Shelley thought of him; what he thought Mrs Shelley thought of him and vice versa; what he thought of Mrs Shelley's step-sister (i.e. that she was a 'damned bitch'), and so on and so forth [. . .] In short, it contained just about everything pertinent to Byron's very personal life-history that has come down to us [. . .]. (17–18)

A crucial position in the process of distilling pieces of information from LB is held by Anna, a research student of Romantic literature, whose task it is to ask LB about the identity of the obscure Thyrza of Byron's poems, "something that even the most conscientious of his biographers may have overlooked" (13).

In this context, the computer program may appear to be merely continuing nineteenth-century Byromania and "the long series of Byronic forgeries and fantasies [. . .] prefigured by the poet's own images and self-images."[8] In Prantera's novel the image of the twentieth-century computer version of Lord Byron, however, is a much more complex one. It may be read as a striking bio-image for the historical link between the 1980s and Byron in particular as well as Romanticism in general. In effect, the very thought of artificial intelligence, artificial human beings as well as computers, bears reference to the Romantic era. In the sphere of literature, one may, for instance, think of E. T. A. Hoffmann's *Der Sandmann* and his shorter narrative "Die Automate." One is also immediately reminded of Mary Shelley's *Frankenstein* and, closely related to it, of Percy Bysshe Shelley's interest in mesmerism and his rendering of the Prometheus myth in *Prometheus Unbound*. Shelley had translated Goethe's *Faust,* and was therefore well enough acquainted with Homunculus, that artificial image of human entelechy. Furthermore, from the fact that in 1822 Shelley and Byron discussed

Goethe and Calderón at great length we may gather that Byron himself must have been absorbed by the topic of Faustian restlessness ("Two souls, alas," says Faust, "are housed within my breast"), Faust's search for knowledge, and the thwarting of his aspirations.[9] In the matter of proto-computers we may recall Melzel's chess automaton, and, most tellingly, we may associate the roots of modern computer science with Byron's own family: Annabella Milbanke, the "Princess of Parallelograms," as Byron derogatorily nicknamed his wife, was a talented mathematician, and their daughter, Ada Lovelace (née Byron), collaborated with the Cambridge professor Charles Babbage, whose work on a difference engine and an analytical engine, a prototype of modern computers, however, was never finished. As late as 1975 the Pentagon had a universally applicable computer language developed named ADA.

Nonetheless, exploiting the computer image for the reconstruction of Byron's life is not without deep, albeit characteristic irony. The connection between Byron and the computer truly mirrors the ill-matched and disastrous marriage of Byron and Annabella: "It was as difficult for her," remarks Leslie A. Marchand, "not to run into abstractions as it was for Byron not to be concrete and direct."[10] In a letter to Annabella dating from September 7, 1814, Byron expresses his bewilderment in the face of her "consistency," which "has been the most formidable apparition I have encountered."[11] LB reproduces a fairly accurate evaluation of 'his'/'Byron's' contempt for digits and numbers in a reminiscence of Ada:

> Illness; pride; an uncomfortable amount of brain: mathematics seemed to have been her downfall — mathematics, and an absurd 'analytical engine' or something of the kind, invented by a Mr Babbage, on which she had spent her energies and a great deal of money. (33)

Byron's/LB's dislike for mathematics and "analytical engines" serves very well as our cue to turn to the second area to which the computer image self-consciously refers in Prantera's novel: literary criticism and epistemology. In this context, it is worth calling to mind that — in order to avoid ambiguity and paradox — computers are programmed and process on *digital* principles. The following example reveals the kind of digital structuring that provides information for LB's memory frames.

*end BE-AFFECTED-BY SUBJ   wife   (SPECIF Annabella Milbanke)
                     OBJ   self   (SPECIF heart, qua seat of
                                    affections)
                     EVENT   separation
                     date   April 21, 1816
                     ref.   Biog. Marchand, vol. II, p. 648.
                     ref.   orig. Letter to Augusta Leigh — Geneva,
                                    Sept 8, 1816 (22)

The fact that there is certainly more to the signifier "heart" than a
digitally programmed signified "seat of affections" ironically emphasizes that language and, especially, literary texts are also equipped with
a symbolic quality, that is, an analogous substratum which goes beyond
digital, uni-dimensional assignments of meaning. It is this substratum
that makes communication and, accordingly, interpretation as multi-
faceted and multi-layered as they are; it actually gives literary criticism
its justification in the first place. Seeing that computer languages are by
definition devised on unmistakable binary oppositions such as
high/low, positive/negative, yes/no, etc., what could be a more suitable analogy for the postmodernist/poststructuralist attempt to go beyond and radically deconstruct a false objectivity grounded on the
building of binary oppositions than ironically making fiction turn to the
computer as a truth-producing instrument? As we have seen, LB is fed
with every retrievable fact and piece of information, that is, every piece
of text available by or on Byron, and, thus, LB 'himself' constitutes
text — and nothing but text. And "the text," as Roland Barthes puts it,
"is not thought of as an object that can be computed."[12]

If LB epitomizes the poststructuralist view of text (or texts), Jakob
Böhme's statement that "In Ja und Nein bestehen alle Dinge" ["all
things consist in yes and no"], which Prantera introduces as the opening motto of her novel, is clearly ironical, too. LB and 'his' relationship
to 'his' interpreter Anna are of a thoroughly deconstructive nature "op-
erating necessarily from the inside, borrowing all the strategic and economic resources of subversion from the old structure,"[13] that is,
Byron's life and his writings. Due to the temporality of all existence,
neither Byron nor LB can constitute biographical essences, in other
words, signifieds based on presence.[14] Quite on the contrary, because
Lord Byron and LB are texts, any attempt to attribute an essential signified to LB's signification is ultimately doomed to fail. In addition, as
we shall see, the more any meaning appears to be captured and attributed to the signifiers, the more such meaning is being deferred. This, of
course, is a metabiographical statement on the impossibility of fully
reconciling the absence of the past *life* in question with the presence of

life-*writing*. The statement renounces logocentrism, the "metaphysics of presence as the exigent, powerful, systematic, and irrepressible desire for such a signified."[15] What is more, it is a notion which problematizes acts of interpretation that are based upon the assumption of objective truth and fixed, closed meanings of texts. *Conversations with Lord Byron* metafictionally addresses this issue by presenting Byron's/LB's writing at variance with our/Anna's reading. Both belong together; none, however, is self-sufficient in the sense of a singular, essential identity. As Hans-Georg Gadamer assures us, hermeneutics intends to capture experience rather than constitute a method to diagnose objective truth ("den richtigen Sinn"). As Gadamer points out, difference lies at the core of identity; were it otherwise, there would be no identity. Likewise, thinking for Gadamer necessarily entails distancing and deferring. Thus, even from a hermeneutical perspective a relationship between life and the rewriting of that life and, consequently, any provisional identity emerging out of this relationship would be characterized by difference.[16]

It would appear that the computer program LB produces digital, unambiguous output — the biographer's dream. LB's status as text, however, takes the meaning of such output to the limits of rationality, indeed, deliberately rendering it paradoxical.[17] And since — as text — LB cannot provide a "self-evident or one-to-one link between 'signifier' and 'signified,'"[18] because all authenticating methods (the program being one of them) fall prey to textuality, Prantera's novel displays a poetics of *différance*, a specifically postmodern aesthetic which, as Linda Hutcheon points out, relishes in "multiplicity, heterogeneity, plurality, rather than binary opposition and exclusion."[19] In this way *Conversations with Lord Byron* accentuates, when analyzed according to Derrida, the nature as well as the possibility of all conceptuality: LB and any other conceivable present rewriting of Byron would necessarily differ from the signified/the original/Byron, or any other concept which would strive towards the reduction of *différance*. Byron as the essential signified shining through Prantera's/LB's writing can only appear as a trace, as a paradoxical presence/absence, as the irreconcilable difference between a historical past and lived experience which sets out to re-write and re-experience it. For that reason, any present signification of Byron must take place "within the hollow of *différance*," and so documents "the enigmatic relationship of the living to its other end, of an inside to an outside."[20]

Biographical Truth and/as
Reader-Inference and Intertextuality

Within postmodern writing such an absence of transcendental signifieds entails play. And just as the author engages in playing by inventing fictions and writing texts, the narrator starts playing whenever he tells a story, and in this context, of course, LB — the second Byron, as it were — exists only in the hermeneutic game called "reading." Anna, the interpreter, and LB, the object of interpretation, are engaged in a game of both searching for and displacing biographical meaning. As the conversations with L(ord) B(yron) are indeed the driving force of the plot, any meaning arises from the researcher's inferences concerning particular details, connections, and continuities in Byron's life and by infinite contextualizations. Evidently, LB's answers to Anna's questions make up the story of the novel. Without these questions — that is to say, without reading — there would be no LB text. Texts, as Barthes underlines, do not exist on shelves in bookshops,[21] their materialization takes place only in the process of reading. The following passage may give a first impression of the game of hide-and-seek Anna and LB are engaged in:

> WHEN DID YOU FIRST MEET EDLESTON?
> OCTOBER 1805.
> HOW OLD WAS HE THEN?
> TWO YEARS YOUNGER THAN MYSELF TO THE HOUR.
> 'Seventeen and fifteen,' she said softly to herself. 'Babies!'
> WHERE DID YOU MEET HIM?
> IF MY MEMORY SERVES ME RIGHTLY, IN TRINITY CHAPEL.
> YOUR FRIEND WILLIAM HARNESS SAYS YOU MET HIM IN
> MORE DRAMATIC CIRCUMSTANCES WHEN YOU SAVED
> HIM FROM DROWNING. IS THIS FALSE?
> IT IS, UNLESS TRINITY CHAPEL IS A BATHING RESORT. (12)

Two things become evident here: firstly, *any* outcome of such questioning by which LB's recalling of 'his'/Byron's life is motivated is linked to the correlation of production and reception rather than being derived from an essential biographical reality. Here, whatever might be taken for such a reality is a construct in a game, which obeys rules chosen according to the relative arbitrariness of Anna's/the researcher's/ any reader's inferences about Lord Byron. If this is the case, LB, like the second Quijote in Jorge Luis Borges's short story "Pierre Menard, Author of the *Quijote*," potentially "exists an infinite number of times, in an infinite number of places, which is every time a reader reads a book and re-writes it in his imagination."[22]

Secondly, the flagrant witticism in LB's answer quoted above (which LB, like Byron, enjoys employing to deceive) illustrates that LB's memory works by analogy, in other words, more like human rather than computer memory. Up to the present day even the most advanced of Artificial Intelligence systems are not intelligent; in other words, they cannot change their functions outside a prefigured, preconceived frame of reference. In much the same way that the monster sets himself free from Frankenstein, LB subverts the presuppositions of 'his' creators, who identify reading with mere consuming when they search for a strategy how to reproduce Byron and, in doing so, reduce LB/Byron to a digital and "passive, inner *mimesis*."[23] Whether, for example, LB "could ultimately *conceal* things, was [. . .] something of an open question [. . .]. Concealing was something that human beings did. A machine could erase or omit, it could not conceal. Problem dismissed" (28). "The facts themselves," Anna is told by one of the assistants, "are finite [. . .] without dragging philosophy into the question" (20). And on the subject of LB's preference for ironical jests:

> 'Joking?' The assistant shut her eyes and muttered something under her breath to check her impatience. 'For God's sake, Anna,' she let out with a sigh, 'I've got high hopes in the program's performance myself, as well you know, but — get this straight in your mind — it can't *joke*. If it asserts that money-lenders are charming, it's because this information is stored inside it somewhere.' (89)

As an expert in Romantic studies, Anna senses that LB is "a bit more complex than that" (13), that "if you wanted it to work for you, you had to mind your manners and avoid treading on its toes" (20). Assuming that LB would resist any reduction to digital one-to-one links (as all texts do), Anna consistently decides to play with LB by entering the analogous field of intertextual reference to the Thyrza poems.

Centering on the years 1805 to 1807, which saw Byron enter into, and escape from, university life in Cambridge, Prantera's fiction and Anna's questioning focus on a bleak yet symbolic slice of Byron's life, a period which was characterized by a strong "sense of being prematurely cast adrift."[24] Characteristically, the exact emotional background and biographical coherence of Byron's melancholy state of mind leave much ground for speculation and constitute a biographical blank, as Marchand points out in drawing on Byron's letter to Augusta of January 7, 1806:

> The specific causes of that melancholy are clouded in mystery. It is possible, however, to make a reasonable surmise from Byron's own statements in his 'Detached Thoughts' and in his later letters dealing

with this period. After speaking of his disgust at the libertinism of Cambridge which threw his heart back upon itself, casting him 'into excesses perhaps more fatal than those from which I shrunk, as fixing upon [one] (at a time) the passions which, spread amongst many, would have hurt only myself,' he says: 'If I could explain at length the *real* causes which have contributed to increase this perhaps *natural* temperament of mine, this Melancholy which hath made me a bye-word, nobody would wonder; but this is impossible without doing much mischief.'[25]

In accordance with Marchand, Anna relates Byron's melancholy to his romantic love for Edleston, the young Cambridge choirboy, by taking Byron's statement to Augusta, "'You know me too well to think it is *Love*'" (66), at face value. Anna also refers to Byron's letter to Elizabeth Pigot, whom he told that "he loved him [Edleston] more than anyone else in the world" (69).[26] It should be noted here that LB functions both in an "input-output" and in an "output-only" mode; in both ways, however, LB is free to "turn itself off if its maximum boredom threshold was crossed" — as it happens, "the Professor was quickest at getting it to do this" (24). While LB memory is continually jogged by Anna's questions, we get an insight into both 'his' output to Anna and 'his' personal thoughts and reminiscences. Interestingly, this takes place on two separate narrative levels: Anna's questioning and LB's answers to her as well as the entire laboratory action are written as a straightforward authorial narrative situation suggesting authority, narrative control, interpretation, commentary, development, and understanding, whereas LB's reminiscences are communicated by means of a figural narrative situation set in free indirect discourse. Constituting a central image of the trace, that is, the ineluctable misunderstanding between text and interpreter, these two narrative situations never overlap. Being reminded of the past, so to speak, LB recalls the whole Thyrza story to 'his' mind; 'he' unintentionally evokes it for *us*, while Anna is kept in total darkness. This lays bare the fact that LB does not only have "a 'richly structured semantics of the self'" (25), 'he' is also thoroughly able to conceal, to lie — in fact, 'he' is even able to "'remember' unrecorded episodes" (26).[27] Highlighting the analogous character of 'his' memory, "a self — to be a self — must be self-reflexive" (27), the figural narrative situation does not only refer back to the nature of fiction, it also allows LB to meet 'his' interpreters with a self-conscious gesture of almost pitying amusement:

> Believe it or not, people were still at him, too, even in this reduced state. Why did you do this? Why did you say that? Did you ever meet so-and-so? Flattering in a way that they were still interested, he sup-

posed, but something of a bore when he couldn't see any of his questioners or make up his mind whether they were worth talking to or not. He had held out on them over the Thyrza/Edleston lark - very properly too: it was none of their business. But perhaps in future it might do to let just a *few* things out of the bag now and again to keep them hopping. It would help while away the time. (170)

To give but a brief survey of 'his' reminiscences, we are informed in much detail about 'his' arrival in Cambridge, the overweight seventeen year-old youth that 'he' was, 'his' lodgings, 'his' Cambridge friends Bankes, Hobhouse, Matthews, and Fletcher, the fateful encounter with Edleston in Trinity Chapel, 'his' falling in love with Edleston, the Cornelian 'he' receives from Edleston and a precious jewel which 'he' buys for Edleston in return — which, as 'he' reports answers for the debts 'he' incurred at that time. Most revealingly perhaps, we learn how deeply the question of homosexuality bore on 'his' conscience, ironically disclosed by an interior dialogue with his moral alter ego, the Calvinist Reverend George Gordon, who warns 'him' that indulging in a homosexual relationship with Edleston will "plummet you down, the pair of you, into dark regions where neither of you will feel at home and from which neither of you — green as you are — will be able to find the exit" (78). And this mixture of feelings of guilt, shame, "love on the grand scale" for Edleston (98), and heed of conventions, makes him forgo sex with Edleston — "pederasty was not for him" (99), 'he' resumes for the time being — and leave Cambridge all of a sudden to become the favourite among London prostitutes and Southwell belles. But, so we are told, 'his' desire for Edleston is stronger, and after a severe diet, a six months' argument with the Reverend, 'he' returns to Cambridge: "Hang the Reverend George. Hang the moralists, and hang prudence and caution along with them: he wasn't going to consider strategy or seemliness any longer" (83), "let the rack pull him the way it listed. If it listed to perversion then to perversion he would go" (118). With nothing but the sexual union with Edleston on 'his' mind, 'he' and 'his' friends go swimming one day, 'he' saves Edleston from drowning, and, while reviving him, finds out what the reader of Prantera's fiction may have guessed on account of such proleptic markers as Edleston's categorical refusal to swim, or Edleston's shrewd remarks that 'he' would see soon that with him it would be "rather different" (85), or that their sexual union "wouldn't be wrong" (100):

> God Almighty! No longer smiling, he drew in his breath with a whistle. For there beneath the thin veil of linen which stuck to the skin like a skin itself, slightly below the pink protuberance of the jewel, as symmetrical to it as the points of an isosceles or what-you-may-call-it

triangle, were two other protuberances: [. . .] Believe it or not, Edleston grew breasts! [. . .]

Well flay me and sunburn me, he thought to himself in stupefaction! [. . .] Edleston was a hermaphrodite. No wonder Edleston sang like a cherub, blushed like a peach and retained a marble-smooth jawline. No wonder he refused to swim in company and kept his shirt on when he did.

[. . .] His hand delved deeper into the secret recesses of Edleston's lower belly and thighs. [. . .] as far as he could make out through the layers of cloth that separated his index finger from what lay underneath, Edleston was not a hermaphrodite, nor even a eunuch: Edleston was a woman. (134–35)

Edleston turns out to be Alba, Royal Princess at one of the highest aristocratic courts in Europe, who is allowed to participate in Cambridge education in man's attire only. The subsequent brief and happy period of their union, LB recalls, makes 'him' able to forget 'his' melancholy, "basking in ray after ray of resplendent sunshine" (143), whilst afterwards "he had never again felt that sense of complete well-being in love" (140). 'He' takes Alba to the South Coast of England, where she passes herself off as one Miss Cameron, debunking the real Miss Cameron as she fashions her name after Boccaccio's *Decamerone*. In a reversal of the obstacles created by Edleston's social ranking, LB is the misalliance here, and as Alba's brother seeks to track them down, 'his' love for Alba becomes dangerous, and LB has to part from Alba and flee to the continent — 'his' partial explanation for Byron's hitherto mysterious and hasty flight from England in 1809.

The somewhat demythologizing theory that "Britain's most renowned womanizer" (13) lost his one-and-only love, whom he could not forget in the arms of many others, would render Byron's psychology almost banally sentimental. Yet LB's assertion that Edleston was a woman could not be further from a serious biographical statement, in fact, it is a uniquely entertaining, metabiographical parody of the very search for such biographical truth. It constitutes just one trace among infinite traces which, after all, are determined by the reader's input. LB's memory of certain topics is pre-structured by numbered ratings scaled "from 1–8 or thereabouts" (18) touching upon interest, sympathy, boredom, and anxiety. Thus, after LB reacts aggressively when asked about Edleston, Anna and the researchers agree on lowering the homosexuality parameter of the program while raising the heterosexuality parameter at the same time. Paradoxically, though, this still does not lead to any clarification of the issue for Anna, as the story remains present for LB and our eavesdropping on 'his' memories, but absent for her: just after LB had found out the true identity of Alba, "Anna yawned. As far as she could see the latest adjustments to the program had not heightened its interest in the opposite sex at all, but had merely made it introspective" (137).

Moreover, the deconstructive parody of biographical truth at work here becomes evident when the text (LB) metafictionally roots the origin of the text (of the history of 'his' love for Alba) in the textual proof of the love between Juan and Haidée described in Canto IV of Byron's *Don Juan*, from which even the swimming metaphor is borrowed loosely, though taken literally/digitally:

> Juan and Haidée gazed upon each other
>   With *swimming* looks of speechless tenderness,
> Which mix'd all feelings, friend, child, lover, brother;
>   All that the best can mingle and express
> When two pure hearts are pour'd in one another,
>   And love too much, and yet cannot love less [. . .]. [My italics][28]

LB therefore rewrites parts of the canto, and 'his' readers/interpreters are asked to look there for "the most sincere portrayal of requited and fulfilled love that he had ever attempted to set to paper" (139). Yet again, this forms but a red herring, for it echoes infinite other passages in Byron's work on the topic of "carnal passion" in a "timeless, flawless world" (139).[29] Besides, LB's rewriting is slightly one-sided in its attempt to read meaning into something as elusive as 'himself'/'itself: however much Canto IV of *Don Juan* evokes the romantic image of fulfilled love, the opening of Canto V immediately retracts, defers, and destroys it:

> WHEN amatory poets sing their loves
>   In liquid lines mellifluously bland,
> And pair their rhymes as Venus yokes her doves,
>   They little think what mischief is in hand;
> The greater their success the worse it proves,
>   As Ovid's verse may give to understand;
> Even Petrarch's self, if judged with due severity,
> Is the Platonic pimp of all posterity.[30]

The intertextual cross-fertilization of Byron's text, LB's metafictional reference to it, and my own account of this reference elucidate that whatever quotes and paraphrases are used in the echo-chamber of *Conversations with Lord Byron*, they can only bear the character of synecdoches that defer the idea of an ontological presence of meaning. Their meaning is the result of the act of reading, conceived of as the entering of the play space of intertextuality which defies a total signified, but implies "the totality of all possible readings" instead.[31]

Free Play, the Absence/Presence of the Signified, and the Triumph of Text

As a way of doing justice to, and fully making use of, such textual indeterminacy, Derrida and Barthes propose a hedonistic approach, characterized by pleasure and *jouissance*.[32] *Conversations with Lord Byron* displays such a playful dealing with the abundance of negotiable meanings even at the simplest, that is, the phonetic, level, creating and deferring meaning by switching letters. LB as an abbreviation for Lord Byron is reminiscent of, but different from, its signified; LB and Albè constitute a phonetic minimal pair, another variation of which, of course, is 'Alba.' Thus, being a mere variation of LB/Albè, Alba becomes a trickster figure, a language game similar to the list "T, DM, S, L, R, E, C, G, A, Z, EB, TM, G, xG, L, xL, F" that LB prints out for Anna as an answer to her question whom 'he' loved best (35). Clearly enough, LB tries to conceal/defer (their) identities, just as 'he' keeps Alba's "awesome and unmentionable surname" (141) to 'himself.' In the same way as LB/Albè/Alba represent trickster figures of/for the text, 'Anna' [A-n(omen)-n(ominandum)-a] may suggest the interpreter, the generalized reader. Apparently, only names are able to provide digital, unambiguous representations of facts, and Prantera's fiction playfully shifts the emphasis from the signified to the signifier by denying denomination.[33] And because there are always further nuances of the signifiers to pursue, it should be noted that LB is both part of, and different from, A[lb]a — both are signs of the trace, the presence/absence of the signified. In 'his' reminiscences, LB links this to 'his' incapacity to say whom 'he' loved best: "All he could truthfully say, to whoever it was who was interested and kept pestering him about it, was that — setting aside the bests and the lasts and the worsts [. . .] — he had certainly loved. Intensely. And often" (34–35). Epitomizing LB's/Byron's desire for fulfilment in love, Alba — like Byron/LB/texts/language — represents and, thus, opts for elusive analogies. To give but one striking example, 'she' counters LB's doubts about contraception by "a famous *Greek* remedy" and by telling 'him' that "the ears [. . .] would do every bit as well in theory, but they are too small" (159).

The self-reflexive nature of the signifier as well as Alba's share in LB's/Byron's ambivalent sexual identity suggest that 'Alba' may be read as a narcissistic projection of something that exists merely as a fantasy, a trace — a reading to which, by the way, LB adds: "Love? Self-Love? Did it matter which?" (140).[34] The narcissistic side is also stressed by Shelley, whom LB recalls laughing at 'him' in Ravenna in 1822: "It's too good to be true: a royal princess dressed up as a choir-boy, beautiful as Antinuous, wise as Athena, and with the flair of a Newton in the bedchamber! You're making the whole thing up!" (160). The self-reflexive image that Alba is, 'she,' like the signifier, gives expression to both the lost transcendental, absolute, essential signified/origin and *différance*:

> There is a void inside me, Shelley, you know. A hunger. A craving. Call it what you will. It made itself felt when I lost Alba, of course it did. But I think it was there before. I think it always was. How far she could have gone towards filling it is anyone's guess. (167)

I have argued earlier that the reaction to *différance* is as important as its diagnosis. Thus, while we cannot know exactly how Byron would have treated the matter, we may imagine that LB as a contemporary rewriting of Byron would construct 'his' meanings on the basis of both nineteenth- and twentieth-century intertextuality. In this, *Conversations with Lord Byron* attributes a proto-postmodernist consciousness to LB/Byron: *différance* and the temporality of existence, it seems, have to be accepted, and "there was little to be gained by moping — not a hundred and seventy odd years later anyway" (171). On the contrary: LB recollects having ironically quoted at Shelley "'no hopes for them that laughs.'" But LB — tongue in cheek — concludes that "Shelley's reply was lost [. . .] in the hoots of laughter that accompanied their progress" (168).

Carnivalesque laughter, *jouissance*, and their aesthetic equivalents of irony, parody, and self-reflexivity are also the ingredients of the final statement that LB/the text makes for the benefit of Anna/the interpreter. This enunciation is not a digital revelation of Alba's/Thyrza's identity, but an analogous poem:

> *I have followed your shadow* (she read softly), *o'erstepping your shade*
> *I have lived, I have loved, that our love would ne'er fade;*
> *And in places grown dark to me, calling your name,*
> *I have courted your likeness, or ghosts of the same.*
>
> *Your voice and your laugh and the curve of your breast*
> *(The one place on earth where my heart has found rest),*
> *I have sought them and found them and lost them apace;*
> *And I'd lie if I said I'd no joy in the chase.*

But believe me, if ever my words have been true,
In the images, traces, and mirrors of you,
In each heart I have plundered, each lip I have kissed,
It was you I was seeking and you that I kissed. (173–74)

The poem's address, "'To A——a,'" is the striking, ultimate *analogy* to the presence/absence of the signified. 'A——a' becomes a cipher of *différance* since, on the one hand, it self-consciously relates to temporality and the unfulfilled desire in LB/Byron's life; on the other hand, it points to a future of further interpretations that resist closure and defer meaning. The reader's associations are required in order to fill the blank — A[llegr/ugust/lb/d/nnabell/mand/nn . . .]a — , in other words, to provide the absent signified that the presence of LB's writing refuses to reveal. Luckily, even Amanda Prantera's first name fits into the 'A——a' pattern, so the author is explicitly included in the textual game of writing/interpreting/contextualizing fiction — the undecided outcome of which is reflected in the radically open structure of the text, whose center as well as fringes are but traces of texts:

. . . ↔ PRANTERA ↔ Byron ↔ LB ↔ A——a ↔ Anna ↔ READER ↔ . . .

Thus, as a piece of writing, the poem "To A——a" comments upon the unquenched desire for meaning via representation and interpretation pertinent to all writing. But apart from such metafictional intentions, 'A——a,' as a trace, becomes a bio-image for the "master tracer"[35] Lord Byron as well as for the asserted void in 'his' life. The desire in language for a meaningful representation of the world and logocentric stability and the desire for an authentic life within life-writing echo Lord Byron's desire for fulfillment in love. *Différance*, thus, becomes the poetological principle of Prantera's biofictional writing, as it makes desire interchange and compete with its deferred fulfillment, a process which — indeed — neither in life or love nor in language nor fiction can ever lead to *"The one place on earth where my heart has found rest"* (174). Rather it plunges LB's/the interpreter's/the writer's desire into the spiral-shaped aporias of time and its representation in fiction. Ironically, however, the fact that within fiction signifiers can no more be fully reconciled with their signifieds than can Byron with his fictional incarnations makes the hermeneutic game of interpretation — and Byromania — go on. In other words, thanks to *différance*, the game of interpreting Byron will never lose its attraction — a statement that testifies to the ultimate superiority of analogous over digital memory, of texts over computers.[36] Exulting in the consequences as well as in the possibilities of *différance*, *Conversations with Lord Byron* — to borrow Byron's phrasing in "The Dream" — does not melancholically "strip the distance of its fantasies"; it turns the fantasies generated by time and *différance* into its triumph.

Notes

[1] Lord Byron, "The Dream," 177–183, in *Poetical Works,* ed. Frederick Page, corr. John Jump (Oxford and New York: Oxford UP, 1986), 93–94.

[2] Jacques Derrida, *Of Grammatology,* trans. Gayatri Chakravorty Spivak (Baltimore and London: Johns Hopkins UP, 1976), 158.

[3] Alan Wilde, *Horizons of Assent: Modernism, Postmodernism, and the Ironic Imagination* (Baltimore: Johns Hopkins UP, 1981), 44.

[4] Leslie A. Marchand, *Byron: A Portrait* (London: Murray, 1970), 399.

[5] Ernest J. Lovell, ed., *Lady Blessington's Conversations of Lord Byron* (Princeton: Princeton UP, 1966), 220.

[6] Cf. Ina Schabert, *In Quest of the Other Person: Fiction as Biography* (Tübingen: Francke, 1990), 3–4, and Annegret Maack, "Das Leben der toten Dichter: Fiktive Biographien," in *Radikalität und Mässigung: Der englische Roman seit 1960,* ed. Annegret Maack and Rüdiger Imhof (Darmstadt: Wissenschaftliche Buchgesellschaft, 1993), 171.

[7] Amanda Prantera, *Conversations with Lord Byron on Perversion, 163 Years after His Lordship's Death* (London: Abacus, 1988) All subsequent page references in the text are to this edition

[8] James Soderholm, *Fantasy, Forgery and the Byron Legend* (Lexington: U of Kentucky P, 1996), 169.

[9] For further background information on Shelley's *Faust* translation, see Timothy Webb, *The Violet and the Crucible: Shelley and Translation* (Oxford: Clarendon, 1976).

[10] Leslie A. Marchand, *Byron: A Biography* (New York: Knopf, 1957), I:172.

[11] Marchand, *Byron,* I: 174.

[12] Roland Barthes, "From Work to Text," in *Image Music Text,* trans. Stephen Heath (London: Fontana Press, 1977), 156.

[13] Derrida, *Of Grammatology,* 24.

[14] See Derrida, *Of Grammatology,* 18–19.

[15] Derrida, *Of Grammatology,* 49.

[16] See Hans-Georg Gadamer, "Frühromantik, Hermeneutik, Dekonstruktivismus," in *Die Aktualität der Frühromantik,* ed. Ernst Behler and Jochen Hörisch (Paderborn: Schöningh, 1987), 260.

[17] See Barthes, "From Work to Text," 157–58.

[18] Christopher Norris, *Deconstruction: Theory and Practice* (London and New York: Routledge, 1991), 24–25.

[19] Linda Hutcheon, *A Poetics of Postmodernism: History, Theory, Fiction* (New York and London: Routledge, 1988), 61. Freeing oneself from a logocentric centre may open up new perspectives: "[. . .] there have been liberating effects of moving from the language of alienation (otherness) to that of decentering (difference), because the center used to function as the pivot between binary opposites which always privileged one half: white/black, male/female, self/other, intellect/body, west/east, objectivity/subjectivity — the list is now well known" (62).

[20] Derrida, *Of Grammatology*, 69–70. Derrida points out that seeking to annihilate *différance* and the trace is characteristic of "all dualisms, all theories of the immortality of the soul or of the spirit, as well as all monisms, spiritualist or materialist, dialectical or vulgar [. . .]" (70–71).

[21] See Barthes, "From Work to Text," 157.

[22] Allen Thiher, *Words in Reflection: Modern Language Theory and Postmodernist Fiction* (Chicago and London: U of Chicago P, 1984), 161.

[23] Barthes, "From Work to Text," 162.

[24] Marchand, *Byron*, I: 101.

[25] Marchand, *Byron*, I: 107–08.

[26] The exact phrasing is: "I certainly love him more than any human being, and neither time nor distance have had the least effect on my (in general) changeable disposition." Letter to Elizabeth Pigot, July 5, 1807, in Thomas Moore, *The Life, Letters, and Journals of Lord Byron* (London: Murray, 1920), 54.

[27] Soderholm's interpretation that "LB prints out its remembrances of things past" is a gross misreading and confusion of the two narrative situations at work in Prantera's text. See Soderholm, *Fantasy, Forgery, and the Byron Legend*, 166.

[28] Byron, *Don Juan*, Canto IV, stanza XXVI, in *Works*, 701.

[29] In the Thyrza/Edleston context one may also point to "'And Thou Art Dead, As Young and Fair,'" "Away, Away Ye Notes of Woe," "One Struggle More, and I am Free," "To Thyrza," "The Cornelian," "To E——," "Epistle to a Friend," and, particularly, to the second canto of *Childe Harold's Pilgrimage*, stanzas IX, IXV-IXVIII; see Marchand, *Byron*, I: 313.

[30] Byron, *Don Juan*, Canto V, stanza I, in *Works*, 712.

[31] Thiher, *Words in Reflection*, 172.

[32] See Barthes, "From Work to Text," 164.

[33] See Christopher Butler, *Interpretation, Deconstruction, and Ideology* (Oxford: Oxford UP, 1984), 86.

[34] On the narcissistic character of all metafictional literature, see Linda Hutcheon, *Narcissistic Narrative: The Metafictional Paradox* (New York and London: Methuen, 1984).

[35] Soderholm, *Fantasy, Forgery, and the Byron Legend*, 170.

[36] See Wolf Kittler, "Digitale und analoge Speicher: Zum Begriff der Memoria in der Literatur des 20. Jahrhunderts," in *Gedächtniskunst: Raum-Bild-Schrift. Studien zu Mnemotechnik*, ed. Anselm Haverkamp and Renate Lachmann (Frankfurt am Main: Suhrkamp, 1991), 404; see also Lachmann's introduction (19).

ANNEGRET MAACK

"The Life We Imagine": Byron's and Polidori's Memoirs as Character Construction

PAUL WEST'S NOVEL *LORD BYRON'S DOCTOR* and Robert Nye's *The Memoirs of Lord Byron* are both concerned with historical figures, Dr. Polidori and Lord Byron respectively, each of whom is given a new life as the author of a fictitious memoir. And both novels presume a reader who is familiar with the literary history of the Romantic movement and with the interwoven biographies of its leading spirits.

Paul West's *Lord Byron's Doctor*: The Relation of Polidori's Memoirs to the Historical Sources

West's novel presents itself as the memoirs of Dr. John Polidori, the physician who at the tender age of twenty accompanied Byron on his continental journey of 1816. The text largely follows the chronology of that journey, describing the sojourn on Lake Geneva, where the travellers met up with Shelley, Mary Wollstonecraft, and Claire Clairmont, the separation between Byron and Polidori, who went on to Italy, and finally Polidori's return to England and his death.

West uses documentary evidence about the historical Dr. Polidori, including his letters and literary works, quotes from Byron's letters and poetry and shows an awareness of the available biographical writing on the Byron-Shelley circle. His detailed knowledge of Byron's works was previously displayed in his *Byron and the Spoiler's Art* (1960); his familiarity with the critical corpus is evident in the volume *Byron: A Collection of Critical Essays* (1963), which he edited.

The dominant pre-text of West's novel is the historically documented diary that Polidori kept between April and December 30, 1816, a work first published in an expurgated version by Polidori's nephew, William Michael Rossetti, in 1911. Rossetti's aunt, Charlotte Lydia Polidori, transcribed the diary, omitting the "peccant passages,"[1] and subsequently destroyed the original, but Rossetti was able to read the diary before this date. His own version refers from memory to the "improper passages" on Byron's and Polidori's sexual adventures, including Byron's escapades with a chambermaid at Ostend. West's fictional memoirs of Polidori begin with this episode,[2] which is used to suggest that they are more authentic than the text of the published diary.

West's novel follows the historical diary in detail, repeatedly quoting short excerpts from it, such as the account of Shelley's age, in which Polidori was first mistaken and which he then took pains to correct (53).[3] Brief diary entries like one on the vaccination of Shelley's son William are given in the memoirs in greater detail (65), and passages that contradict historically established facts are also included. One such is the account of Shelley's career; that, for instance, "he had married a girl merely to let her inherit his money. [. . .] At fourteen he published a novel for thirty pounds. His second work earned him a hundred" (63). Where Rossetti in his commentary points out factual discrepancies of this sort,[4] in the novel Byron is given the task of explaining the errors as a romantic fiction created for the benefit of the gullible doctor: "He [Shelley] is romancing you, Polly. Remember the novelist in him. He sees you as easy meat. His novel *Zastrozzi* came out when he was seventeen or eighteen" (63). With passages such as these, the author of the memoirs communicates a greater knowledge than the historical Polidori possessed. Likewise, there is nothing in the diaries that corresponds to Polidori's opium-induced fantasies, his conversations with the poets or his wide ranging, self-destroying doubts, all present in the novel.

The novel is mainly concerned with those days in June 1816 — often described — that saw the genesis of Mary Wollstonecraft's *Frankenstein*, Byron's "Fragment" and Polidori's *The Vampyre*. The historical Polidori's account of events in the Villa Diodati conflicts with Mary Shelley's account in her foreword to *Frankenstein*,[5] while the fictional Polidori's memoirs present two different accounts. One is given by the Countess of Breuss, who is said to have told Polidori of Byron's planned ghost story and who was the historical recipient of the doctor's own manuscript.[6] Polidori, therefore, recreates himself fictionally here: "Thus did Polly write about Polly" (84). The second and more detailed account follows the historical diary and describes in the following terms the agreement made on June 16 by Shelley, Byron, Polidori, Mary

Wollstonecraft, and Claire Clairmont that they would all write ghost stories:

> Each looking at the other as if seeing some unspeakable being behind the other's shoulder, and aghast at the view; then each in turn seeing the ogre behind all the others' backs, mouthing and slavering even as, too drenched in hideous imagining to turn back, we vowed to invent monsters of our own to frighten others with, until the whole race leapt into the sea to save its reason. (80–81)

Polidori reports on the progress of the ghost stories. Mary Shelley has told him about her tale of "the piecemeal man" as follows: "I keep seeing a creature, found among the ice floes or the jungles, long abandoned, whom some devout scientist has pieced together [. . .] all from human cadavers" (90). But it was not Byron's "Fragment," it was his poem "Darkness" that Polidori understood as a ghost story: "The ghost therein was that of our very own world" (93).

In West's novel, Polidori gives detailed information about the genesis of his *Vampyre*, telling how he rejected the original idea of "a skull-headed woman punished for watching through a keyhole something so unspeakable"[7] and commenced a tale "envisioning the departure of two friends from England, one of them dying in Ephesus, after getting from his companion an oath, never to mention his death" (82). To that extent Polidori's plot coincides with Byron's "Fragment," published later. But the fictional Polidori suggests that the parallels between the stories begun by Byron and himself in the Villa Diodati were accidental: "How Byronic, I thought, even if superficially akin to my own narrative. After all, how many basic plots were there for authors to employ?" (94). Thus Polidori emphasizes the independence of his own narrative without excluding the question of influence: "my own was my own and the better tale [. . .]. We had all been playing at mental incest. But who knew what had or had not criss-crossed our conjoint minds [. . .]" (143).

The Memoirs as Polidori's Search for Identity

Polidori defines himself by means of Byron; that is already clear from the title of the novel, which names him only in his function as the young nobleman's doctor. His memoirs begin with the commencement of the journey in April 1816 and suggest that Polidori's literary existence was initiated in an act of name-giving. "Polly," the novel's opening word, is not only the name Byron gave his doctor; it also describes his other, non-medical role as the parrot whose duty it is to repeat and to confide to his diary what has been said and done. Byron's publisher, Murray, had already promised 500 pounds for a diary of the journey. But Polidori sees himself not just as doctor, diarist, and memoir-writer, but as "socialite, rake, friend, lover, traveller, Englishman, or boor" (113; cf. 123). The question of his identity runs right through the memoirs and always in relation to his employer; although he also provides character sketches of Shelley, Mary Wollstonecraft, Claire Clairmont, and Thomas Love Peacock, his self-portrait is first and foremost a portrait of Byron, and one not calculated to flatter the myth of the great Romantic.

From the moment they meet, Polidori sees himself in competition with the aristocrat, whom he describes as "the most famous rake in England" (3), but whose feats, sexual and otherwise, he is unable to equal. Right at the beginning he asks Byron "'what is there, excepting poetry, that I cannot do better than you?'" (8).[8] Byron's answer makes clear his own feeling of superiority: he is the better shot, the better swimmer, and could give Polidori a thrashing if he chose to. Later questions yield similar replies (69). Polidori wants to put himself on an equal footing with Byron; he would be the mirror image of the famous Lord. He copies Byron's appearance: "I would dress Byronic" (144); he seeks to imitate Byron's sexual mores, even to the point of contracting venereal disease; and he manages to slip on a hill-path and sprain his foot, an adventure that endows him at least temporarily with a Byronic limp (76).[9] His relation to Byron is mirrored, too, in his vampire story, whose protagonist, Lord Ruthven, takes his name from the Byron figure of Lady Caroline Lamb's *roman-à-clef, Glenarvon,* and whose young companion-figure, Aubrey, reflects his own position in the *ménage.* But his utmost exertions fail to raise him to the literary eminence of his master and, realizing this, he sighs: "Now, if only I had written 'Darkness,' but I did not, nor could I have" (143).

The five parts into which the memoirs are divided, with their mottos from the writings of the historical Polidori, establish a structure that reminds one of a classical five-act tragedy. The brief introductory section lists Polidori's duties and inaugurates the theme of competition between him and Lord Byron. Part II deals with the journey up to the arrival at Lake Geneva and describes both the influence of Byron on Polidori and the latter's emulation of his ideal: "we were no longer lord and liegeman but Don Quixote and Sancho Panza, Mephisto and Faust, each of us both of them turn and turn about" (39). The long third part is devoted to the events at the Villa Diodati up to Polidori's departure. While Byron and Shelley continue to grow in mutual understanding, Polidori feels snubbed by the two poets, who make no secret

of their scorn for his attempts at drama. Part IV covers Polidori's stay in
Italy, where he meets Byron again both in Milan and in Venice before
finally separating from him. Byron's companion knows he cannot
achieve fame with his diary, for many before him have tried their hand
at the hero's biography: "the Hobhouses, the Leigh Hunts, not to
mention a host of women" (229). Part V, with its motto "On the
Punishment of Death," is a preparation for that event and, quite consistently, it ends with Polidori's suicide through taking poison, a process which, however, he reports in the following terms: "Now Charlotte,
at ten to noon, enters to open the shutters and hears me groaning
[. . .] I linger for ten minutes" (277). One must here, at the very latest, ask who the author of these memoirs really is. For not only does
Polidori report his own death but also the verdict of the coroner's jury,
which is not suicide but death "by the visitation of God" (277).

Apart from the account of his death, Part V also tells of Polidori's
return to England and of his visits to Byron's mistress, Claire Clairmont, who is living with the Shelleys in Bath. He relates how he expects to be called to help her in her confinement, and tells of the letter
to Byron in which she breaks the news of the death of her step-sister
Fanny; Polidori also speaks of Shelley's reaction to the suicide of his
wife: "I was there, I saw him age and falter" (253). But Fanny Imlay's
death in October 1816, Harriet Shelley's suicide in December 1816,
and the birth of Byron's daughter Allegra in January 1817, all took
place while Polidori — as is clear from Part IV — was still in Italy. He
did not leave that country until April 1817.[10] Such bilocation can only
be explained on the assumption that Polidori has become "a ghoul, a
revenant" (244) who, like the vampire of his story, can transmute into
a deathless voice bound neither by time nor place. That voice continues
to speak of death, even reporting the death of Claire Clairmont, which
did not occur until 1879: "I saw her, long after we were all dust, an old
lady with white curls" (153; 253).

Forewarnings of Polidori's nature can be found earlier in the book.
Thus, he knows that his sister Charlotte will expurgate his diary (33;
168); he speaks of the deaths in the Shelley circle that will take place
after his own death in August 1821 (146); and his knowledge of
Byron, too, far exceeds what the historic figure of the doctor could
have imagined:

> He [Byron] wished to be a force, I thought: a star, a peak, a wind,
> untrammelled by intercourse. If he was not the last man in the world,
> as in the poem he was writing, he was the last man *of his kind*, and he
> knew it, as like to have a thousand imitators (Polidori included) as to
> die unique: deformed, misanthropic, pretty. (147)

The text is full of allusions to the poets' vampire-like being, long before the members of Byron's circle began to write their ghost stories.[11] Polidori sees Byron's hunger for life as making him into "a life-swallower, a devourer" (6), who nourishes himself from the energies of others. "He took his energy from others" (86); he was "a shadow, a ghost, not really present among us" (101). The doctor imagines Byron creeping into his bedroom "crouching at my hand to lap its blood while I slept, almost vampyrelike" (74); in his view Byron resembles Mary Shelley's monster: "And, in a weird way, he seemed to have come out of Mary Shelley's head: the ghoul, patched together from a thousand misdemeanours, failed lives, wasted loves, atrophied parts. He was a scarecrow of rumours [. . .]" (188).

More frequently still, Polidori sees himself as a vampire. In his opium-induced dreams he experiences "how closeness to death would feel" (150), and he moves as if deathless. From the beginning he lives on Byron, and in a metaphorical sense he becomes the vampire of the Byron-Shelley circle: "I was the Vroucolocha of the set" (143).[12] Lifting sentences from his own ghost story to describe his "real" experiences, he becomes, finally "a [literary] vampyre to myself" (97).

Many too are the discussions about the reawakening of the dead — or of dead matter — to life. Polidori fantasizes about dissection and about himself as the born pathologist: "my natural bent was [. . .] to find matters of live lie st interest in cadavers" (37). During the first stage of the journey Byron and his doctor indulge themselves in "warping the usual ideas of life and death" (39): "Could the defunctus be brought back? [. . .] by focussing the mind, say, or even a bolt of lightning?" (17); "Could not the created being itself create life? Create it from something dead?" (79). As Viktor Frankenstein awakens the parts of corpses, so does Polidori, the writer of memoirs, awaken the historical figures of the Byron-Shelley circle to a new and different literary life: "Now we too were a Frankenstein monster" (161). Changing a few details of a poem, he shows too how he can give "a new lease of life" (58) to old texts.

But the process of literary dissection goes further. In literature Polidori finds the sources for an understanding of his own life: he is as unimportant for Byron and Shelley as the player who represents Wall in Shakespeare's *Midsummer Night's Dream* (58). And he describes his inner tensions in terms of two such opposed characters as "the sexually successful jester-cum-Lothario, and the washed-up drowned man whose eyes the crabs had taken" (243). Riding to Claire at night, he sees himself as one of Dante's "infernal lovers" (250), and it is from Goethe's *Werther* that he takes the inspiration for his suicide (251).

Byron's "Darkness" provides him with the truest description of his role, that of the faithful dog belonging to the "last man" in the Byronic vision of the end of time: "the last unselfish act coming from a dog who guarded his master's body until his own death" (85). Polidori's life is one with these texts.

In the final part of his memoirs Polidori succeeds in resuscitating the figure whom the biographers have treated with least respect: Claire Clairmont, a woman so unimportant that she could be called "Polidora" (154). Making her his own mistress, Polidori sustains to the end his relationship with the man he had served; in his relationship with Claire, Byron's mistress and the mother of his child, he is a surrogate for Byron himself. And her situation mirrors his own: "We had both been rejected, so we should combine our thrown-off natures and make ourselves a wholly wanted person, each half infatuated with the other" (237).

West's Double Portrait: Byron and Polidori

Like Byron, Polidori is "too many men in one" (28), but unlike the poet, he cannot live with paradox and contradiction — an element in Byron's portrait that West's critical work confirms. "I agree with Wain," West writes, "when he says flatly that Byron 'did not, in the deeper sense, have a self.'"[13] While West's Polidori prepares the poison draught that will kill him, he cites as a magic formula a passage from Canto III of *Childe Harold's Pilgrimage* in which Byron is concerned with the workings of the creative process on the poet. Only in poetry is the formation of identity possible:

> 'Tis to create, and in creating live
> A being more intense, that we endow
> With form our fancy, gaining as we give
> The life we imagine, even as I do now.[14]

In the following lines, which Polidori does not quote, Byron writes of his relation to his fictive Childe Harold. The lines could with equal justification be applied to Polidori and Byron. They would describe a search for identity that the Polidori of the memoirs could only achieve in relation to his master:

> What am I? Nothing: but not so art thou,
> Soul of my thought! with whom I traverse earth,
> Invisible but gazing, as I glow

Mix'd with thy spirit, blended with thy birth,
And feeling with thee in my crush'd feelings' dearth.

Robert Nye's *Memoirs of Lord Byron*: Inconsistent Identity

After Byron's death his literary executors tore up and burned the manuscript of his memoirs.[15] Byron's friend John Cam Hobhouse, one of the few who had read the memoirs, wrote in his diary: "'The whole Memoirs were fit only for a brothel, and would damn Lord Byron to everlasting infamy if published.'"[16] Nyc's novel is a fictional reconstruction of this text. As in *Falstaff* or *Merlin*, the author again uses "literary ventriloquy"[17] to approach a historical figure through stylistic imitation. This is apparent even in the way the book is set, with Roman numerals being used for the page numbers — a common convention in the Regency period.

Nye's Byron begins his memoirs in Venice in July 1818, in order, as he says, to overcome boredom. He begins "with the beginning," with the death of his father when he was three, and proceeds on a broadly chronological basis to recount his life: early childhood, school, first loves, his relationship with his mother, the inheritance of the title and of Newstead Abbey, the beginning of his poetic career, his marriage to and separation from Annabella, his departure from England and his continental journeys. The sojourn on Lake Geneva, so fully described by Polidori, is only touched on here, and Polidori's irrelevance for Byron is evident in the fact that his name is not even mentioned — not even in connection with those events that Polidori treats both in his historical memoirs and in West's reconstruction, for instance the seduction of the chambermaid at Ostend, the journey to Lake Geneva, and the famous agreement of the Romantics to write ghost stories. Byron dismisses this in a single sentence:

> We tried our hands at composing ghost stories, though only Mary persevered in the attempt, writing a fine piece of nonsense about a monster created by a Dr. Victor Frankenstein (in which I always thought that the doctor bore a distinct resemblance to her husband, and the monster to me). (169–70)

Byron's recollections are continually interrupted by things happening in the present: conversations with his daughter Allegra, the attentions of his current, sex-obsessed mistress Margarita, letters, and visitors, notably the Shelleys. He comments on the process of composition, which continues up until May 1819, and on his reasons for attempting an autobiography at all. Realizing how deceptive a subjective view can be, he soon despairs of his initial intention "to represent or enact me *as I am*" (73). "Impressions of one's friends," he observes, may well be "truer than the faces in one's own private mirror" (73); what is important is not just how we see ourselves, but "how others see us" (93).

The fictional Byron of this portrait knows that the image he presents cannot be consistent, for his character is marked by irreconcilable oppositions: "If I am sincere with myself (but I fear one lies more to one's self than to anyone else), every page should confute, refute and utterly abjure its predecessor" (121). He enjoys these contradictions, to the point of raising discordance to a conscious attitude: it is his "favourite mode, in life as in literature" (84). And he cultivates this mode not only within his self-portrait, but in the relation of this to his public image as a libertine and rake. Thus, he loves solitude (96); his favourite occupation is "lying on my back and turning the pages of a book at regular intervals" (83); and his "innermost being" is depicted most faithfully in those verses from *Lara*: "a stranger in this breathing world, / An erring spirit from another hurl'd . . . . " (156). But he rejects with equal vigour the allegation that he is some sort of chameleon, for his constant changing indeed serves only to direct public attention to his figure: "I take not their [i.e. the surroundings] colour on myself to hide myself, but *from* their colour all I need to display myself" (189).

Reporting his "minor loves" he at the same time wonders how to treat the "one unquestionable major" love of his life (51), his relationship with Augusta, about which he writes in a chapter that has no other inscription than the sign for incest: "XXX" (151). The misogynous attitude revealed in the account of his various dalliances and also of his marriage — "I have not quite made up my mind that women have souls" (139) — contrasts with the true love he experiences for his sister. Chapter Thirteen begins with the "Stanzas for Music" written in 1814, verses which Nye alters and extends to accommodate the revelatory character of this chapter. Thus, instead of "I speak not, I trace not, I breathe not thy name,"[18] Nye's Byron writes:

> I speak not — I breathe not — I write not that name —
> There is grief in the sound, there is guilt in the fame . . . .
> We have loved — and oh, still, my adored one we love!
> Oh the moment is past, when that Passion might cease. —
> We repent, we abjure, we will break from the chain, —
> We will part, we will fly to — unite it again! . . .
> The thought may be madness — the wish may be guilt!
>
> (146)

The lines added (2, 3 and 6–7) speak of the poet's passion, which is tantamount to an admission of incestuous love.

Literature as a Model of Life

Byron's judgements on poetry, both his own and that of others, provide an accurate picture of his development. Here too, contradiction is an essential element. At the beginning of his career he was "half in love with the idea of poetical fame," but now he has "no great esteem for the pursuit of poetry" (55). His first work, *Fugitive Pieces*, he condemns as "a thin bad volume" (55), and he considers *Hints from Horace* more important than *Childe Harold* (102). Nor does he make any attempt to conceal his dislike for Wordsworth and Keats, unmercifully mocking "Turdsworth and his Lakeland tadpoles" (102), despite the fact that his concept of poetry as "the lava of imagination [. . .] the expression of *excited passions*" (42) bears a close resemblance to Wordsworth's celebrated definition. For Keats's aestheticism he has nothing but scorn, calling *Endymion* the "onanism of poetry, piss-a-bed stuff by a crybaby" (197). On the other hand he admires the "intellectual" Romantics Coleridge and Shelley and considers himself to have done a service to English poetry when he recommended to his publisher Murray the printing of Coleridge's "Christabel" and "Kubla Khan" (144). The catalogue of contradictions is completed by his assertion that the Neoclassicists Pope and Dryden were his poetic forebears (102).

Literary critics and historians may have established the dictum that Byron made poetry of his life, but Nye's Byron asserts the contrary: his life was modelled on literature, and not just the literature of his own creating. Like Dante and Beatrice, Byron fell in love with Mary Duff at the tender age of eight (43). His relationship with Mary Chaworth resembled that of Romeo and Juliet; their families too were at loggerheads. Mary incorporated for him the ideal of womanhood, for in her his imagination reached its first perfection (46). His sojourn at Newstead Abbey was "like living in the intellectual and emotional landscape of one of my early poems" (77). The fictional figures of his narrative verse are more real for him than the woman he loves (92), and Caroline Lamb's true character is only apparent to him when he conceives of her as the heroine of a romance (113). Byron describes himself and Augusta as "a wicked Hansel and a wanton Gretel" (150); he sees her as the reincarnation of Shakespeare's Cleopatra, so beautiful is she, so changeable and so full of intrigue (152). An autobiography in which Byron were to suppress the major love of his life would be like "the

tragedy of *Hamlet* at a country theatre recited 'with the part of the
Prince left out by popular demand'" (52). His own forced departure
from England seems to him like Adam's expulsion from Paradise. It enables him, however, to become in his journeyings the hero he himself
had created in the characters of Cain or Manfred, "a soul in outer
darkness howling dismal" (164). Nye's Byron is in love with his own
fictions (46).

The Fascination of Death

Nye's Byron ended his memoirs in May 1819. In 1822 he added two
chapters as postscript, reporting in them the deaths of his daughter Allegra and of his friend Shelley. An epilogue foretells his own death and
the destruction of the memoirs.

A preoccupation with transience and death runs through Nye's
book like a *leitmotif*. One cannot, however, always distinguish the
light-hearted from the serious: Byron's attitude is again one of discordance. The motto from *Don Juan* set at the head of the memoirs immediately invokes the theme of transitoriness: "I would to Heaven that
I were so much clay / As I am blood, bone, marrow, passion, feeling — ."[19] Citing these lines in the context of Chapter Nine, the fictive
Byron, however, contradicts their tenor and asserts that he merely
wants to impress the reader. Again, when he comes to speak of his "finest and least affected poem," "So we'll go no more a roving / So late
in the night . . . " (177), he emphasizes not the noble attitude of departure and denial the poem suggests but a powerful will to live.

The thought of death, the poet says, is constantly before him. The
happiest hours of his schooltime at Harrow were spent reclining on a
grave: "I would lie there for hours and hours, sometimes devouring for
my own pleasure books of travel and shipwrecks" (26). In Venice he
goes in search of a suitable grave and a suitable inscription for it (40);
on another occasion he designs a gravestone for his dog, who is to be
buried in the ruined chapel at Newstead Abbey (79), and next to
whom he hopes one day to lie himself. Using his servant's name, he
writes a letter to Hobhouse announcing his own death, and he inserts
as a quotation into his memoirs the epitaph he writes in Patras where
he is suffering from malaria (95). For his daughter, too, he designs a
gravestone, even though the thought — later elaborated by Poe — that
"female beauty should be subject to death" fills him with fear (193).

While Byron is himself the defining model for West's Polidori, for
Nye's Byron it is Shelley who directs the poet's thoughts and feelings.
He formulates his own position in relation to the person of Shelley and

his works. Shelley is "the least selfish and mildest of men" (38); he admires his poetry and "the sublime glitter of his mind" (169). But in contrast to the younger poet Byron has no great esteem either for poets or for poetry. He does not believe that poets are "the unacknowledged legislators of the universe" (42), and he is convinced that ever since Plato "the wiser part of mankind" knows that poets lie (91). Byron maintains that in *Adonais* Shelley foretold his own death. His fascination with the process of death is evident in his account of the burning of Shelley's body on the beach at Viareggio. This chapter reads like an excerpt from the Gothic novel that Byron never wrote. In grotesque detail he relates how the poet dissolved before his eyes in a "magma of putrid slime" (209), his skull split, his heart alone enduring the fire like "a big rotten prune" (211).

Shelley, whom Byron loved unselfishly, is the mirror in which he would dearly like to see himself. Although Shelley's mind is "just about the opposite of" his own, Byron discovers there "an undercurrent or depth of harmony" (170) between the two. In this relationship, too, however, the poet remains a deeply torn personality, unable even in his memoirs to construct for himself a coherent identity.

Carlyle recommended the study of biography as a gateway to history, although he considered the life of every individual unfathomable. It was in this sense that he warned against the notion that history could ever be finally understood.

> History is the essence of innumerable Biographies. But if one Biography, nay, our own Biography, study and recapitulate it as much as we may, remains in so many points unintelligible to us; how much more must these million, the very fact of which, to say nothing of the purport of them, we know not, and cannot know![20]

West and Nye present in their novels the reading of an individual life. As far as facts and dates are concerned, both follow the standard biographies. The character projected by the fictive Byron demonstrates, however, that the search for *the* facts and *the* truth is illusory. The autobiographies are fictions: postmodern fictions that follow the convention that their characters are composed by texts. Only in literature — in every sense of that word — do their characters live. Nye shows how "the very act of writing kills the *I* who writes it."[21] We think that we hear in his Byron the "true speaking voice" (dust-cover blurb), and West's Polidori, too, becomes a voice without a body. In these reconstructions the historical writer can be understood only as a revenant assuming the form of a "verbal construct," a "fictional ghost."[22]

Notes

[1] *The Diary of Dr. John Polidori 1816: Relating to Byron, Shelley, etc,* ed. William Michael Rossetti (London: Elkin Mathews, 1911), 11.

[2] Paul West, *Lord Byron's Doctor* (Chicago: U of Chicago P, 1989), 3; all subsequent page references in the text are to this edition; cf. Polidori, *The Diary*, 33.

[3] Cf. also Polidori, *The Diary*, 101.

[4] Polidori, *The Diary*, 109.

[5] Cf. James Rieger, "Dr. Polidori and the Genesis of *Frankenstein*," *Studies in English Literature* 3 (1963): 465.

[6] Rieger, "Dr. Polidori and the Genesis of *Frankenstein*," 462.

[7] Cf. Mary Shelley, *Frankenstein or the Modern Prometheus*, in *Three Gothic Novels*, ed. Peter Fairclough (Harmondsworth: Penguin, 1968), 261.

[8] The autobiographies report the details of this competitiveness.

[9] Polidori, *The Diary*, 136.

[10] Polidori, *The Diary*, 10.

[11] Cf. David W. Madden, *Understanding Paul West* (Columbia: U of South Carolina P, 1993), 96–97.

[12] Cf. "the living vampyre, elsewhere known as Vroucolocha" (135).

[13] Paul West, *Byron and the Spoiler's Art* (London: Chatto, 1960), 12; cf. John Wain, "The Search for Identity," in *Byron: A Collection of Critical Essays*, ed. Paul West (Englewood Cliffs, NJ: Prentice Hall, 1963), 158, 159.

[14] Canto III, Stanza vi; Byron, *Poetical Works*, ed. Frederick Page, corr. John Jump (London: Oxford UP, 1970), 210; cf. West, *Lord Byron's Doctor*, 273–74.

[15] Cf. "The Burning of the Memoirs," in Doris Langley Moore, *The Late Lord Byron* (London: John Murray, 1976), 12–56.

[16] Quoted in Robert Nye, *The Memoirs of Lord Byron: A Novel* (London: Hamilton, 1989), 215. All subsequent page references in the text are to this edition.

[17] Neil Berry, "Dominated by the sex," *Times Literary Supplement* 17–23 Nov. 1989: 1271.

[18] Byron, *Poetical Works*, 75.

[19] Cf. Byron, *Poetical Works*, 635 (Canto I, Fragment).

[20] Thomas Carlyle, "On History," in *A Carlyle Reader*, ed. G. B. Tennyson (New York: Random House, 1969), 57.

[21] Nye, *The Memoirs*, 121.

[22] Christine Brooke-Rose, *Stories, Theories and Things* (Cambridge: Cambridge UP, 1991), 176.

PETER PAUL SCHNIERER

In Arcadia Nemo:
The Pastoral of Romanticism

I

"PASTORAL" IS A DIRTY WORD THESE DAYS. CRITICS have shown us the pernicious tendencies of the pastoral mode, and reviewers, ignoring the critics, have gone on equating it with nostalgia and sentimentality. To write pastoral today, the consensus seems to say, is at worst to deceive and at best to embarrass.

Thus, the anti-pastoral has been the only feasible permutation for some time now. In Edward Bond's play *Restoration: A Pastoral* (1981), for instance, the country yokels are hunted down, jailed and hanged by an aristocrat and an industrialist, both of whom are town-dwellers. These oppressor figures are not of Bond's invention. In fact, they are every inch as vulgar and as successful as the money-lender in Horace's Second Epode, published around 30 BC; he, too, returns to town in the end, the rural setting serving merely as a refuge from the strains of extortion. The pastoral, established two and a half centuries earlier by Theocritus, was thus already identified as irresponsible and rebarbative.

Considering this troubled history, it seems ingenuous of Tom Stoppard to entitle his play about Byron *Arcadia* in 1993 without delivering the ritual debunking of the bucolic that one has come to expect. Here are no murdered peasants, as Stephen Greenblatt detected them in a previous *Arcadia*, Sidney's of 1590.[1] Stoppard's is much closer to the title's even earlier incarnation, Jacopo Sannazzaro's *Arcadia* (1480/1502), which reintroduced the term and practice to an audience already receptive to Greek and Roman prototypes. Stoppard's play dramatizes the end of that development, the displacement of a classical aesthetics by a romantic one, and the pastoralization of the former. In a different but parallel movement, his twentieth-century characters collect fragments of information on Byron's life and reassemble from them a meaningful narrative. This biography is necessarily fictional and can be described in terms of pastoral as well.

II

Sannazzaro still worked with an undisputed definition of pastoral: the literature of idealized country life. This definition has itself acquired idealizing overtones: not only are there no longer happy, melancholy, or at any rate unproblematic shepherds (the impossibility of their existence at the time and place of writing is essential to pastoral), but the genre recalling them has itself become impossible. The nymphs and swains have long since departed, and even saying so has now become an obsolete gesture.

This is the result of a process that took centuries and began, if one follows the argument outlined above, almost at the beginning, with Horace's reworking of the model purveyed by Theocritus. It was only in our century, however, that three major literary critics tried to finish off the genre altogether.

The most recent of these attempts, Raymond Williams's *The Country and the City*,[2] avoids the term "pastoral" almost completely, but the axis along which it aligns its topography is familiar enough. Country and city, the ideal landscape or the *locus amoenus* versus whatever the reader experiences as her or his reality, these are the oppositions it generates and exploits. A history of these oppositions in literature would have to include *The Tempest, Robinson Crusoe, Stalky & Co.*, indeed, the entire colonial canon written for those at the center. Any Arcadia belongs here; it is in fact the archetype of the "other" place.

The second axis along which pastoral ideals can be aligned is temporal rather than spatial. Arcadia's isomorphic territories, the genetic Eden and the apocalyptic New Jerusalem that initiate the Old Testament and conclude the New, are defined not by their being somewhere else, but by being not any more or not yet. One shades off into creation myths, the other is the model for utopian discourses. In the former there is no conflict, no alienation yet, in the latter conflicts have at last been successfully resolved; there is no alienation any more. W. H. Auden is this alignment's most persuasive critic: he first drew attention to the neat dichotomies it makes possible, and he saw the sedative power of Edenic narratives (which he calls Arcadian) as well as the dehumanizing potential of Utopian ones.[3]

William Empson's questioning of the pastoral, written in 1935 and entitled *Some Versions of Pastoral*, is the earliest of the three, and the most radical. The title of his study alone indicates the pluralization of a once straightforward concept. For Empson, the genre's structural axis is neither spatial nor temporal, but societal. He uses the term "pastoral" to encompass all literature designed to bridge the gaps between classes and reconcile the have-nots with the haves.

> [The] essential trick of the old pastoral, which was felt to imply a beautiful relation between rich and poor, was to make simple people express strong feelings (felt as the most universal subject, something fundamentally true about everybody).[4]

According to Empson, the opposition activated in pastoral is therefore not between social groups, but between a society with social divisions and one without; it makes use of the reader's inevitable experience of social inequality and insists on a society where people are free and equal. This does not imply the absence of social differences, but these are shown to be "natural" and unproblematic. Here is the genre's tranquillizing potential, here its affirmative and hence deplorable function. No later disapproval of pastoral has really progressed beyond this point.[5]

Yet for all his determination to finish off pastoral as a viable form of art, Empson's versions can be made to multiply, not as ever more insidious ways of anaesthetizing the working class, but as structures similar to those identified by him, by Auden and by Williams. "Pastoral" as a sharply delimited term does not exist in our current critical discourses, as has become evident. Thus, faced with a loss of its original meaning (no shepherds have been in sight for a long time now) and a proliferation of new explanations, a more basic and at the same time more precise definition is within reach.[6] The spatial, temporal, and societal axes are not the only ones that can be applied to any kind of literature with a potential for pastoral, several others are conceivable that widen the range of evasions that can be described as pastoral.

For evasion is at the heart of the pastoral mode as it will be defined here: to be somewhere else, before our time, in the ages to come, at court or in the shepherd's hovel, but never on the middle ground occupied by the reader.[7] This evasion need not even be desirable: the Golden Age was never more than a rhetorical construct, and the pastoral of the ghetto is as powerful as that of the palace.

The pastoral of childhood — the term is Peter Marinelli's[8] — has already been identified by Empson in his final chapter on "The Child as Swain." By extrapolation in the opposite direction on the biological axis we can add the pastoral of old age. Adam in *As You Like It* gives an example of such pastoral cosiness projected onto an unlikely screen: "my age is as a lusty winter / Frosty, but kindly."[9] Another evasive strategy yields the pastoral of the soul, by locating identity either in some external astral body unlimited by the constraints of our quotidian existence, or deep within oneself, in a place that is constructed in the heart, as Friedrich Schiller has it: "In des Herzens heilig stille Räume / Mußt Du fliehen aus des Lebens Drang."[10] The social axis with its extremes of solipsism and mass identity and the political one demarcated by anarchy and totalitarianism are further alignments made possible by these metaphors.

Such a view can make evident some strategies that otherwise very different texts have in common, without sacrificing the critical potential Empson and Williams have made available. The usefulness of such a model lies both in its triadic approach and in its flexibility: by placing the reality of author and reader in the center, it avoids the dichotomy inherent in the tradition of pastoral literature, and by identifying structures rather than trappings, it does not require the presence of Theocritan devices. There is no need for shepherds frolicking or mourning in a landscape without rain.

III

Lord Byron (not Tom Stoppard's absentee, but the historical author, whose existence nobody denies) once wrote that

> An indoor life is less poetical;
>   And out of door hath showers, and mists, and sleet,
> With which I could not brew a pastoral.[11]

Stoppard, as if setting out to prove that he can do what Byron could not, signals the expendability of traditional pastoral equipment by means of a stage direction at the very beginning of *Arcadia*. He describes the interior of the room that is to be the play's only setting, and continues:

> *Nothing much need be said or seen of the exterior beyond. We come to learn that the house stands in the typical English park of the time. Perhaps we see an indication of this, perhaps only light and air and sky.*[12]

The vagueness is intentional, and it is significant coming from an author whose fastidiousness over stage directions has always been remarkable. Pastoral drama may conventionally show the *locus amoenus*; on stage the virtual may become tangible, but Stoppard insists on the absence of his Arcadia. "Absence" is neither synonymous with nonexistence nor identical with the cover-all term that was fashionable in critical theory from the 1960s.[13] It is, rather, absence as the precondi-

tion of pastoral: an absence that is a presence elsewhere or at some
other time. Stoppard's Arcadia is tantalizingly close, just outside our
field of vision and about to be destroyed, as Lady Croom, one of the
nineteenth-century characters, realizes:

> Here is the Park as it appears to us now, and here as it might be when
> Mr Noakes has done with it. Where there is the familiar pastoral re-
> finement of an Englishman's garden, here is an eruption of gloomy
> forest and towering crag, of ruins where there was never a house, of
> water dashing against rocks where there was neither spring nor a stone
> I could not throw the length of a cricket pitch. My hyacinth dell is be-
> come a haunt for hobgoblins, my Chinese bridge, which I am assured
> is superior to the one at Kew, and for all I know at Peking, is usurped
> by a fallen obelisk overgrown with briars — (12)

Lady Croom's catalogue of horrors is the twentieth-century index of
the Romantic picturesque, of course, and thus merely a new version of
pastoral. Stoppard's choice of items is intended to trigger this recognition in the reader or spectator, but, again, there is no support from the
scene: "*The landscape outside, we are told, has undergone changes. Again,
what we see should neither change nor contradict*" (15). The phrase "we
are told" is indicative — Arcadia is a mere tale, and any reference to it is
filtered by the teller. This foreshadows Stoppard's later treatment of
Lord Byron himself, a further absence in the play who becomes the
metonymic figure for yet another pastoral evasion.

Arcadia is set in a single room in a stately home in England, but in
two different centuries: the action shuttles between 1809 and the present. It revolves, in the nineteenth century, around one Septimus
Hodge, tutor to the child prodigy Thomasina, and lover of Mrs.
Chater. He is also a merciless reviewer of Chater's husband's literary
efforts and friend to Lord Byron, who lives a day's ride away. In the
twentieth century, Hodge's place at center stage has been taken by
Bernard Nightingale and Hannah Jarvis, two Byron scholars and merciless reviewers in their own right. They attempt to make sense of the
snatches of information about Byron which can be unearthed in the old
house's archives and in libraries elsewhere.

Much can be made of *Arcadia*'s intertwining of modern academe
with nineteenth-century education, of its detached passions, and of
Stoppard's dramatization of the Second Law of Thermodynamics —
there is the typical admixture of high comedy and scientific and philosophical ideas for which Stoppard is known.[14] As in his *Travesties*
(1974), the title *Arcadia* signals the literary device that is subjected to
scrutiny by the play itself as well as by the characters in it. Lady Croom

continues her complaint quoted above with a rejoinder that displays a
remarkable sense of artistic decorum:

NOAKES: [. . .] Irregularity is one of the chiefest principles of the
               picturesque style —

LADY CROOM: But Sidley Park is already a picture, and a most amiable
               picture too. The slopes are green and gentle. The trees are
               companionably grouped at intervals that show them to
               advantage. The rill is a serpentine ribbon unwound from
               the lake peaceably contained by meadows on which the
               right amount of sheep are tastefully arranged — in short, it
               is nature as God intended, and I can say with the painter,
               'Et in Arcadia ego!' 'Here I am in Arcadia,' Thomasina.
                                                                      (12)

Lady Croom defines the loss of her classical garden as a loss of the
pastoral ideal, and she uses all the right terms: "amiable," "gentle,"
"peaceably," and indeed "sheep." Her last statement shows her to be
aware of Nicolas Poussin's 1630 painting but unaware of its title's sinister double meaning ("I, Death, am even in Arcadia"). Her words are
in themselves a display of pastoral innocence.

IV

The particular loss Lady Croom is about to experience is irreversible,
but what is depicted is not the moment where pastoral innocence is lost
forever, but rather a replacement: one version of pastoral is supplanted
by another, and the "modern" aesthetics that destroys Lady Croom's
Eden will itself become Edenic. Stoppard drives home that point with
the help of the metonymic figure of Lord Byron, who features so
prominently in *Arcadia* without ever being seen or heard. The fragments of Byron's life that are constructed in the play and by the play
are part of an illimitable pastoral regress: they are never complete and
never verifiable, but they fulfill an escapist function similar to the older
versions of pastoral. Such pastoralization, Stoppard implies, may be applied to Romanticism as a whole.

     The first time we hear of Byron in the play it is in a significantly in-
direct way: Bernard reduces the *Complete Works* of Caroline Lamb, as
about to be edited by Hannah, to "simply [. . .] a document shedding
reflected light on the character of Lord Byron" (21). The word "reflected" is significant: the light that can be had from such a source is
not even direct. A body of fictional texts by another author, yet to be

rearranged by a modern editor, allows no immediate access to Byron's "character."

A few moments after Bernard's speech Hannah complains about the reception of her last book on Byron:

HANNAH: [. . .] All the academics who reviewed my book patronized it.

BERNARD: Surely not.

HANNAH: Surely yes. The Byron gang unzipped their flies and patronized all over it. (22)

Again, Byron is the ostensible subject of Hannah and Bernard's exchanges. Actually, however, we get the reaction of some modern readers to a book on Byron, and Hannah's reaction to that reaction. Byron is present only as a text in the present, and, at another remove, as secondary literature. A few minutes later, Stoppard turns the screw once more. Bernard is now referring to a book on Byron that does not even exist yet, based on "facts" that are manifestly wrong:

BERNARD: Comic turn, fiddlesticks! *(He pauses for effect.)* He [Byron] killed Chater!

HANNAH: *(A raspberry)* Oh, really!

BERNARD: Chater was thirty-one years old. The author of two books. Nothing more is heard from him after 'Eros.' He disappears completely after April 1809. And Byron — Byron had just published his satire, *English Bards and Scotch Reviewers*, in March. He was just getting a name. Yet he sailed for Lisbon as soon as he could find a ship, and stayed abroad for two years. Hannah, *this is fame*. Somewhere in the Croom papers there will be *something* — (31)

The "Croom papers," another repository of revelations just around the corner and never quite attainable, are only the last in a sequence of texts that are made to serve a meaningful fiction.[15] They are props for the construction of a not-here-and-now: in other words, a pastoral according to the present definition.

The characters in the play's twentieth century have no means of verifying what was going on two hundred years earlier. The more they try to make sense of their biographical project, the more they have to rely on written evidence. Access to Byron is only within textuality, and thus requires an interpretation of signs. Any such interpretation can and will go wrong, even if it is not quite as spectacularly misguided as the one Bernard opts for — Byron as the killer of his neighbor's guest.

We, in contrast to the characters in the play's twentieth century, seem to have the means of bypassing the interpretation of signs. Stoppard has given us a window on history in the scenes set in the nineteenth century. Yet, we cannot see Byron either: Stoppard, a part of our present, elects to keep him ephemeral. By maintaining, even emphasizing, Byron's absence, Stoppard turns him into a screen for our projections. He dramatizes not just absence, but the principal impossibility of presence. Once permanent absence is established, and with it the certainty that no more authoritative versions of reality can intrude henceforth, the absent becomes capable of being pastoralized. Thus, Byron must be demonstrated as evanescent, unreachable by any disinterested, reliable, unmediated account (for such accounts are themselves absent). A "Biography fiction," in Aldous Huxley's term,[16] must take the places of these accounts and of Byron himself; only then can the process of pastoralization begin. Like the irregular garden of the Romantic Age that began as a revolutionary concept and ended up as Arcadia itself, Romanticism as embodied by Byron loses whatever impetus it once had and becomes a point on yet another axis of bucolic evasion: the pastoral of literary history.

No ambiguity is intended here. Romanticism itself had enough pastoral characteristics to allow us to describe much of the period's literary output as pastoral. A trawl through Ernest Bernbaum's splendid catalogue of definitions of Romanticism yields: "The return to nature," "The cult of the extinct," "An effort to escape from actuality," "Vague aspiration," and so on.[17] What is at issue here, however, is not Romanticism as a source of pastoral, but Romanticism as pastoral.

There is no need to define "Romanticism" with any degree of precision — indeed, the very nature of the evasive action demands that such a definition remain hazy and adaptable at a moment's notice. The vague figure of Byron that emerges in Stoppard's play is *pars pro toto*, a metonymy of the equally murky concoction that is the play's version of Romanticism and the landscape it engendered:

> English landscape was invented by gardeners imitating foreign painters who were evoking classical authors. The whole thing was brought home in the luggage from the grand tour. Here, look — Capability Brown doing Claude, who was doing Virgil. Arcadia! And here, superimposed by Richard Noakes, untamed nature in the style of Salvator Rosa. It's the Gothic novel expressed in landscape. Everything but vampires. (25)

Hannah, the modern literary critic who speaks these words, perceives the process by which a hermeneutical model replaces a reality that is beyond her (and our) grasp, but she stops short of taking the second step, the application of such fictionalization to all her scholarly endeavors. She can speak of the "whole Romantic sham" (27), but she does not see the irony of her own words:

It's what happened to the Enlightenment, isn't it? A century of intellectual rigour turned in on itself. A mind in chaos suspected of genius.
In a setting of cheap thrills and false emotion. The history of the garden says it all, beautifully. (27)

Such a lament is equally applicable to what she and Bernard are doing;
Stoppard's characters involuntarily and unconsciously analyze their own
epistemology. They do not get beyond the first step, that of analyzing
pastoral as a mode: theirs is the lament for innocence lost, the mourning for a way of organizing a landscape, a requiem for an ideology they
prefer to the current one. In a world that offers them deconstructions,
they escape into wholeness.

We, on the other hand, can take the second step. By treating
Arcadia as a landscape that, far from being lost, has to be traversed over
and over again, we can read Stoppard's and any pastoral as process.
Arcadia, the Enlightenment, Byron, all are irretrievably gone for Stoppard's complaining scholars; they can only reconstruct them as pastoral,
made whole and meaningful, perhaps for the first time. By seeing them
at it, we may detect the pastoral impulse in our own efforts. We may
resist our urge to wholeness and keep up, if we are so inclined, the
work of deconstruction, the academics' anti-pastoral.

Yet behind such necessary efforts the outline of a third step becomes
discernible, and vague as it is, it is hard to resist. Stoppard gives us reasons to assume that in a few centuries it is our heirs' turn to remember
us wrongly or rightly as the last dwellers in Arcadia. That is a place we
cannot see ourselves: it is only where and when we are not. Although
nobody ever is in Arcadia, everybody will have been there once.[18]

Notes

[1] Stephen Greenblatt, "Murdering Peasants: Status, Genre, and the Representation of Rebellion," in *Learning to Curse: Essays in Early Modern Culture*
(New York: Routledge, 1990), 99–130.

[2] Raymond Williams, *The Country and the City* (London: Chatto & Windus,
1973).

[3] W. H. Auden, "Dingley Dell and The Fleet," in *The Dyer's Hand and
Other Essays* (London: Faber, 1948), 407–28.

[4] William Empson, *Some Versions of Pastoral* (Harmondsworth: Peregrine,
1966), 17.

[5] Cf. the excerpts in Brian Loughrey, ed., *The Pastoral Mode: A Casebook*
(London: Macmillan, 1984).

[6] Paul Alpers, in *What is Pastoral?* (Chicago: U of Chicago P, 1996), attempts to reclaim the term and argues against such extensions as the one that will be outlined here.

[7] For a discussion of pastoral's fictionality, see Wolfgang Iser, *Das Fiktive und das Imaginäre: Perspektiven literarischer Anthropologie* (Frankfurt am Main: Suhrkamp, 1991), 52–157.

[8] Cf. Peter V. Marinelli, *Pastoral* (London: Methuen, 1971), 75–82.

[9] William Shakespeare, *As You Like It*, ed. Agnes Latham (London: Methuen, 1975), I, iv, 52–53.

[10] Friedrich Schiller, "Der Antritt des neuen Jahrhunderts," in *Werke*, ed. Herbert G. Göpfert, Vol. 2 (Munich: Hanser, 1966), 822–23 (823).

[11] Byron, *Don Juan*, in *Poems*, Vol. 3 (London: Dent, 1948), 400 (Canto 14, XXX, 1–3).

[12] Tom Stoppard, *Arcadia*, rev. ed. (London: Faber, 1993), 1.

[13] Peter W. Graham puts it to good use nevertheless: "In a postmodern play absence echoes as loud as presence; and with a gesture both theatrically effective and ideologically appropriate to our day of celebrating the marginalized, Stoppard excludes from both past and present scenes most of the characters who could be termed figures of power or authority" ["Et in *Arcadia* nos," *Nineteenth Century Contexts* 18 (1995): 311–319 (314)].

[14] For a full bibliography of Stoppard's works and some material on *Arcadia*, see Paul Delaney, ed., *Tom Stoppard in Conversation* (Ann Arbor: U of Michigan P, 1994). Mel Gussow, *Conversations with Stoppard* (London: Nick Hern, 1995), also contains some references to the play. A useful earlier monograph is Katherine E. Kelly's *Tom Stoppard and the Craft of Comedy: Medium and Genre at Play* (Ann Arbor: U of Michigan P, 1991).

[15] Cf. Joachim Zelter, *Sinnhafte Fiktion und Wahrheit: Untersuchungen zur ästhetischen und epistemologischen Problematik des Fiktionsbegriffs im Kontext europäischer Ideen- und englischer Geistesgeschichte* (Tübingen: Niemeyer, 1994).

[16] Aldous Huxley, *The Genius and the Goddess* (London: Chatto & Windus, 1955), 7.

[17] Ernest Bernbaum, *Guide through the Romantic Movement* (New York: Ronald Press, 1949), 301–02. Bernbaum gives occasional names, but not his exact sources. For a recent discussion of the pastoral potential inherent in Romanticism, see Aidan Day, *Romanticism* (London and New York: Routledge, 1996), 39–64.

[18] For suggestions, proofreading, and patience, I am grateful to Lothar Fietz, Werner Huber, Svenja Kuhfuß, David Matley, and Martin Middeke.

FRANCES WILSON

"A Playful Desire of Imitation": The Ghost Stories at Diodati and *A Single Summer With L. B.*

IN 1831, FIFTEEN YEARS AFTER WRITING *Frankenstein*, Mary Shelley was asked by Henry Colburn and Richard Bentley, who were including her famous book in their Standard Novels series, to "furnish them with some account of the origin of the story." Mary Shelley therefore wrote an introduction to *Frankenstein's* third edition in which she tried to please her public by giving them "a general answer to the question, so very frequently asked me — 'How I, then a young girl, came to think of, to dilate upon, so very hideous an idea?'"[1] The tale her introduction tells of the ghost story contest (although the idea of a "contest" was never mentioned by any of those concerned) proposed at Lord Byron's villa during a "wet, ungenial summer" on the shores of Lake Leman, near Geneva, is as strange as her novel itself. The exiled Byron, his doctor, John Polidori, Mary Godwin — as she then was — , her common-law husband, Percy Shelley, and her step-sister, Claire Clairmont (who is not mentioned in the introduction), were "confined for days to the house" due to "incessant rain," and what went on in the Villa Diodati has become an integral part of the *Frankenstein* myth. Indeed, Mary Shelley's introduction serves as one more frame to *Frankenstein's* multi-framed structure, in which the stories of Robert Walton, Victor Frankenstein, and the Creature are contained within one another. If *Frankenstein's* most unsettling effect is the way in which its narratives accumulate so that the novel is enfolded in the tale of its own construction, the concentric circles do not stop here. Mary Shelley's autobiographical account of writing her story has itself become enclosed by fictions of biography, one of which is Derek Marlowe's 1969 biofiction, *A Single Summer With L. B.*[2] Marlowe is continuing a tradition of biofictions generated by the events at Diodati, of which Mary Shelley's introduction is an important part. For while the stormy weekend of June 15–18, 1816, has been subsequently fictionalized, fiction at Diodati was already standing in for experience.

In a bizarre imitation of *Frankenstein*'s subject, Mary Shelley saw her book as a monstrous creation from which she wanted to sever all links and break free. She concluded her 1831 introduction with the command, "and now, once again, I bid my hideous progeny go forth and prosper."[3] *Frankenstein* has since reappeared, transfigured and transformed, in stripped-down versions of the plot which omit most of the story and its narrative structure to focus on the generation of the creature alone. In a bizarre imitation of both the book's subject and its history, the contest which gave rise to *Frankenstein* has also broken free of its authors and produced its own late entrants with their own transformations and omissions. Thus, the June weekend resulted not only in *Frankenstein*, in Byron's own terse "Fragment" of a vampire story which he published at the end of *Mazeppa*, and in Polidori's tale, *The Vampyre* (whose blood-sucking milord would serve as the model for Bram Stoker's debonair Count Dracula), but also in *A Single Summer With L. B.*, where the contest itself becomes the ghost story. So not only does Derek Marlowe add another frame to Mary Shelley's introduction — he joins in the competition.

Ghost stories are frame narratives *par excellence*. They traditionally begin with an audience framing a blazing fire, and the narrator's acknowledgment that the story about to be told is only an imitation of the original and therefore not to be thought his own. Ghost stories circulate: they are returned to, repeated, and passed on, and the stories which are told about Diodati are not concerned to end the cycle of retellings but rather to find the origin of the tales and begin them again. Returning to the origin of the ghost story contest at Diodati, Derek Marlowe's novel is uncanny in the literal sense. *A Single Summer With L. B.* is both strange and familiar: the reader feels that he has been here before, and Marlowe is keen to remind us that his is a story that has already been written. The beginning of the book is preceded by an author's note which states that the tale and much of the writing are not even his: "Apart from John Polidori's letters to Florence, which are the author's creation, all quotations and much of the dialogue are taken solely from the letters and journals of the personages involved, or extracted from contemporary sources."[4] But there is nothing new in Marlowe's claim of unoriginality, for Mary Shelley's introduction to *Frankenstein* was also concerned to prove just this, and she claimed that her novel was the product of a conversation between Byron and Shelley — a point to which I shall return. Marlowe's desire to sever his story from himself is imitative not only of Mary Shelley's relation to her "hideous progeny," but also of the anxieties expressed by the other ghost story writers at the Villa Diodati.

Byron and Polidori, too, went to great lengths to distance themselves from their creations, and they located the origin of their tales in each other. Polidori said that there was nothing original in *The Vampyre*, that it was "founded upon the ground-work upon which [Byron's] fragment was to have been continued,"[5] had the poet not discarded the tale soon after it was begun. The responsibility for *The Vampyre* lay at Byron's door, but the story was written up later that summer "at the request of a lady" with whom he left the manuscript. Polidori claimed that the story was produced "in the course of three mornings,"[6] a boast which suggests he was imitating the rapid composition of Byron's fragment. The manuscript was passed on to the publisher, Henry Colburn, whose "hands" it "fell" into, along with an accompanying letter (published as *Extract of a Letter from Geneva*) stating that the sender had been passed the "outlines" of the other tales written at Diodati and was in turn passing them on to Colburn. This "letter" was published with Polidori's story and its introduction — which is the first retelling of the ghost story contest — along with an entirely fictional account of "Lord Byron's Residence in the Island of Mitylene."

The strange mixture of fact and fantasy in the three texts that frame *The Vampyre* make them the earliest biofictions to have been born of the Diodati weekend. Polidori's manuscript circulated like a ghost story, moving further and further away from its origins, and when it was published in 1819, it was in Byron's name. Meanwhile, Byron insisted that there was nothing creative about his own highly original "Fragment"; that his vampire story was printed for the sole purpose of disassociating himself from Polidori's, which was assumed to be not only by but *about* Byron himself. He sent it to John Murray to show his own publisher just "how far it resembles Mr Colburn's publication."[7]

A Single Summer With L. B. tells the tale of the first six months of Byron's exile through the person of the precocious and tragic Polidori. Chapter seven, "Laudanum and Vampyres," is — like the monster's speech in *Frankenstein* — at the heart of Marlowe's novel, encircled by the surrounding fourteen chapters. "Laudanum and Vampyres" describes those few nights in June 1816, when, as Mary Shelley's introduction puts it, "some volumes of ghost stories, translated from the German into French, fell into our hands," after which Byron proposed that "'we will each write a ghost story'"[8] in imitation of the ones just read. While Mary Shelley and Polidori struggled to think of a suitable idea, Shelley quickly discarded his, "founded on the experiences of his early life,"[9] Claire Clairmont declined to join in, and Byron began the tale which would remain unfinished. Chapter seven repeats and develops Mary Shelley's attempt to "furnish" her readers "with some account of the origin" of her novel, and Marlowe is also concerned to account for the origins of the two other stories conceived over the weekend. In order to furnish my own readers with an account of the origin of Marlowe's story, I am therefore imitating *A Single Summer with L. B.* by returning to the terms of *Frankenstein*'s introduction. But then imitation and return describe the circular dynamic of the writing that began at Diodati, anticipated by Mary Shelley's 1818 preface to *Frankenstein,* which states that the German ghost stories, "excited in us a playful desire of imitation."[10]

The structure and appearance of *A Single Summer With L. B.* is an imitation of Mary Shelley's novel and its introduction. The story is a compendium of diversions and different styles and is compiled from historical sources which are sometimes acknowledged in a footnote and sometimes not, sometimes printed in italics, and at other times simply interpolated into the body of the text. "Laudanum and Vampyres" has a different typographical appearance from the rest of the novel because here the sutured narrative style is exacerbated. In this chapter more quotations from letters and journals are crudely sewn into the fictional reconstruction of events, and the narrative flow is broken more often by "factual" notes that comment, *ad hoc,* on some of the anecdotes and information used. There are four curiously irrelevant footnotes that serve as odd appendages to the story: the first quoting lines 755–768 of Byron's poem, *The Giaour,* which refer to vampires (105); the second noting that Lady Caroline Lamb was the source for Lady Mercer in Polidori's story and adding that Lamb dressed as a page and adored Byron (111); the third outlining the complicated publishing history of *The Vampyre* and quoting from Byron's letter to John Murray, denying any right to the work (112); the fourth claiming that "Certain authorities suggest that Shelley may well have been a laudanum addict" (113). Throughout the chapter, Mary Shelley's introduction to *Frankenstein* is broken up and scattered, to appear either paraphrased or quoted in randomly italicized extracts. The text is made to look even more jagged by the introduction of dramatic form for Polidori's contribution to the ghost stories.

POLIDORI   (*boldly*) The heroine of my story is a lady

CLAIRE   (*pertly*). As heroines usually are.

POLIDORI. I mean the protagonist, though I have only random ideas and
it is not quite formed. But (*a clearing of the throat*) my heroine
is in league with the devil. She is the devil's mistress who is
unfaithful to him and returns to earth in mortal shape. (106)

The story that follows is what Mary Shelley described as "Poor Polidori['s] [. . .] terrible idea about a skull-headed lady who was so punished for peeping through a key-hole — what to see I forget —
something very shocking and wrong of course [. . .]."[11] In her introduction, it is *Mary* who is presented as the Peeping Tom spying into
someone's conversation, and it would seem that this terrible idea was
her own, as in Polidori's account of the contest there is no evidence
that this was his plot. Instead, the introduction to *Ernestus Berchtold*,
Polidori's 1819 novel about two incestuous siblings, states that the
"tale here presented to the public is the one I began at Coligny, when
Frankenstein was planned and when a noble author having determined
from his lofty range, gave up a few hours to a tale of terror, and wrote
the fragment at the end of Mazeppa."[12] Polidori's introduction is interrupted by a footnote as long as the introduction itself, in which he denies responsibility for the idea behind *The Vampyre* and for its delivery
to a publisher under Byron's name. As with "Laudanum and Vampyres," it is difficult to see whether Polidori's tale lies in the body of his
text or in its digressions.

The result of Derek Marlowe's repetitions, selections, and insertions
is that the ghost-story chapter of *A Single Summer With L. B.* resembles
nothing less than the patched-up and ill-fitting form of Victor Frankenstein's monster himself. Both "Laudanum and Vampyres" and Mary
Shelley's creature are constructed from parts more beautiful than the
finished whole. While one of the anomalies of the monster is that,
having been made up from an assortment of handsome limbs, he
should turn out to be ugly, "Laudanum and Vampyres" takes the best
literary anecdote of the last two centuries, supports it with some of the
most intriguing and beguiling writing by Byron, Shelley, Polidori, and
Mary Shelley, and from this fascinating material Derek Marlowe puts
together such a heavy-handed, cumbersome creature as this.

In Mary Shelley's own version of the Diodati weekend, events are
rewritten, figures are blanked out, and chronologies are skewed.[13] Apart
from attributing to Polidori a tale he did not tell, the presence of Claire
Clairmont is omitted altogether ("there were four of us"); Shelley's
considerable contributions to the manuscript of her novel are erased ("I
certainly did not owe the suggestion of one incident, nor scarcely of
one train of feeling, to my husband"); the ghost stories that she recalls
the party reading, whose "incidents" are "as fresh in my mind as if I

had read them yesterday," are misremembered; and the length of time it took for her to begin her story is extended.[14] A comparison of this belated introduction with Polidori's diary extracts reveal two entirely different perspectives on the same activities. Polidori's diary is also a catalogue of confusions: he does not get Claire Clairmont's name right until June 16; Shelley's age is noted as twenty-six when he was in fact twenty-four; although he realized that Claire was "*L. B.*'s," Polidori believed the relationship between Shelley "and the two daughters of Godwin" (only Mary was Godwin's daughter) to be a threesome, which indicates that he thought incest was involved.[15] In his brief and functional daily recordings we can assume Polidori was more accurate, and he noted that on June 17, the morning after Byron's proposition on the night of June 16, "the ghost stories are begun by all but me."[16] This conforms to the date on Byron's "Fragment," which was started and left off on that day. Mary Shelley, however, recalled that she had not started writing this soon, having had several mornings of "blank incapability of invention" until the conversation between Shelley and Byron about galvanism inspired the dream which led to her story.

From whatever angle it is looked at, the ghost story contest simply cannot be got into focus, and Derek Marlowe's own rendition of events is equally askew. He relies on both Polidori and Mary Shelley as sources but mirrors along with Thomas Moore's *A Life of Byron* and Edward Dowden's *Life of Shelley* — the fuller and more atmospheric description of the latter's more easily available introduction.[17] And this is because Marlowe's book attempts, in straightening the story, to tell it as it really was, which assumes that the events at Diodati were straight to begin with.

Mary Shelley's, Polidori's, and Derek Marlowe's are not the only distorting frames around the goings-on at Diodati: Byron described years later to Thomas Medwin how the entire scene was framed by the twisted perspectives of local visitors who turned what they saw into their own horror story: "There was no story so absurd that they did not invent at my cost. I was watched by glasses on the opposite side of the lake, and by glasses too that must have had very distorted optics [. . .]. I believe they looked on me as a man-monster."[18] The identification of Byron with Mary Shelley's monster is in keeping with the merging of fiction and non-fiction that was to be one of the most ghostly features of the ghost story contest. Even Byron's proposition that they each write a ghost story came from the ghost stories themselves, which suggests that the contest was already framed in fiction. The first story in the *Phantasmagoriana* begins, "everyone is to relate a story of ghosts [. . .]."[19] Thus the publisher's claim on the book's back cover that *A*

Single Summer With L. B. narrates the dizzying events of that summer
"using only biographical fact" rests uneasily alongside these other
crooked perspectives. The comfort and security of solid "biographical
fact" stands in marked opposition to the dynamics around Villa Diodati, where verifiable statements about individual and unique lives can
be seen to dissolve into fictions. In Marlowe's insistence that his fiction
is factual, whose version of the facts is he going to tell? For Shelley,
Mary Shelley, Polidori, and Byron all told a different tale, and at their
hands any "facts" we have concerning the writing of the ghost stories
consistently give way to other stories.

Not only did the optical frames of voyeurs distort the facts: fictions
about the party at Diodati began circulating during the summer itself.
Derek Marlowe includes in his novel Lord Glenbervie's cross-eyed diary
entry for July 3, 1816:

> *Among more than sixty English travellers here, there is Lord Byron who is
> cut by everybody. They tell a strange story of his at Dejean's Inn. He is
> now living at a villa on the Savoy side of the lake with that woman who it
> seems proves to be a* Mrs Shelley, *wife to the man who keeps the Mount
> Coffee-House* (93; his italics).

Marlowe notes that Lord Glenbervie's "assumption was farcical, to say
the least," because Byron was involved with Claire Clairmont and not
Mary Shelley. But this is only one of the distortions. Christopher Frayling explains how the final sentence of Lord Glenbervie's information
"gets every single detail hilariously wrong,"

> Byron was not living with 'a Mrs Shelley', who in any case was still
> called Mary Godwin at the time. The man who kept the Mount Cof-
> fee-house was John Westbrook, the father of Harriet Westbrook, who
> was Shelley's first (and at that stage only) wife. So Lord Glenbervie's
> diary entry manages to confuse Mary Godwin with both 'Claire'
> Clairmont *and* Harriet Westbrook, Percy Shelley with Harriet's father,
> and, above all, Shelley with Lord Byron.[20]

The narrative frames that surround Diodati reflect the events and accounts of the events like a series of fairground mirrors, and never more
so than in the relationship between *Frankenstein*'s introduction and its
preface. The description of *Frankenstein*'s "origin" that Mary Shelley
dutifully gives in her 1831 introduction returns to the account given in
the brief 1818 preface to the novel's first edition, which also outlines
"the event on which this fiction is founded."[21] Both the earlier preface
and the later introduction recall how stormy weather kept the party of
travellers indoors and led to their reading the collection of ghost stories
which inspired them to attempt their own. Both tell how a conversa-

tion gave Mary Shelley the theme of her novel; the 1818 preface recalling simply that the "circumstance on which my story rests was suggested in casual conversation,"[22] and the 1831 introduction more specifically remembering that she was not a participant in the conversation but its observer.

> Many and long were the conversations between Lord Byron and Shelley, to which I was a devout but nearly silent listener. During one of these, various philosophical doctrines were discussed, and among others the nature of the principle of life, and whether there was any probability of its ever being discovered and communicated. [...] Perhaps a corpse would be reanimated; galvanism had given token of such things: perhaps the component parts of a creature might be manufactured, brought together, and endured with vital warmth.[23]

Frankenstein is therefore immediately framed by two accounts of its origins. The second, in the 1831 introduction, repeats and develops the description presented in the first, while the picture Mary Shelley gives in the later introduction of her novel's origins residing in Byron and Shelley allows her to distance herself from the scene of creation: the monstrous birth of "so very hideous an idea" had nothing to do with the author, who was merely an amanuensis for an abstract idea discussed by Byron and Shelley. In the event that the novel might still be regarded as *her* creature, Mary Shelley then claims that following her companions' conversation, the vision on which her story was founded, of "the pale student of unhallowed arts kneeling by the thing he had put together,"[24] came from a "waking dream" which was no more related to her than the exchange she had overheard. She described being "possessed" by her dream as if she were not the dreamer but the dreamt: "My imagination, unbidden, possessed and guided me, gifting the successive images that arose in my mind with a vividness far beyond the usual bounds of reverie."[25] The similarity between this "waking dream" and the one that inspired Coleridge's *Kubla Khan*, which, he said, was published at Byron's request, cannot go unremarked.

Frankenstein was therefore born of trance-like looking, and yet Mary Shelley too must have had very distorted optics, for the order of events is awry. According to Polidori's journal, the conversation "about principles — whether man was thought to be merely an instrument,"[26] which must be the same conversation as that which inspired Mary, occurred on June 15, the night *before* the ghost story contest began, and not, as she remembers, two nights afterwards when she was busying herself "*to think of a story*."[27] Polidori further recorded that the discussion was between Shelley and *himself*, and not Shelley and Byron. So Mary Shelley began her story before the beginning on June 16, and

Frankenstein's origins in Byron and Shelley give way to other origins in Shelley and Polidori. Beginnings and origins continually erase and supplant one another, creating a veritable *mise-en-abyme*. In "Laudanum and Vampyres," Derek Marlowe twists the perspective even further, describing the overheard conversation as between Byron and Polidori and taking place three days later, on June 18, on the same evening as Shelley's hysteria after hearing Coleridge's *Christabel*. In Marlowe's account it is Shelley listening silently in the corner and Byron who asks Polidori, "if a tree, why not a corpse? [. . .] A Corpse. Why could a man not bring a corpse to life if he had power?" (115). Byron and Shelley; Shelley and Polidori; Polidori and Byron: in every version of the coupling from which *Frankenstein* was conceived, the setting remains the same but the players shift around. The figures of this midnight scene have become indistinguishable and interchangeable, as do the authors of *The Vampyre*, and as will Mary and Percy Shelley.

In the 1831 introduction, Mary Shelley "recollects" how the 1818 preface, like the conversation which inspired her novel, also had nothing to do with her, being "entirely written by" Percy.[28] This makes the introduction to the later edition her *first* and not her second description of the novel's origin. The original 1818 version of the origin of *Frankenstein* therefore undermines the very idea of an origin by being a false start: the concept of the beginning as something which comes first is simply dissolved in the interplay between *Frankenstein*'s introduction and its preface. Thus, Mary Shelley, halfway through her introduction, pauses to note — no doubt with Shelley's preface in mind — that every beginning is always preceded by another. "Every thing must have a beginning, to speak in the Sanchean phrase; and that beginning must be linked to something that went before."[29] Her introduction was linked to a beginning that went before; so too was the start of her story, which began before its beginning. It is in keeping with this ghostly economy that the author's note at the beginning of *A Single Summer With L. B.* connects Marlowe's novel to accounts of the contest which came earlier.

Ghost-written, the 1818-preface to *Frankenstein* is an imitation of the author's voice and not the real thing, and as such it anticipates the confusion of imitations and origins that characterize the other stories inspired by the contest, not least Derek Marlowe's. In his preface, Shelley imitates Mary's voice, but he also recounts the tale of reading the ghost stories as if he were imitating the opening lines of a ghost story itself: "The season was cold and rainy, and in the evenings we crowded around a blazing wood fire and occasionally amused ourselves with some German stories of ghosts, which happened to fall into our

hands."[30] It is Percy Shelley and not Mary who therefore describes how
the ghost stories drew them all into a "playful desire of imitation," as if
the loss of one's voice in the imitation of another's were their most un-
nerving effect. From Polidori's tale onwards, this "playful desire of
imitation" will dictate how the ghost story contest is to be described:
Derek Marlowe's account is an imitation of Mary Shelley's, which is an
imitation of Shelley's, which is itself an imitation of the beginning of a
ghost story. Polidori's tale, which imitated the circulation of a ghost
story, is an imitation of Byron's tale and was thought to be Byron's
imitation of himself. In her own account of the beginning of her story,
Mary Shelley imitated Shelley's imitation of a ghost story, and in her
introduction she describes the conversation between "Lord Byron and
Shelley" and the "waking dream" that possessed her as if she were
writing a gothic horror. She gives us the night-time stage, the sleep-
lessness, the zombie-like state of the victim being taken over by
thoughts not her own: "Night waned upon this talk, and even the
witching hour had gone by, before we retired to rest. When I placed
my head on the pillow, I did not sleep, nor could I be said to think."[31]

Just as the narrator of a ghost story is presented as telling someone
else's tale, Derek Marlowe begins "Laudanum and Vampyres" with an
account of other peoples' ghost stories. He frames the events at Diodati
in a factual observation about Gothic fiction and its imitations:

> It was the age of Gothic horror. Since Walpole had written his *Castle
> of Otranto* in 1764, countless tales of the supernatural had flooded the
> bookshops of England, most of them poor imitations of each other,
> but popular nevertheless. The formula was all much the same — an-
> cient abbey, panelled corridors, virgin on the grass glimpsed by
> moonlight, screams from the tower, master's hair turned white. (102)

Marlowe follows this up with the insertion of an italicized quotation
from the *Quarterly Review* of May 1810, in which the critic argues that
"I heartily disapprove of the mode introduced by Mrs Radcliffe and
followed by Mr Murphy and her other imitators, of winding up their
story with a solution [. . .]" (102). In his desire to frame his fiction
with facts, Marlowe imitates the 1818 preface to Frankenstein, which
begins with Shelley's remark that this fiction has a possible factual basis:
"The event on which this fiction is founded has been supposed, by Dr
Darwin, and some of the physiological writers of Germany, as not of
impossible occurrence."[32] It is only after his literary context has been
established that Marlowe begins his own story in the traditional fashion: "At Diodati, on the night of the 15th, the stories [. . .] were read
around the blazing fire [. . .]" (102). Where he starts his account of

the ghost story contest with a flippant retelling of other people's stories, so too did Mary Shelley's introduction digress from telling the tale
of her own story's birth to telling — or mistelling — the ghost stories
which "fell into their hands," much as Polidori's discarded tale would
"fall into the hands" of a lady in Italy. Marlowe's narrative style is cut-
and-paste, and he interjects Mary Shelley's faulty renditions of these
German tales as if they were facts. "There was the history of the Inconstant Lover, recalled Mary years later, who when he thought to clasp
the bride to whom he had pledged his vows, found himself in the arms
of the pale ghost of her whom he had deserted" (102). Ghost stories,
like Chinese whispers, shift and change in their endless repetition and
recitation. Mary Shelley passed these stories on and Marlowe followed
suit. This playful imitation, like the desire to be severed from one's tale
and have it off one's hands, conforms entirely to the logic of the ghost
story.

Had there been a contest on June 16 it was for who could start
their story last and discard it first, and Derek Marlowe was drawn in on
these terms. The introduction to *Frankenstein* stresses not only how
Mary Shelley's "hideous idea" was not hers to tell, but how she could
not begin to tell it.

> I busied myself *to think of a story* [. . .]. I felt that blank incapability
> of invention which is the greatest misery of authorship, when dull
> Nothing replies to our anxious invocations. *Have you thought of a
> story?* I was asked each morning, and each morning I was forced to re-
> ply with a mortifying negative.[33]

Byron and Shelley had "speedily relinquished their uncongenial task"[34]
before Mary had started: both of Byron's stories he discarded and left
unfinished, one of which was picked up by Polidori as his own, to be
begun months later and dropped; Shelley discarded his idea before it
began. Polidori's diary claims that he began his tale — presumably
Ernestus Berchtold — twice, each beginning, like the preface and introduction to *Frankenstein,* negating the other. He wrote on June 18,
"began my ghost story after tea," and again on June 19, "began my
ghost story."[35] "Laudanum and Vampyres" documents this contest
with precision, having Byron release Polidori from his writer's block by
giving his doctor his own tale to tell: "'Take mine. You can take my
story of the Vampire. Write that'" (110). Which returns us to the
author's note at the start of *A Single Summer With L. B.,* where Marlowe describes how he too was given his story by the other participants.
Marlowe has Mary Shelley finish last: throughout the chapter "invention [. . .] passed her by" (112), and the beginning of her story is only

reached in the closing sentence, which states that "the story conceived so horrendously by this polite, shy, eighteen-year-old girl, was none other than *Frankenstein*" (119). But it is Derek Marlowe who really wins the ghost story contest by discarding, like Shelley, his own hideous progeny before it has even begun.

In the play of imitations, chronological disturbances, and authorly exchanges that frame the ghost stories at Diodati, it comes as no surprise to find, at the end of the 1831 third edition, a spectral anticipation of Marlowe's mimicry of Shelley. Shelley's ghost-written preface is concluded with the signature: Marlow, September, 1817.

Notes

[1] Mary Shelley's introduction to the third edition (1831) in *Frankenstein or, The Modern Prometheus*, edited, with variant readings, an introduction, and notes, by James Rieger (Chicago and London: U of Chicago P, 1974), 222.

[2] Other fictionalizations of the Diodati weekend include Ann Edwards, *Haunted Summer*, Brian Aldiss, *Frankenstein Unbound*, Howard Brenton, *Bloody Poetry*, Liz Lochhead, *Blood and Ice*, Paul West, *Lord Byron's Doctor* (see elsewhere in this volume).

[3] Shelley, introduction, 229.

[4] Derek Marlowe, *A Single Summer With L. B. The Summer of 1816* (Harmondsworth. Penguin, 1973). All subsequent page references included in the text are to this edition. In America this was published as *A Single Summer With Lord B.* (New York: Viking Press, 1970).

[5] John Polidori, introduction, *Ernestus Berchtold; or, The Modern Oedipus* (London: Longman, Hurst, 1819), v.

[6] Polidori, introduction, vi.

[7] *Lord Byron: Selected Letters and Journals*, ed. Leslie Marchand (London: Pimlico, 1982), 196.

[8] Shelley, introduction, 224–25.

[9] Shelley, introduction, 225.

[10] Mary Shelley, preface, in *Frankenstein*, ed. James Rieger, 7.

[11] Shelley, introduction, 225.

[12] Polidori, introduction, v.

[13] See James Rieger's "Dr Polidori and the Genesis of *Frankenstein*" in his *The Mutiny Within: The Heresies of Percy Bysshe Shelley* (New York: Braziller, 1967) for a full account of the "almost total fabrication" of the "received history of the contest in writing ghost-stories at Villa Diodati" (237).

[14] Shelley, introduction, 225, 229, 224.

[15] *The Diary of Dr John William Polidori*, introd. William Michael Rossetti (London: Elkin Mathews, 1911), 101.

[16] *Diary of Polidori*, 125.

[17] Both Thomas Moore and Edward Dowden treat Mary Shelley's 1831 introduction as documentary evidence in their biographies of Byron and Shelley, and they recall her account of the weekend verbatim.

[18] Thomas Medwin, *Conversations of Lord Byron*, ed. Ernest J Lovell Jr. (Princeton: Princeton UP, 1966), 11.

[19] See Christopher Frayling, *Vampyres: Lord Byron to Count Dracula* (London: Faber, 1991), 13–14.

[20] Frayling, *Vampyres,* 10.

[21] Shelley, preface, 6.

[22] Shelley, preface, 7.

[23] Shelley, introduction, 227.

[24] Shelley, introduction, 228.

[25] Shelley, introduction, 227.

[26] *Diary of Polidori*, 123.

[27] Shelley, introduction, 226 (her italics).

[28] Shelley, introduction, 229.

[29] Shelley, introduction, 226.

[30] Shelley, preface, 7.

[31] Shelley, introduction, 227.

[32] Shelley, preface, 8.

[33] Shelley, introduction, 226 (her italics).

[34] Shelley, introduction, 225.

[35] *Diary of Polidori*, 128.

CHRISTINE KENYON JONES

Poetry and Cyberpunk:
Science Fiction
and Romantic Biography

IN 1822 THOMAS MEDWIN RECORDED Lord Byron's prophecy that

> we shall soon travel by air-vessels; make air instead of sea-voyages;
> and at length find our way to the moon, in spite of want of atmos-
> phere [. . .] Who would not wish to have been born two or three
> centuries later? We are at present in the infancy of science [. . .] Who
> knows whether, when a comet shall approach this globe to destroy it,
> as it often has been and will be destroyed, men will not tear rocks
> from their foundations by means of steam, and hurl mountains, as the
> giants are said to have done, against the flaming mass?[1]

Such "proto-science fiction" themes are not far to seek in Romantic
writing, and Byron may also be credited with having originated one of
the genre's favourite time-travel devices — the idea of current objects
becoming the museum pieces of the future — when in an 1823 canto
of *Don Juan* he imagined a post-catastrophe generation unearthing the
remains of a well-known and hugely fat figure of his own time:

> When this world shall be *former*, underground,
>   Thrown topsy-turvy, twisted, crisped and curled,
> Baked, fried, or burnt, turned inside-out, or drowned,
> [. . .]
> Think if then George the Fourth should be dug up!
>   How the new worldlings of the then new East
> Will wonder where such animals could sup!
> [. . .]
> *How* [. . .] will these great relics, when they see 'em
> Look like the monsters of a new Museum?[2]

Percy Shelley, too, was fascinated by the imaginative games that could
be played by looking back at one's own life and times with the odd and
slanted angle of vision bestowed by a viewpoint in the far future, and,

in December 1819, he addressed his fellow poet Thomas Moore by en-
visaging an era

> when St Paul's and Westminster Abbey shall stand, shapeless and
> nameless ruins, in the midst of an unpeopled marsh; when the piers of
> Waterloo Bridge shall become the nuclei of islets of reeds and osiers
> and cast the jagged shadows of their broken arches on the solitary
> stream [. . .][3]

Then, Shelley predicted, "some transatlantic commentator will be
weighing in the scales of some new and now unimagined system of
criticism," the respective merits of Moore's work and that of William
Wordsworth, whose verse Shelley unmercifully satirizes in *Peter Bell the
Third*, to which this is the preface.

What neither Byron nor Shelley could have predicted in their wild-
est flights of fancy was that, nearly two hundred years later, the fame of
their own work and that of their male fellow-poets would be outshone
in popular culture by the creations of Percy Shelley's wife Mary — by
Victor Frankenstein and his monster. Nor could they have foreseen that
not only would "a new and unimagined system" of narrative — science
fiction — flower from the eighteen-year-old Mary's first novel, but that
the time would come when their own lives would be reinterpreted
through this genre and even, perhaps, become better known by this
biofictional means than through the medium of their own works.

The notion of an affinity between science fiction and the lives and
works of the Romantic period would have appeared, indeed, an odd
and unlikely one until not very long ago. But it has now become almost
an established convention which — unlike Frankenstein's monster —
has been able to father and give birth to vigorous and autonomous
progeny of its own, not only in criticism but also in fictional works. In
this paper I want to trace the beginnings, the *raison d'être*, development, and nature of this link, and to indicate why this association
should have become an appealing, meaningful, and inspiring one for
writers in a postmodern era and at the end of a millennium.

As one of science fiction's best-known writers and historians, Brian
Aldiss, has pointed out, "before I wrote, almost no one paid any attention to that old pre-Victorian novel of Mary Shelley's."[4] Aldiss's *Billion
Year Spree*, published in 1973, certainly was enormously influential, not
only in identifying the Gothic or post-Gothic as the characteristic mode
of science fiction, and in arguing for the status of *Frankenstein* as the
first true science fiction narrative, but also in drawing attention to the
imaginative depth of Mary Shelley's novel and in claiming its right to
be the object of serious literary study.[5] Aldiss's promotion of the work

and the author coincided with the rise of critical feminism, and the growth in Mary Shelley's reputation may owe more to the latter than to the former, but it is nevertheless true that the effect of her rediscovery in the last two and a half decades has been an astonishing one: not only changing the way in which the history of science fiction is perceived, but also contributing to a redrawing of the mental map of Romanticism itself.[6]

Aldiss expressed his imaginative as well as critical interest in Mary Shelley in the form of a 1973 novel, *Frankenstein Unbound*, in which a twenty-first-century American ex-president, Joseph Bodenland, travels back in time to 1816 and has a sexual encounter with the author of *Frankenstein*.[7] He meets not only Mary and Percy Shelley, Dr. John William Polidori (author of *The Vampyre*) and Lord Byron, but also the offspring of Mary's imagination, Victor Frankenstein, and the illicit creature of *his* envisioning, the monster himself. This blurring in a fictional setting of the line between historical personages and imagined ones, biographical and fictional personalities, and the associated exploration of the nature of reality and consciousness, are explicit features of Aldiss's novel which I shall return to discuss later. *Frankenstein Unbound* is an evident precursor for two of the other works I want particularly to look at here: Tim Powers's *The Anubis Gates* (1983) and Powers's more extended bio-fantasy of 1989, *The Stress of Her Regard*.[8] Both these novels are substantially set in the Romantic period and feature Romantic poets as protagonists with traits that hark back to Aldiss's work.

Also to be considered here as belonging to the neo-Romantic family ancestored by Aldiss is William Gibson and Bruce Stirling's *The Difference Engine* (1990).[9] The steam-powered, computerized nineteenth-century London, whose story Gibson and Stirling present as having been generated by one of its own machines, provides the established "major" Romantics with alternate, but wittily appropriate, non-poetic bit-parts. As Percy Shelley is secondary in importance to Mary in Aldiss's novel, so Lord Byron appears in *The Difference Engine* primarily as the father of Lady Ada Byron, "the Queen of Engines, the Enchantress of Numbers," and also as a Prime Minister who owes his real power to his wife. (In this version of events, Lady Byron has decided not to leave her philandering husband, enabling Byron to maintain a rather shaky hold on respectability and thus to become a Victorian English gentleman.)

"P B Shelley" has been executed by Byron before the novel opens, in retribution for his activities as an ultra-radical conspirator, whose followers, "fired to a phrenzy by the furious polemics of the atheist," attacked and looted Establishment churches.[10] "Professor Coleridge" and "Reverend Wordsworth" are the utopian leaders of the "Susquehanna Phalanstery": an extrapolation from the real Pantisocracy project, which absorbed Coleridge and Robert Southey in the 1790s, when they planned to emigrate and set up an egalitarian community in New England.[11] John Keats appears as a "kinotropist" — a creator of steam and computer-driven moving pictures — who "tends to somewhat excessively fancy work" and suffers from a nasty cough.[12] Of the canonical Romantic "big six" only William Blake is still allowed to be a poet, and he illustrates his own books of poems because he "can't find a proper publisher." In this world where poets have turned into politicians, prime ministers are recast as full-time writers: Benjamin Disraeli has become a hack journalist and the role of the "fine poets of England" has been taken over by such as John Wilson Croker (in reality the MP and Tory politician who critically attacked Keats).[13]

The Difference Engine has some extremely well-informed reworkings of early nineteenth-century preoccupations, including the theory of Catastrophism, which is what lends the work of the real Percy Shelley and Lord Byron much of its proto-science-fiction flavour.[14] As expounded in James Parkinson's *Organic Remains of a Former World* (1804–11) and Baron Cuvier's *Recherches sur les ossemens fossiles de quadrupèdes* (1812), with their exploration of the significance of the dinosaur bones then beginning to be unearthed, Catastrophism posited that the world had been destroyed — probably by the impact of a comet — and recreated many times before, and that previous worlds had been dominated by non-human species which might well have been superior in intelligence and achievement to human beings.

Percy Shelley's response to these ideas was mainly political. The ending of former worlds was believed to have been sudden and brutal, and he envisaged that the political revolution he longed for might begin in this way, and thus celebrated the destructive force of autumn in the words of the famous "Ode to the West Wind": "If Winter comes, can Spring be far behind?" Shelley's Panthea in Act Four of *Prometheus Unbound* (1819) describes

> The wrecks beside of many a city vast,
> Whose population which the earth grew over,
> Was mortal, but not human [. . .][15]

Byron, meanwhile, in the 1823 preface to *Cain* speculates "that the pre-Adamite world was also peopled by rational beings much more intelligent than man, and proportionately powerful to the mammoth," and the visions of *previous*, as well as future, universal catastrophes that he communicated to Medwin evidently owe their origin to this theory.

Gibson and Stirling pick up these ideas in *The Difference Engine*, making their main protagonist Edward Mallory a geological Catastrophist, who is led by this theory to "his greatest personal triumph: the discovery, in 1865, of continental drift."[16] Mallory also applies Catastrophism outside the strictly geological sphere: "History works by catastrophe! It's the way of the world, the only way there is, has been, or ever will be. There is no history — there is only contingency!"[17] This claim supports the fiction on which the whole novel is founded, since the narrative premises an alternative nineteenth century based on contingencies creating events that are supposedly just as plausible as the ones that occurred in reality.

In Gibson and Stirling's novel the portraits of the Romantic poets are highly ingenious, but they extend to little more than thumb-nail sketches. This topos has, however, been worked out on a much larger scale in the work of Tim Powers, and it is Powers's two biofictions or fantasies — *The Anubis Gates* and *The Stress of Her Regard* — that I want to discuss in the second part of my paper. I shall do so by relating them to a much more dominant sub-genre of late-twentieth-century science fiction: cyberspace and cyberpunk.

At first sight, it would seem difficult to find anything more different from the subject matter of the cyberculture novels of authors such as William Gibson, K. W. Jeter, Richard Kadrey, Melissa Scott, and John Shirley than the fantastic biofictions of Tim Powers. Cyberculture novels deal with a determinedly non-historical world, where referents can only be sustained with difficulty over hours or days — let alone years, decades or centuries — because the speed of change is envisaged as being exponentially faster than that of our own time, and where all culture, which is based on history, is imagined as being subjugated to the machine. Biofictions and fantasies, on the other hand, are apparently entirely preoccupied with the historical and the personal: they start from the premise of a given individuality and what they construct on this basis only makes sense if the details of the biographical foundations are known to the reader to some degree.

But such a simplified description of their subject-matter misses out the point that the two sub-genres exist side by side in time, written within a community of discourse and a genre that is notably or notoriously self referential, and that they are sometimes, as in Gibson's case, the product of the same word-processor. As Percy Shelley pointed out:

> There must be a resemblance, which does not depend upon their own will, between all the writers of any particular age. They cannot escape

from subjection to a common influence which arises out of an infinite combination of circumstances belonging to the times in which they live [. . .].[18]

In fact, I hope to show that the small handful of Romantic biofictions share with the much more extensive and widely-read volumes of cyber culture novels a fascination with exploring the organization and disorganization of self, a compulsion to test the nature of their authors' contemporary, postmodern world, and a desire to reflect upon the texture and meaning of science fiction itself: a preoccupation of late-twentieth-century science fiction writers, which, as Edward James has remarked, may either be taken as a sign of the maturity of the genre or as one of its decadence.[19]

Damien Broderick, in *Reading by Starlight* (1995), selects from Fredric Jameson's analysis of the postmodern some features that are particularly apposite to science fiction:

'a flatness or depthlessness' [. . .] a waning of affect, or feeling, linked to the (alleged) loss of a discrete subjectivity [. . .] the end of personal, unique style and a sense of history itself, and their replacement by *pastiche* [. . .] [and] the fragmentation of artistic texts [. . .] which takes the form especially of collage governed by 'differentiation rather than unification.'[20]

Many critics (including Jameson himself) have identified these features in cyberculture novels, particularly William Gibson's hugely influential *Neuromancer* of 1984, which some have seen as quintessentially postmodern.[21] Tim Powers's *The Anubis Gates*, which won one of science fiction's most prestigious prizes, the Philip K. Dick Award, the year before, does, I believe, respond in very much the same way to postmodern influences, despite its nineteenth-century setting and its plot, which ranges from Romantic biography to ancient Egyptian magic, from Piranesian Gothic to the Dickensian underlife of beggars.

The story centers around a character called William Ashbless, who is presented as a canonical Romantic poet. But Ashbless is actually fictional in more than the straightforward sense, since the novel itself narrates the fictionality of his creation: he is in fact a combination of the personality of Brendan Doyle (a twentieth-century academic who travels back in time partly to research Ashbless and gets stuck in the year 1810) and the body of another twentieth-century time-traveller who is the victim of a body-change werewolf. Ashbless is therefore a collage, in Jameson's terms, whose physical entity is made up from fragments, and whose poetry and biography are fictions created by Doyle from his own memory of reading them in the twentieth century. Doyle/Ashbless is destined to live out every detail of his own remembered life, lacking "a discrete subjectivity" until the very end of the book when he unexpectedly kills his *Doppelgänger*, thus hoodwinking his fictional biographer into recording Ashbless's own death, and liberating Doyle/Ashbless to live on into the unknown future, unrestricted by any previously recorded life-story. *Doppelgängers* are an important feature of the novel: the young Lord Byron appears in it only as a *ka*, or replicant, while another character exists in three different versions simultaneously: the "original," his double, and the ravaged version of that double who has been almost destroyed during a time-travel episode.[22]

There is perhaps a link here with Aldiss's *Frankenstein Unbound*, where, at the end, "dual moons sailed in the sky," indicating a state of multiple possibilities, and where Bodenland feels that his "original personality had now almost entirely dissolved, and the limbo I was in seemed to me the only time I knew."[23] But in Aldiss's novel, although a concern with the disintegration of individuality is strongly prefigured, it is as yet mainly a side-effect, brought about by time-travel and encounters with alternate fictions and realities. The main theme of the book is firmly stated and is quite different, being to show Mary Shelley's *Frankenstein* as "the archetype of the scientist, whose research, pursued in the sacred name of increasing knowledge, takes on a life of its own and causes untold misery before being brought under control."[24]

Powers's 1983 *Doppelgänger*, however, along with his surgically created monsters and his biofictional and fabricated personalities, share with Gibson's 1984 cyborgs — personality constructs and human/machine hybrids, different as they appear to be on the surface — a much more central involvement with the fragility of personal and biographical identity, and a preoccupation with defining individuality at the very limits of the possible that is recognizably postmodern in its development.

In *The Anubis Gates* literary achievement seems to be revered and privileged (although, the fabrication of a "new" canonical Romantic poet in the novel draws satirical attention to critics' ability to resurrect and almost to "invent" certain authors, among whom one might include Mary Shelley). At the end of the novel a sympathetically drawn Samuel Taylor Coleridge — whose lecturing is the ostensible reason for the time-travel in the first place — interprets the whole of the villains' Gothic edifice and its monstrous inhabitants as creatures of his own imagination: a sort of anachronistic Ballardian inner space. He assumes in a distinctly post-Freudian way that the building and its prisoners — "mistakes" created by experiments on living human flesh — are embodiments of his own duties, vices, and virtues which he has imprisoned in his unconscious, and he politely requests some "Thought or Whimsy or Fugitive Virtue" to "direct me to the waking levels of my mind."[25] As in Aldiss, where "the poets had always been on the side of the people," and in Gibson's *Neuromancer*, where it is the strong humanity of the Zionites that makes them able to write poetry, while the personality construct of the Dixie Flatline is sentient but "ain't likely to write you no poem," contact with poetry acts as a touchstone to define the inherent sympathy or moral worth of a character.[26]

In Powers's *The Stress of Her Regard*, however, the use of biofiction applies itself to an attack on the poets and on the idea of literary individuality. The younger Romantic poets were in many ways the apogee of literary individualism: the cult of the poet as a remarkable and unconventional personality reached its peak with them, and a close link was perceived between inspirational biography and literary output, a link that has never been so significant before or since. Powers's later novel turns this on its head by reducing Byron's, Percy Shelley's and Keats's poetic inspiration to nothing but the effect of playing host to the vampire-like Nephelim, who are brilliant musical and poetic creators, but who harbor murderously jealous intentions toward the poets' families. "I wonder how many of the world's great writers have owed their gift to the [. . .] ultimately disastrous attentions of the nephelim," Powers's Byron ponders, "and how many of them would have freed themselves, if they could have."[27] When Keats, Shelley, and Byron at last find the strength to cast off their supernatural muses they cease to be poets but become fully human instead.

Powers effectively deploys this myth, with rigorous attention to accuracy with respect to the biographical "facts" of the Romantics' lives (although keen Romanticists will spot that he does make a few mistakes!). In *The Anubis Gates* Byron's actual life is described as "appalling thoroughly chronicled," and in his later novel Powers determinedly shoe-horns into the interstices of Byron's, Percy Shelley's and Keats's well-documented lives a Gothic science fiction plot that completely subverts the meaning and authority of the biographies while leaving the surface patterns intact. The effect is that of a structure that has tremendous complexity and intricacy, but which in fact is not "original": it relies on what Jameson identifies as pastiche and collage, or more accurately, on *bricolage* — not quite in Lévi-Strauss's terms, but as a reuse of existing materials to create something new.

Here again, despite the entirely nineteenth-century setting, there are many resemblances to cyberspace and cyberpunk. One of the characters has a "mechanical mode," very reminiscent of a robot, into

which she reverts when the going gets too tough for her "real" person
ality to cope. There is an episode where Byron and the novel's main
protagonist Crawford share and exchange consciousness and bodies in a
way that readily recalls Case using "simstim" to access Molly's experiences in *Neuromancer*. The Nephelim can create visual phantasms
similar to Riviera's mental holograms, and "elective surgery" of the
type favored by streetwise gangs in Gibson's work is necessary in Powers's book to create the hybrid creature Werner von Aargau, who unites
the human and nephelim species by having a stone child implanted into
his abdomen. Crawford in *The Stress*, like Case in *Neuromancer*, can see
making physical love in two contradictory ways at once: as both "the
flesh, the meat the cowboys mocked" and as a uniquely human and
powerful experience.[28]

Gibson's novel, as the earlier of the two, must be accepted as the
originator of these nova, but Powers deploys them in distinct and inherently convincing ways so that there is no sense of borrowing or
copying. The effect is rather that of using very different material —
about as different as it *could* be within the confines of science fiction
and fantasy, although Gibson does include distinctly Gothic elements
in his description of the Tessier-Ashpool dynasty — to explore the same
themes and preoccupations. While Gibson and his cyberculture col-
leagues are exploring ways of deconstructing the human essence in a
technology-dominated world, Powers and the other creators of biofiction are taking that most human of artefacts, a biography, and subject-
ing it to forces that crack it open and rebuild it in quite a different
form.

Biofiction and science fiction may not immediately appear to be
productive partners, but it seems to me that in fact biographical material can be very successfully adapted for science fiction. Karl Kroeber
has suggested that science fiction plots must tend towards the functional, because science fiction aims to convince by using scientific discourse which requires an absolutely straightforward relationship
between cause and effect to demonstrate proof.[29] Scott Sanders has described science fiction as a genre "centrally about the disappearance of
character," and it is a common perception that the creative energy of
science fiction writing goes not into plot or characterization but into
the novelty of the treatment.[30] Critics have nevertheless expressed disappointment with the predictability of Gibson's plots and characters
and called for "a radically different formulation of human agency and
action" to go with the exciting surface of cyberpunk.[31] The biofiction
novels of Powers and the other writers I have explored suggest that biography and biofiction might provide a way of meeting this need, by

offering a ready-made framework — of both character and plot — onto which science fiction can be woven, allowing the maximum possible scope for ingenuity and originality within carefully defined limits.

Romantic biographies are particularly appropriate for use in this way. The life stories of the Romantic poets are especially gripping in their own right, and their association with Mary Shelley, the writer who was arguably the founding mother of science fiction, adds to their attention. As a setting, the turn of the eighteenth and nineteenth centuries offers possibilities because it is at the crossroads between eras of magic and superstition on the one hand and those of modern science and technology on the other: a time when, as John Clute has it, "any experiment might well bear fruit, any dream might become reality."[32] This was also the great age of biography — including Samuel Johnson's *Lives of the Poets* (1779); James Boswell's *Life of Johnson* (1791), the Comte de Las Cases' life of Napoleon (1821–23) and Thomas Moore's life of Byron (1830) — and thus the first era to find a literary means of celebrating personality and cultivating individuality. We seem now to be at the end of this era — to have arrived at a point where the cult of personality has gone full circle and is being broken down again by forces defined as postmodern. Romanticism and postmodernism are the two ends of an arch celebrating human individualism which has spanned two centuries. William Gibson's *Neuromancer* — or "New Romancer" — begs the question as to who or what the *old* romancer is. The novels I have presented here supply an answer to that question by both celebrating and driving a postmodern stake into the heart of Romantic biography.

Notes

[1] Thomas Medwin, *Conversations of Lord Byron noted during a residence with His Lordship at Pisa, in the years 1821 and 1822* (London: Henry Colburn, 1824), 226–28.

[2] *Don Juan* IX: stanzas 37–40, quoted from *Lord Byron: The Complete Poetical Works*, vol. 5, ed. Jerome J. McGann (Oxford: Clarendon Press, 1992), 420–21. For museums in science fiction, see Robert Crossley, "In the Palace of Green Porcelain: Artefacts from the Museums of Science Fiction," in *Fictional Space: Essays an Contemporary Science Fiction*, ed. Tom Shippey (Oxford: Blackwell, 1991), 80–89.

[3] Percy Bysshe Shelley, *Poetical Works*, ed. Thomas Hutchinson, corr. G. M. Matthews (Oxford: Oxford UP, 1970), 347.

[4] Brian Aldiss with David Wingrove, *Trillion Year Spree* (London: Gollancz, 1986), 18.

[5] Brian Aldiss, *Billion Year Spree: The History of Science Fiction* (London: Weidenfeld and Nicolson, 1973).

[6] Aldiss does sometimes overemphasize Mary Shelley's originality. He describes her short story, "Transformation," as one which "throws light on the events of Frankenstein's wedding night" (*Trillion Year Spree*, 36). In fact "Transformation" (published after 1828) owes its plot and its theme to Byron's unfinished play *The Deformed Transformed*, which was written in 1822–23, some six years after *Frankenstein*, and copied out by Mary Shelley for Byron in 1823. Both the story and the play feature the exchange of bodies between the hero and a misshapen Mephistophelian dwarf, who succeeds in wooing the woman the hero loves.

[7] Brian Aldiss, *Frankenstein Unbound* (London: Triad, Granada, 1982). The title of Aldiss's novel is, of course, an allusion to Percy Shelley's poem *Prometheus Unbound*, which is echoed in *Frankenstein*'s own subtitle: "The Modern Prometheus."

[8] Tim Powers, *The Anubis Gates* (London: Harper Collins, 1993) and *The Stress of Her Regard* (London: Grafton, 1993).

[9] William Gibson and Bruce Stirling, *The Difference Engine* (London: VGSF, 1995).

[10] Gibson/Stirling, *The Difference Engine*, 358.

[11] Gibson/Stirling, *The Difference Engine*, 262.

[12] Gibson/Stirling, *The Difference Engine*, 111.

[13] Gibson/Stirling, *The Difference Engine*, 271.

[14] The two poets' interest in Catastrophism is discussed by William D. Brewer in *The Shelley-Byron Conversation* (Gainesville: UP of Florida, 1994), 31–35.

[15] Shelley, *Prometheus Unbound*, IV: 296–98, in Poetical Works, 261.

[16] Gibson/Stirling, *The Difference Engine*, 288. In reality, the theory of continental drift did not receive serious attention until the publication of Alfred Wegener's *Die Entstehung der Kontinente und Ozeane* in 1915.

[17] Gibson/Stirling, *The Difference Engine*, 271.

[18] Shelley, Preface to *The Revolt of Islam*, in *Poetical Works*, 35.

[19] Edward James, *Science Fiction in the Twentieth Century* (Oxford: Oxford UP, 1994), 201. I have not included here Amanda Prantera's novel, *Conversations with Lord Byron on Perversion, 163 Years after His Lordship's Death* (London: Abacus, 1987), because it is discussed elsewhere in this volume. But, with its breakdown of the dividing line between "real" and computerized biography and its playing with the nature of individuality and personality, this work too could be considered in the context of cyberculture writing and postmodernism.

[20] Damien Broderick, *Reading by Starlight: Postmodern Science Fiction* (London and New York Routledge, 1995), 104; and Fredric Jameson, *Postmodernism, or, The Cultural Logic of Late Capitalism* (London: Verso, 1991).

[21] William Gibson, *Neuromancer* (London: Harper Collins, 1995).

[22] In a letter to John Murray of 6 October 1820, Byron recounted how several people claimed to have seen him in London in 1810, when he was in fact in Greece and Turkey. See *Byron's Letters and Journals*, ed. Leslie A. Marchand, 13 vols. (London: John Murray, 1973–1994), 7: 192.

[23] Aldiss, *Frankenstein Unbound*, 133, 139.

[24] Aldiss, *Frankenstein Unbound*, 47.

[25] Powers, *Anubis Gates*, 450.

[26] Aldiss, *Frankenstein Unbound*, 58; Gibson, *Neuromancer*, 159.

[27] Powers, *Stress*, 176.

[28] Gibson, *Neuromancer*, 285.

[29] Karl Kroeber, *Romantic Fantasy and Science Fiction* (New Haven: Yale UP, 1988), 28.

[30] Scott Sanders, "The Disappearance of Character in Science Fiction," in *Science Fiction: Its Criticism and Teaching*, ed. Patrick Parrinder (London: Methuen, 1980), 131.

[31] Claire Sponsler, "William Gibson and the Death of Cyberpunk," in *Modes of the Fantastic: Selected Essays from the Twelfth International Conference on the Fantastic in the Arts*, ed. Robert A. Latham and Robert E. Collins (Westport: Greenwood Press, 1991), 53.

[32] John Clute, *Science Fiction, the Illustrated Encyclopaedia* (London: Dorling Kindersley, 1995), 110.

CHRISTOPHER INNES

Elemental, My Dear Clare:
The Case of the Missing Poet

ONE OF THE MORE INTERESTING — BUT LEAST known — poets from the Romantic era to resurface in contemporary literature is John Clare, who was born just one year after Shelley and died in 1864, thirty years after Coleridge. Historically a very different type of artist from the other Romantic poets, the way he is portrayed and the thematic use made of his figure is also distinct from the modern literary treatment of other poets from the Romantic period.

The first appearance Clare makes is in Edward Bond's play *The Fool*, performed at the Royal Court Theatre in 1975; and he reappears almost twenty years later in John MacKenna's *Clare: A Novel*, published in 1993. Even if the same characteristics are recognizable from one depiction to the other, and each overlaps the other in the details presented from Clare's life, yet he is used to represent strikingly different things. This, of course, could be seen as a natural consequence of the gap in age and nationality between the two authors, as well as reflecting their education and individual artistic aims. Bond, born in 1934, has a London inner-city working-class background — MacKenna is Irish and was born in County Kildare in 1952. But the difference between Bond's characterization and MacKenna's also represents an ambivalence towards Clare himself that echoes the type of critical attention his work has received — both during his lifetime and since his death in 1864. In addition, the contrast between the two versions of Clare's life can be used to measure the changing political climate over a generation. However, before exploring such issues, it is necessary to take into account the generic differences between the novel and drama and their divergent literary history. The page and the stage are not simply separate media, but bring contrasting contextual assumptions — particularly where portraits of authors are concerned — that are directly reflected in the focus on the art form or aesthetic questions that such characters invariably carry with them in their baggage.

Literary self-reference has become one of the hallmarks of postmodernism in novels that expose the mechanics of story-telling, intersect with another published text, or deconstruct the figure of the author. Since the late 1960s it has signalled a rejection of standard ways of story-telling for the novelist. In the theater, however, this is a highly traditional and long-established approach; and the European repertoire is filled with plays that break down illusion, foreground performance, take the audience backstage, or deal with characters whose profession is that of an actor or a playwright. Overt theatricality was already an integral part of the earliest secular drama, with Moliere's use of the commedia dell'arte conventions, or Shakespeare: take for example the acting troupes in *A Midsummer Night's Dream* (incompetent amateurs) and in *Hamlet* (professional tragedians) — who are shown in the dressing-room or at rehearsal, displaying their skills as rhetoric and discussing the nature of their art, as well as acting out a play for a highly critical on-stage audience. And these plays-within-the-play not only mirror the drama within which they are performed, but also incorporate passages and pastiches of earlier Elizabethan plays: all the postmodern attributes, in fact, that are evident in contemporary plays like David Mamet's *A Life in the Theater* or Tom Stoppard's *The Real Thing*.

Indeed backstage drama has been a staple of English theater from the beginning of the twentieth century, with Pinero's *Trelawney of the 'Wells'*, which also included a recognizable portrait of a mid-Victorian playwright as its romantic hero. Osborne's *The Entertainer* displays the decaying Music Hall as an image of Britain in decline. Michael Frayn's *Noises Off* transforms the production of fashionable West End comedy into farce. In Alan Ayckbourn's *A Chorus of Disapproval* the off-stage lives of the actors in provincial repertory copy their roles in *The Beggar's Opera*. In each of these plays, theatrical performance merges with reality — and all have been highly popular. In fact, the appeal of behind-the-scenes portrayal of the world of drama is such that two of the most popular American musicals of the last twenty years, *A Chorus Line* and *42nd Street*, have been set back-stage.

The open exploration of internal form in the novel can also attract a wide readership, as with John Fowles's *The French Lieutenant's Woman* or A. S. Byatt's *Possession*. But the comparative novelty of such metafiction means that critical attention tends to focus on the stylistic aspect, as examples of a new literary movement. A play like David Hare's *A Map of the World* is very much the equivalent of metafictional novels. The action switches between "filmed" scenes, which turn out to be only "acted" reproductions of past events that are very different in the memories of the participants (who include a fictional novelist — though one who bears some resemblance to Salman Rushdie) and thus destabilize the audience's sense of reality. Yet in contrast, the metatheatrical level of David Hare's play was accepted as a far more standard technique carrying thematic meaning, and most critical discussion concerned the political commentary in the play.

This difference in genre forms the context for any investigation into the portrayal of a poet such as John Clare, whose figure appears both in a novel and on the stage. Authors have, of course, been the subjects of one particular type of novel — the *Bildungsroman* — from Goethe's *Wilhelm Meisters Lehrjahre* to James Joyce's *A Portrait of the Artist as a Young Man*. But there the focus is always on the subjective education of a writer; and that writer, although fictionalized to some degree, is always the author himself. The theater also has such oblique self-portraits, as in *The Masterbuilder*, where Ibsen projects his own guilt, artistic aims and sexual relationships into the Faustian and doomed Solness, whose architectural career parallels the phases of Ibsen's development as a dramatist — or Shaw's *Man and Superman*, where the protagonist is a very Shavian writer of political manifestos. But these are a very small minority compared to the dramatization of artistic lives that are in no sense autobiographical. Characters based on real-life actors have been striding onto the stage from Alexandre Dumas's *Kean* in the early nineteenth century right up to Terrence McNally's *Masterclass* (which centers on Maria Callas) or, most recently, *Barrymore* (a work premièred in Canada in the summer of 1996 and still on the road to Broadway). Writers are equally common; and although some are purely fictional figures, again the vast majority are clearly identifiable and well-known historical figures.

In *The Seagull* Chekhov establishes his new theatrical principles through fictional representatives: a young poetic dramatist, a hack novelist, and two contrasting actresses. The isolated and marginalized single voice of *Krapp's Last Tape* embodies the writer as existential clown in the universal terms typical of Beckett's work, as does the displaced poetess of Stoppard's recent play *Indian Ink*. Sam Shepard's *True West*, which takes its title from a journal dedicated to cowboy-fiction, splits the writer (in this case a no less characteristically American Hollywood screenwriter) into archetypal alter egos. However, particularly on the British stage over the last thirty years, such generalized figures are far outweighed by real-life counterparts. Edward Bond indeed is one frequent employer of dead writers, with Shakespeare as his protagonist in *Bingo* and the Japanese Haiku poet Basho in both *Narrow Road to the Deep North* and *The Bundle* — in addition to Clare in *The Fool*. Along the same lines Stoppard gathers Tristan Tzara, James Joyce, and Lenin (as the writer of polemics on art and imperialism) in *Travesties*, while Brenton's *A Sky Blue Life* deals with Gorky, as does Robert Bolt's *State of Revolution*; and David Edgar's *The Shape of the Table* presents a thinly disguised picture of Vaclav Havel: the writer as successful political activist. There is a noticeable distinction between these two groupings. The imaginary figures, while almost always set in contemporary society, are used in order to deal with general artistic issues such as the representation of reality or the nature of creative inspiration. By contrast, actual writers — even though usually taken from history — are turned into models for political action or commentary on immediate public issues.

This is particularly true of the way the Romantic poets — the most numerous of all writer-figures in British drama — are treated on the stage. The Romantic age is seen by post-1960s political dramatists as having clear analogies to the present. Both periods are characterized by long wars, extensive social unrest, and the birth of radical ideas. The French Revolution is used as a parallel to the student revolution that swept Europe at the end of the 1960s, but ultimately failed to change the social order. The rise of industrialization (Blake's "satanic mills" defacing "England's green and pleasant land") during the lifetime of the Romantics marks the beginning of modern capitalism, while the Peterloo massacre (in which dragoons slaughtered a group of striking labourers in 1819) appears as a concrete image for less tangible contemporary repression. On the other hand, it was also then that the "Rights of Man" were proclaimed and today's socialist values first articulated. Above all, the Romantic poets, in validating subjective experience, laid the basis for political equality and the primacy of the individual against corporate and state hegemony. Iconoclasts and rebels in their own time, they stand as an ideal for left-wing playwrights in the generation immediately following Osborne, who had been radicalized by the 1969 student movement.

The favourite figures among the Romantic poets are Shelley and Lord Byron, who appear together as outcasts sacrificing themselves for their political principles in Howard Brenton's *Bloody Poetry*. The tone was first struck by Ann Jellicoe's *Shelley, or the Idealist* in 1965; and in more ways than these playwrights perhaps recognized, Shelley and Byron were prototypes for their own experience: university-educated, distanced by middle-class backgrounds as well as professional status from the working masses for whom they saw themselves as speaking. Shelley and to an even greater extent Byron had won significant public followings and established reputations as major poets during their own lifetimes. Both poets can also be seen as martyrs for their ideals, burning in the "great big, bloody, beautiful fire" of metaphorical poetic inspiration, or dying in a successful struggle for liberation.[1] All this, of course, makes them attractive alter egos for modern political dramatists. However, John Clare, the peasant poet, was a complete contrast on almost every level. Even the simplicity of his name — compared to, say, Percy Bysshe Shelley's — sounds unromantic.

A self-taught farm-labourer, living in extreme poverty all his life, and writing in dialect with his language butchered by his well-meaning publisher, Clare was ignored by the reading public after the brief success of his first collection of poems (the fashion for "peasant poets" having passed with Burns, who died just three years after Clare was born). Not only politically impotent, Clare was also clinically insane for the last twenty-seven years before his death at the age of seventy-one. In short, Clare can hardly be seen to correspond either to the hopes or personal experience of young urban radicals like Howard Brenton or David Hare. Clare's poetry contains passages of powerful protest against social injustice and the exploitation of the poor — but in many ways his vision is conservative, reacting against change and arguing for the restoration of a traditional status quo, since the major problem for people in the rural villages of the early nineteenth century was the expropriation and enclosure of common land and the consequent degradation of independent peasants into hired labourers. Clare's poetic inspiration was intimately connected with his local landscape, and it is specifically the physical alteration of the countryside that resulted from the Act of Parliament enclosing the area around his Northamptonshire village of Helpstone in 1809 that aroused much of his anger. The intensely personal tone of his poems, and even more his agricultural focus, were alien to urbanized playwrights looking for historical models to animate their attack on the growing dominance of Thatcherism.

In addition, Clare was the least well-known of all the Romantics. Out of print and unread until the first collected edition of his poems in 1939 — seventy years after his death — with only the most lyrical of his work anthologized, his relevance was almost unrecognizable. The first studies of his work appeared only in the 1970s; and it was not until a decade later, when books on his life and work multiplied, that Clare could truly be said to have been rediscovered.[2]

So when Edward Bond took Clare as a protagonist for *The Fool* in 1975, very few of the Royal Court audience would even have recognized his name. A biography had recently appeared (Anne Tibble's *John Clare: A Life*, a revised version of a long-out-of-print study initially published in 1932), from which Bond took the general facts of Clare's life. Yet Clare still lacked wide recognition; and this is reflected in the play.

Some of the themes of Clare's poetry are introduced in the first scene — but from the opposing political viewpoint, by a highly reactionary parson:

> In this year of our lord eighteen hundred and fifteen England is beset by troubles. The tyrant Bonaparte has been put down. But we are entering a new age. An iron age. New engines, new factories, cities, ways, laws. The old ways must go. The noble horse and the hand are slow. Our land must be better used. Forests cut down. Open spaces put to the plough . . . We must work for the common good.[3]

Clare himself is presented as simply one of the starving and embittered villagers to whom this is said, indistinguishable from the others in dialect and attitude. The first mention of his writing comes after a popular insurrection and the condemnation of his friends to death in prison. Against this context it seems indeed almost irrelevant ("scribblin' come t'summat"); and only in Scene Five — over half-way through the play — is his status as a poet brought to the fore. Even then, the discussion of his literary work is literally upstaged by a brutal prize fight. Although there are parallels between the demands of Clare's literary backers (Lord Radstock and Mrs. Emmerson, both identifiably based on actual patrons who supported — and censored — Clare) and the sadistic group betting on the boxers, the emphasis is on the economic exploitation of the working classes, in the graphic image of the fight:

> FIRST BACKER. Blood on his gob! Pump the fella's tummy up in his mouth.
>
> JACKSON *is half unconscious.* POTER *knocks him down. He sways slowly to his feet, like a half-drowned man forcing himself to make useless gestures. He's unable to give up . . .*
>
> FIRST BACKER. Collect my winnin's.
>
> THIRD BACKER (*To* JACKSON). A hundred guineas on you! Borrowed money.[4]

The boxer's battering is an obvious metaphor for Clare's mental fate; and the next scene applies the economic lesson specifically to poetry.

Representatives of the establishment, Mrs Emmerson, Lord Milton (the local landowner), and the parson, bring bags of Clare's remaindered books, for him to buy "at cost price" and sell to his neighbours: "Publishing is business. Printing, advertising, copies for critics — . CLARE. Hev the world gone mad?" Without any income from his writing (his publisher is demanding money for printing) and with neighbours who are completely illiterate, the incongruity of such "help" is simply another blow. Unread, rejected, unable to feed his family, let alone pay the rent on the country cottage that his visitors find so idyllic (seeing only "this beautiful view," "full of peace and stillness"), Clare has been beaten down by the system to the point where he is no longer capable of writing. Interpreting his problem as insanity, the establishment figures forcibly remove Clare to an asylum, which for him is merely another form of imprisonment. After a brief interlude, when he escapes, the final scene, twenty-three years later, shows him reduced to "*a bathchair. A shrivelled puppet. His head nods like a doll's. His face is white.*"[5] He has even lost the ability to speak, though significantly one of the other lunatics can understand and interpret the sounds he makes.

For Bond the issue is Clare's refusal to compromise, which is spelled out in an exchange with the landowner — the longest speech given to Clare in the play — immediately before he is taken away to the asylum.

CLARE   ... You had a poet in your field my lord. Wrote first poem when I were a boy pickin' up stones in your field. Took a stone in me hand an' poem come in me head ...

MILTON.   Read us a poem.

CLARE.   I hev — but you on't know how t'listen. On't write for you. On't be a poet then. No more'n his carpenter's a carpenter. He touch a piece of wood an' it turn t'coffin. His corn's grass. His men are animals ... what I wrote was good. Yes. Worth readin'. Shall I step in line now? No. I on't labour in your fields n'more. You cut your fields up small so you could eat 'em better. I've eat my portion of the universe an' I shall die of it. It was bitter fruit. But I had more out the stones in your field than you had out the harvest.

The image of eating is central to *The Fool*, which is subtitled "Scenes of Bread and Love" and plays on the Biblical resonance of substituting stones for bread. We are also introduced to another Romantic poet, Charles Lamb, whose mentally unbalanced sister compulsively buys mounds of food, which she believes spoiled before she can carry it home and leaves "rotting on the floor. Is she afraid of starving? Is it some punishment?" And in the scene where Clare, completely famished, is walking home after breaking out of the asylum, one of the figures he meets is physically incapable of eating. This is a ghost from Clare's past, his wife's brother, who was hanged for stealing earlier in the play and reappears as a boxer, broken and blinded in the ring, with a burn mark on his neck from the rope of the noose. He is offered stolen bread by another ghost, Clare's lost love Mary, now "*a tramp. Grotesque, filthy, ugly.*" Although he can taste the bread, his twisted neck makes swallowing impossible. He spits the chewed crumbs out all over the stage floor, unable to assuage his eternal hunger; and Bond has Clare spell out the symbolism: "I dreamt I saw bread spat on the ground . . . I'ld hev teach him how to eat. I am a poet an' I teach men how to eat. Then she on't go in rags. He on't blind. And I — on't goo mad in a madhouse."[6]

As Bond remarks in his introduction to the published text of the play, the asylum is intended to correlate to the "insane world of nineteenth-century Europe" — which explains the inversion of sense and madness in the final scene, where Clare's utterance is perfectly plain to a madwoman while appearing meaningless to the characters who find their society "normal" as well as to the contemporary audience who live under the same system. And in discussing the opposition of culture to capitalism (which he sees as inherently irrational, its only "rational" form being fascism) Bond implies a connection between modern views of art as an elitist or subjective expression and the industrialization and land-enclosure of Clare's lifetime that marked the birth of the capitalist system. When Bond declares "art is usually taken as a very private experience. This goes back to the nineteenth century, the first age that tried to take art away from the masses of people," he is attacking the leading Romantic poets; and shortly after completing *The Fool* he rejected Wordsworth's vision of nature as depersonalizing the landscape by omitting the labourers who worked on the land and turning the displaced peasants into picturesque objects of curiosity.[7] Such a view of the Romantic aesthetic is common among modern left-wing playwrights — and indeed the figures of Wordsworth, Keats, and Coleridge are noticeably absent from the British stage, clearly indicating the almost exclusive degree to which dramatists present the Romantics for their politics, not for their poetry.

The Fool or "Scenes of Bread and Love" is one in a series of four plays, to each of which Bond has given linking subtitles: "Scenes of Money and Death" (*Bingo*, 1974), "Scenes of Right and Evil" (*The Bundle*, 1978), and "Scenes of Freedom" (*The Woman*, 1978). All are experimental in form, with *The Fool* being episodic and including a traditional Mummer's play. All also focus on the intersection of literature and politics. Two others besides *The Fool* have poets as their protagonists, while *The Woman* is a rewriting of Euripides' *Trojan Women*.[8] However, both the other poets are object-lessons about writers who sell out to their unjust societies. Shakespeare commits suicide in *Bingo* because he is no longer able to reconcile his artistic principles with his pursuit of wealth, which has led him to write plays absolving exploitation and justifying injustice. In *The Bundle* the classical Japanese poet

Basho is presented not merely as the apologist of oppression, but its active agent: a wealthy provincial governor whose position can only be maintained by soldiers killing those who rebel. Destroyed by revolution, Basho's authorship of elitist Haiku poetry is analogous to SS officers listening to Mozart in Auschwitz. Only Clare refuses to compromise; and though he pays for his integrity by being forcibly silenced by society, in resuscitating him Bond is asserting the possibility of politically engaged art. The censorship of Clare's work — which has effectively remained in force for over a century since his death, and thus represents the continuance of the same oppressive system — is broken by the public performance of the play.

Bond, who stresses his own working-class background and lack of advanced education ("not going to grammar school was the making of me [. . .] Once you let them send you to grammar school and university you're ruined," since "education is nothing less than corruption, because it's based on institutionalizing the pupil"), identifies closely with Clare, to the extent of appending a selection of "Clare Poems" to the play: poems that Clare might have written and that declare Bond's own principles:

> Poetry destroys illusions — it doesn't create them
> And hope is a passion that will not let men
> Rest in asylum's peace.[9]

To increase the parallels, he presents Clare as a "natural" talent without any education at all and minimizes the rural setting that is the basis of almost all of Clare's poetry, a setting that becomes a false "paradise" envisioned by the wealthy who refuse to see the poverty and despair of the workers who live in it. Bond also heightens Clare's political involvement, making him a participant in a peasant uprising and giving him a direct relationship with one of its hanged leaders ("Darkie," whose green coat Clare symbolically wears after the execution). Clare actually contributed articles for a radical newspaper; and one of his radical friends, a Stamford publisher, was badly beaten for his political opinions. But the Luddite riots and popular risings against industrialization and land-enclosures between 1811 and 1830 occurred in distant parts of the country.

John MacKenna, too, in his *Clare: A Novel* changes the circumstances of Clare's life, though for quite different thematic reasons. The most significant alteration of fact in MacKenna's work relates to Clare's patrons, here combined into a single fictional woman, Lady Kettering. MacKenna reduces the motives of the historical Mrs. Emmerson and Lord Radstock to an entirely corrupt selfishness. (Radstock was in actuality the author of an evangelical tract entitled *The Cottager's Friend*, in which he insisted that Clare delete his denunciations of social injustice from poems such as "Helpstone"; Radstock's demands undoubtedly came from moral principle.) A bored and intensely snobbish aristocrat, Lady Kettering is only concerned to help Clare because of a perverse sexual attraction to "the earthiness of one who otherwise might never have entered our drawing rooms" and whose sense of "a deeper, darker side to this man" excites her use of him to "supply the intrigue and stimulation then absent from my life."[10] When Clare rejects her seduction, she humiliates him socially and sexually, and her demands that all radical sentiment be cut from his poems are seen as the revenge of outraged pride. MacKenna also omits almost all the broader social scene. We never follow Clare to London, and while the defacing of the countryside that came with enclosure is stressed, the poverty and political commitment that form the center of Bond's portrayal are consistently downplayed.

In fact, although both works share the main outline of Clare's life, the two interpretations are so completely different that the protagonists in the play and the novel appear to share practically nothing but the same name; and the contrast is summed up in the cover pictures for the two published texts. The photograph on the front of the Methuen edition of *The Fool* shows Tom Courtney as a hollow-eyed, glowering Clare with a basin of potatoes he has been peeling beside his elbow, clenching a blank sheet of paper. The cover of *Clare: A Novel* carries a colour reproduction of *The Magic Apple Tree*, one of Samuel Palmer's most glowingly luminous paintings of the idyllic landscape in his mystical valley of vision, complete with shepherdess and dreaming sheep.

In response to this quality in the novel, reviews of MacKenna's work bore titles like "Romanticizing the Romantic" — though they also treated it as "faction," claiming "it can be read, quite legitimately, as [. . .] biography." In addition, where reaction to *The Fool* overlooked the formal aspects of the play to focus exclusively on Bond's political agenda, reviews of *Clare: A Novel* are largely concerned with its presentational technique as stylistic innovation. Building on the oral tradition that Clare had learned from his father, whom he described as "illiterate to the last degree,"[11] and himself used in his ballads, MacKenna presents his text as dialogue spoken to an anonymous and unseen interlocutor. The fictional form is the tape-recorded interview from which the interviewer's questions have been edited out: an exploration into the life of a famous figure through the memories of four people who knew him. The text is full of statements beginning "I recall [. . .]" or "I remember he told me [. . .]" and the immediacy of the telling is continually stressed. For instance, one of the speakers presents a letter from Clare: "in learning it and going over the letters, I have got to know the words. I have it here, look. It says [. . .]," and the recordings close with the comment: "I do not want to talk or think again of the vicissitudes of our lives with my father. I need never talk of him again. I have told you all that I recall [. . .]."[12]

These speakers are placed in chronological order to cover Clare's life from childhood to his funeral; and reviews of the novel highlighted the multiplicity of differing perspectives that result from this technique of narration.

Significantly all four speakers are women — Clare's sister, his wife, his daughter, and Lady Kettering. There is also a fifth woman, Mary Joyce, to whom all the speakers refer. The subject of several deeply felt love poems by Clare, a childhood love who had refused to marry him and vanished completely from his life five years before his first poems were published, Mary becomes the absent center of the novel. Although in the fifth and final section of the novel we hear from Clare himself, this is only a short letter; and it is not only written to the long-dead Mary, but also about her treatment of him. Since each speaker is fully individualized, what we primarily learn when they speak of Clare is his effect on them; and the focus becomes the source of Clare's poetic inspiration. In each case — most obviously with Lady Kettering — he has disappointed their expectations, because his commitment to his art meant that he could not act as a childhood companion, a breadwinner, or a paternal protector and role model. Poetry is set against the ordinary obligations of social life, particularly family responsibilities. Indeed, it destroys the happiness and even the existence of the poet himself. As his daughter comments, speaking of her ability to read and associating Clare's voracious reading with his writing of poetry:

> I am grateful for that gift, though I am grateful, too, that it did not impinge on my acquaintance with normality. My father paid an extortionate price in his own life and lived to regret it [. . .]
> But I was not the only one affected by his illness. All of us were dealt blows of our own.[13]

And this connection between Clare's poetic vision and insanity is central in the novel.

Right from Clare's birth, MacKenna has Clare's sister say, "there was a strangeness about John" that is externalized in the form of epileptic fits when he lies as if dead, but with his eyes open; and the doctor who runs the asylum is reported as "blam[ing] my father's illness on years 'addicted to poetical prosings.'" Clare is repeatedly described as out of place, "removed from the world about him" and, whether in London or the country, "wanting to be somewhere else and something else and [. . .] never happy." Social displacement is clearly an analogy for visionary experience; and MacKenna sets poetry as the antithesis of "normality" and life, showing his Clare obsessed by death. Picking up on the fact that Clare was a twin, whose twin-sister only survived their birth by a few days, MacKenna offers this as a metaphor for the poet's striving after a spiritual reality: "His other breathing half was dead." This role is taken over by Clare's lost love. Mary becomes the poetic muse; and the novel focusses on the women in Clare's life, because they represent substitutes that test his artistic calling. The poet must rise above human love, particularly sexual desire (which is the all-consuming basis of Clare's relationship with his wife), to pursue a passion of the soul. As Clare's daughter comments, he is

> a man always waiting for Mary Joyce and never being quite fulfilled by anything within his life. In seeing that as I have seen, beyond doubt, none of us failed him in any way. Nothing we could have done within the family could have made his life in any way better or sweeter [. . .][14]

The writer becomes a secular Job (whose story is Clare's favourite passage from the Bible, according to his sister), tormented by false images in his commitment to the divine force of art.

In the novel everything reduces to poetry. Even the political repression and enclosure of the land are presented primarily as factors that "would curb [poetic] freedom and imagination."[15] Clare's vision and the rejection of human relationships it requires may be seen by the women as insanity. But the asylum, where Clare continues to write reams of poetry, is the only place in an unfeeling society where he can fully follow his calling. The effect is a universalization in which historical details themselves become an equivalent for the physical relationships that Clare learns to dismiss as distracting illusions. In addition, the form MacKenna has chosen necessarily gives at best only an oblique view of Clare himself. The women's personalities come across vividly, but in a very real sense they are marginal to the novel's focus, since none have any understanding of Clare as a creative artist. Although the poet is the exclusive subject of all four interviews, as in modern sub-atomic physics, his presence can only be detected by its effect on surrounding elements.

As does Edward Bond, MacKenna clearly associates himself with Clare, whose generalized experience stands as a model for any created writer. In contrast to Bond's inclusion of his own poems as the works of his protagonist in *The Fool*, MacKenna reprints one of Clare's poems as a preface to his novel. Yet this poem itself speaks of the withdrawal of the poet from the world: "I am — yet what I am, none care or knows [. . .]." And in excising his own presence as the interviewer/author from the novel, MacKenna duplicates Clare's absence.

The striking thing is the way that the title figure in both these contemporary depictions of Clare is almost literally a "missing person." Although on the stage in every scene in Bond's play, he is secondary to the activities depicted, subordinated to the social analysis. Thus, in the Hyde Park scene, Clare's dialogue with his patrons is on the sidelines, carried out between each round of the boxing-match. During the uprising, when Darkie and the other peasants are stripping the parson (demonstrating that his rolls of fat have nourishment "stolen" from the starving workers), Clare is off in the bushes searching for his girl. In the asylum scene he is reduced to an inarticulate and unmoving object. MacKenna carries this even further. In his novel Clare is deliberately kept outside of the narrative frame, with his absence as such carrying central thematic weight. When he does appear, in the final section headed "John Clare," it is not as a living voice but as a recovered document — the letter, which follows the account of his death and funeral — indicating that as a poet he exists only through his writings.

At the same time, both contemporary authors identify themselves with Clare and use him as a projection of their own views of art. Thus, on the one hand, he becomes the model for rational, politically committed writing that has the potential to change the social system, and his oppression is presented as proof of the injustice that requires such change. On the other hand, he epitomizes the irrationality of art conceived as divine inspiration, and he is used to demonstrate that a writer has to cut himself off from social ties in order to create. Such completely different, even antithetical portraits may have been determined by the differential in development between modern drama and the contemporary novel. But the contrast also indicates the actual irrelevance of historical fact. In each case, while the fictional context may evoke the Romantic period, the focus is on the twentieth-century present. And (despite Bond's exaggeratedly archaic dialect) the picture of Clare that emerges is a marginalized figure, increasingly abstract as one moves from the 1970s to the 1990s. But then, this simply marks the essential polarity between fiction and biography. Clare may offer an extreme example, yet the same would be true of all other contemporary renditions of the Romantics. They are no more than masks for the modern writers themselves.

Notes

¹ Byron's response to Shelley's funeral pyre in Howard Brenton, *Bloody Poetry* (London: Methuen, 1985), 77.

² Although a biography was published during Clare's lifetime, the first major critical study was John Burrell, *The Idea of Landscape and the Sense of Place, 1790–1840: An Approach to the Poetry of John Clare* (Cambridge: Cambridge UP, 1972). Then in the 1980s an increasing number of books began to appear on Clare, including: Timothy Brownlow, *John Clare and Picturesque Landscape* (Oxford: Clarendon Press, 1983); Tim Chilcott, *'A real world and doubting mind': A Critical Study of the Poetry of John Clare* (Hull: Hull UP, 1985); Edward Storey, *A Right to Song: The Life of John Clare* (London: Methuen, 1982).

³ Edward Bond, *The Fool & We Come to the River* (London: Eyre Methuen, 1976), 7.

⁴ Bond, *The Fool*, 28, 45.

⁵ Bond, *The Fool*, 53, 55, also 52, 68.

⁶ Bond, *The Fool*, 57, 45, 60.

⁷ Introduction, in *The Fool*, xvi, xiii; Bond in conversation with the author, 1978, see "Edward Bond: From Rationalism to Rhapsody," *Canadian Theatre Review* (Summer 1979): 182. For a comparable comment from another Marxist dramatist, see the Canadian George Ryga: "Nowhere in 'I wandered lonely as a cloud' do we find that there was a man who went there and cultivated the daffodils. The Wordsworthian assumption is a bourgeois one — to deal with the scene and eliminate the providers of it" (interview 1980), quoted in Christopher Innes, *Politics and the Playwright: George Ryga* (Toronto: Simon & Pierre, 1985), 80.

⁸ There are also internal links between the plays. For instance Darkie, the name given to the rebellious brother of Clare's wife, is clearly related to "the dark man" whose assassination of the Greek dictator in *The Woman* leads to the establishment of a utopian society.

⁹ Bond in Malcolm Hay and Philip Roberts, *Edward Bond: A Companion to the Plays* (London: TQ Publication, 1978), 7, 43–44; Bond, *The Fool*, 73.

¹⁰ John MacKenna, *Clare: A Novel* (Belfast: Blackstaff Press, 1993), 108, 111.

¹¹ *Irish Literary Supplement* (Fall 1994): 9; Clare, quoted in John Lucas, *John Clare* (Plymouth: Northcote House/The British Council, 1994), 5.

¹² MacKenna, *Clare*, 78, 114.

¹³ MacKenna, *Clare*, 142.

¹⁴ MacKenna, *Clare*, 6, 159, 82, 47, 170.

¹⁵ MacKenna, *Clare*, 136.

RAMONA M. RALSTON AND SID SONDERGARD

Biodepictions of Mary Shelley:
The Romantic Woman Artist
as Mother of Monsters

WHILE POPULAR CULTURE ENCODES THE ROMANTIC writer iconi-
cally as male, a poet, and a character of excess — whether a Byronic libertine (a nineteenth-century Jim Morrison) or a Coleridgian
drug visionary (a nineteenth-century William S. Burroughs) — the text
that figures in pop culture consciousness as the quintessential Romantic
literary work is Mary Shelley's *Frankenstein*. The latter association has
been perpetuated by over twenty film treatments of the novel or its
characters since director J. Searle Darley's sixteen-minute adaptation,
produced by Thomas Alva Edison, in 1910. Though there have been
no "biopics," or explicitly biographical film narratives, created to
dramatize the life of Mary Shelley, in addition to the many adaptations
of her novel, male filmmakers have constructed narratives that employ
her as a character in a gendered analogy of the technological fears that
have been extrapolated from *Frankenstein* to form its mythos in popular culture. Whereas most adaptations of the novel treat the "increasing
mechanization of the human and humanization of the machine, a process moving toward an ultimate end in which the machine is god and
the human is reduced either to slavery or obsolescence,"[1] the films we
examine here transcode this metaphor as a gender conflict, wherein
mechanization signifies "masculinization," humanization "feminiza-
tion," human "woman," and machine "man." That is, the challenge to
conventional male hegemony over authorship represented by Mary
Shelley's composition of *Frankenstein* is viewed not merely as masculine (signified by Mary's confidence, resourcefulness and independence)
but also as unnatural in the portraits of her as character.

The conventional association of Frankenstein with his creature, and
of the creature as a *Doppelgänger* of its creator, "the dark side of the
self [. . .] assuming its own independent form,"[2] is turned to the service of fictionalizing the relationship of Mary Shelley to her novel — the

very act of creating which is Promethean in its threat to the power of the male literary canon. In retribution for the audacity of this act, Mary as creator is demonized both through the monstrosity of the *Doppel-gänger* she has brought into existence and through concerted gender typing that depicts her variously as a fortune-teller or medium who functions as a conduit for the male Romantics rather than as a creative source; as a witch who dares to dabble with powers she cannot hope to control, ultimately condemning herself and others through her over-reaching; as a mother of monsters (that is, of children who are fated to die, of Frankenstein's monster, and of the other Romantics who behave as a monstrous brood); and as an ahistorical anomaly: the nineteenth-century "modern woman."

The fundamental inspiration for these filmmakers, consequently, comes not from biographies of Mary Shelley, but from her introduction to the 1831 edition of her novel. In response to the question raised by her publishers, Henry Colburn and Richard Bentley, "how I, then a young girl, came to think of, and dilate upon, so very hideous an idea," she traces *Frankenstein*'s genesis to the Villa Diodati in Switzerland during the "wet, ungenial summer" of 1816, where she joined Lord Byron, Percy Bysshe Shelley, John William Polidori, and Claire Clair-mont (not mentioned in the preface) in a "ghost story" competition at Byron's behest.[3] Her response has been of interest to filmmakers primarily as a source of *dramatis personae* and an exotic setting; the resulting narratives have balanced the question of how a young woman could write a novel of *Frankenstein*'s intellectual influence with cautionary speculation about the emotional cost of that creative act. The male fascination with *Frankenstein*'s iconoclasm and notoriety, expressed by the publishers of the 1831 edition, then, has invited filmmakers to remove the boundaries separating Mary Shelley's life from her fiction, to project their own aesthetics (and gender politics) onto constructions of Mary as character that reconcile her (female) authorship with the enduring power and popularity of her art.

Mary the Medium: Channeling the Anxieties of Male Influence

One Mary construction posits that the imaginative power behind *Frankenstein* ultimately issues from the artistic influences of Byron and Shelley — with the author complicit in this identification, writing in her 1831 introduction that "many and long were the conversations between Lord Byron and Shelley, to which I was a devout but nearly silent listener" (280). This attitude of self-effacement is recorded in director James Whale's *The Bride of Frankenstein* (1935) to signal Mary's function as a passive reflector of the wit of her male companions. The pseudo-historical prologue attached to the sequel to Whale's successful *Frankenstein* (1931) introduces three character icons to the audience: the bombastic, larger-than-life Lord Byron (fashioned as "England's greatest sinner") acting as master of ceremonies; the studious Percy Bysshe Shelley (authorized by Byron as "England's greatest poet"), who is writing even as we meet him; and the sweetly domestic Mary, author in this scene of nothing more audacious than a piece of needlework. Elizabeth Young sees this "angelic persona" serving both "to promote and to defuse her narrating powers; she occupies the important position of author, but here only as the conduit for a story passing between two men."[4] As Byron and Shelley condescendingly tease her about her as-yet-unpublished narrative, Mary defensively asserts that the publishers who have turned down her manuscript "did not see that my purpose was to write a moral lesson of the punishment that befell a mortal man who dared to emulate God." Despite this attempt to pass off her story as a cautionary tale, its narrative power is rooted in the terror it evokes: Mary begs Byron, "don't remind me of it tonight," and pricks herself in terrified response when he embarks on a synoptic voice-over of stock footage from the 1931 film. In contrast to the image of Percy writing, signifying legitimate, that is, male authorship, Mary, acquiescing to the men's insistence, continues her tale of Victor Frankenstein *orally*. The effect is to reduce "the stark reality of *Frankenstein*" to "a fantasy world pouring from the mind of the author to — in effect — entertain some friends on a dreary evening."[5]

Ivan Passer's *Haunted Summer* (1988) offers more explicit evidence that Mary Shelley is not the sole inventor of *Frankenstein*, arguing that she derives the novel's central action largely from Byron's tirade that "one day scientists will move beyond the natural boundaries of human knowledge and instruct us how to propagate ourselves without coupling. [. . .] Man will create himself in laboratories with the aid of electricity and chemicals." Byron's influence here problematizes the question of Mary's authorship even of her own nightmare: the sounds of Byron's limping are transformed into the halting, uneven footsteps of an approaching monster that shares the face of the incubus in Fuseli's painting *The Nightmare*, recently acquired by Byron and explicated by him as an allegory of revenge and rape.[6] When Mary and Polidori attempt to achieve a degree of vengeance against the arrogant Byron, they succeed in frightening him with a mask worn by Polidori — though his fear is heightened by an opium epiphany that leads him to identify with the monster and its "great longing and sadness." The semiosis of the film is that Byron's is the greater creative intellect, and through fascinating Mary he impregnates her mind with the germ of the novel, supplying the outline of the plot, providing the archetype for Victor Frankenstein's cruelty towards the monster and his inability to consider the welfare of others, as well as suggesting the monster's lonely solipsism.[7]

The most curious variant of the film narratives challenging Mary Shelley's role as the creative imagination behind *Frankenstein* is Jack Smight's 1973 *Frankenstein: The True Story*, in part because the commercially released version of the film excludes the crucial introductory scene of Christopher Isherwood and Don Bachardy's teleplay, which features Mary in the company of the male contingent of the Diodati personalities.[8] The first lines of the film were written to be Mary's voice-over: "I am Mary Shelley. Here I sit demurely beside my husband. But in my head is a story of horror and you shall hear it," and she is quickly denoted as the only one of the four to take up the "ghost story" challenge with both enthusiasm and success. Polidori's attempt is laughably bad, Shelley admits that he was "too lazy" to write anything, and Byron confesses to progressing "no farther than page two." Quickly Mary begins reciting her story (as in the *Bride of Frankenstein*, implying that she can "tell" her story more effectively than "write" it), assigning roles to each of them: Shelley becomes Victor Frankenstein, Byron both Henry Clerval and the monster (the "perfected" monster is initially beautiful, but decays with time), and Polidori an antagonist named Polidori who is reminiscent of Dr. Praetorius in *The Bride of Frankenstein*. Shelley, performing as Frankenstein, is suddenly able to swim, and when Byron objects to Mary that he had better go after Shelley in case he "forgets he's Victor," Mary coldly insists, "I am not Mary. My name is Elizabeth." This intriguing metamorphosis of fiction into biography, however, is seemingly contradicted both by Elizabeth's death in the narrative[9] and by the story's dominant focus on Victor's succession of male relationships with Clerval, then with Polidori, and finally with the monster created from the dead Henry. In terms of biographical speculation, this seems a doubly appropriate choice of tales for Mary/Elizabeth to tell: it dramatizes anxieties Mary might have felt related to Byron "seducing" Shelley away from her, and it punishes Byron, a rival for Shelley's affection, first by characterizing Clerval as socially inept and unattractive to women, and then by grafting his brain into an initially beautiful but rapidly deteriorating body. As in *The Bride of Frankenstein*, however, the glory belongs to the male Romantics, and the "true story" asserted by the title here is a homage by Isherwood and Bachardy to gay director James Whale — the "true" love story of males living and dying together gloriously.

Mary the Witch:
The Female Author as Overreacher

It is a critical commonplace that, as George Levine has written, "*Frankenstein* echoes the old stories of Faust and Prometheus, exploring the limits of ambition and rebelliousness and their moral implications,"[10] yet Ellen Moers points out that "Mary Shelley's overreacher is different. [. . .] He defies mortality not by living forever, but by giving birth."[11] Some of the male filmmakers constructing biofictional narratives about Mary Shelley have adapted this formula by configuring Mary as a pattern for her own Victor Frankenstein. By daring to compete with the male Romantics for literary fame, she oversteps the bounds of female propriety, neglects her authentic sphere of domestic nurturance, and so creates, and becomes, a monster. This exercise of autonomy is so dangerous a threat to conventional male hegemony that it must first be perverted, and then punished. In the prologue to *The Bride of Frankenstein*, Mary Shelley is portrayed as a demure figure who nevertheless contains the hidden power to "thrill the blood" of even a debauched libertine like Byron "with icy creeps." That this incongruous capacity is deemed monstrous is confirmed by actress Elsa Lanchester's recollection that James Whale insisted she play the part of the "female monster" as well as "sweet and docile" Mary Shelley.[12]

In contrast to this explicit encoding of *Frankenstein*'s author as monstrous, *Remando al viento* [*Rowing with the Wind*] (1988) more insidiously develops Mary Shelley's monster as a product of her own neuroses, strengthened and made concrete rather than exorcized or dissipated by the process of writing. She comes to believe that through completing and publishing her novel she has brought the creature, the embodiment of her fears, to life and that its incarnation is the punishment for her audacity, as it proceeds to cause the deaths of those for whom she cares. This extensive examination of Mary Shelley's life, written and directed by Gonzalo Suárez, extends chronologically from her courtship by Shelley to the death of Byron and beyond, using historical fact selectively to emphasize similarities between the author's biography and the plot of her novel.[13] Whether the monster portrayed in the film is an objective correlative of her fears and guilt, a metaphorical corrective for female overreaching, or a purely delusional manifestation, Mary suffers by taking responsibility for the monster's agency in the deaths of John William Polidori, Shelley's wife Harriet, Mary's half-sister Fanny, Mary's son William, Allegra Byron, Percy Shelley, and Byron himself. She blames herself for having something aggressive inside her that "killed my mother when she gave birth to me" and for releasing that power again through writing her novel, "against the laws of nature." When she declares *Frankenstein* "nothing but the fruit of my pretension and pride," we assume her self-condemnation includes her aspiration to become an author and her satisfaction in her artistic accomplishment.

Remando al viento confirms Mary's culpability in the tragedies surrounding her by corroborating her self-castigation. Byron feeds her ego by stating he would like to publish something jointly with her some day, but follows with the injunction that they all write ghost stories to divert Percy Shelley — because he has been frightened by a vision of Mary which depicted her independence ("Your thoughts were no longer my thoughts"). She becomes so absorbed in writing her tale, as soon as Byron and Percy Shelley leave on a sailing trip to Chillon, that she refuses to respond to the despondent Polidori's pleas and howls outside her door. This choice of literary ambition over nurturing compassion to her "little brother" (as she calls him) heralds the emergence of the monster into her world and, consequently, Polidori's (anachronistic and inaccurate) suicide. Following the death of William, a scene in which Mary rejects Shelley's intimate attempts to console her ("I do not want any more children. We have no children, only death. I do not want to see a creature born that is destined to die") is preceded by a scene in which she is distraught over a negative review of *Frankenstein*. When Percy Shelley postulates a society without critics, she wails, "and who would talk about us then?" The implication is that she has rejected the orthodox mode of female reproduction for the conventional male method, authorship, and once the unholy choice has been made, it is irrevocable. Paradoxically, the efforts of the film to elevate its characterization of Mary Shelley to the mythic status of her creations, Victor Frankenstein and the monster, have the corollary effect of insinuating that a woman who presumes to write a work of art is either mad or monstrous, and that Mary somehow deserves the sufferings she endures in the loss of her children, her husband, and her friends.

Mother Mary: The Tale of a
Most Contrary Child, or
The Dysfunctional Romantic Family

Anne Mellor describes Mary Shelley during her temporary residence at
Lake Geneva as "an exhilarated but anxiety-prone girl" fascinated by
Byron "as well as by the range of topics covered in their conversations,"
nervous about "Percy's continuing allegiance to Claire," and feeling "a
deep need to belong to a stable family."[14] This confluence of factors
matches the portrayal of Mary Shelley in Ken Russell's 1986 film *Gothic*
though with some typical Ken Russell exaggerations and additions such
as Byron's homosexuality and vampirism, Percy's laudanum addiction
and subsequent hallucinations, Polidori's religious perversions and homosexual jealousy of Percy, and Claire's nymphomania and hysterical
fits. Mary's greatest fear, called up during a séance in *Gothic*, springs
from anxiety about motherhood; recalling a dream about the revival of
her dead first child, she fears her maternal instincts are so strong she
would "do anything to bring my baby back to life." Throughout the
film Mary provides a voice of maturity, common sense, and love and
compassion for the Diodati ensemble — components of a good
mother, exercised in a desperate attempt to mediate and to give meaning to the communal experience of a hideous brood whose parlor
games and storytelling entertainment go awry and give physical form to
their collective fears. As the mother figure, she exhibits the courage to
smash the skull that supernaturally channels their dread, "killing death"
(again replicating the act of her fictional protagonist) in an attempt to
protect them all. This act allows her to acknowledge her anxieties in a
waking dream — and as the mother who preserves the memory of her
culture, she remembers it the next day when the others, her "children,"
seem untouched by their nightmarish experience. She reproduces this
memory, yet another generation of offspring, in *Frankenstein*.

Mellor's observation that Mary Shelley idealized "the nuclear family
as a community of mutually dependent, equally respected, and equally
self-sacrificing individuals"[15] is interestingly deformed in *Haunted
Summer*. Mary, Percy, and Claire, on their way to Switzerland, are en-
coded as children of nature: unafraid (their carriage hanging at the
cliff's edge), uninhibited (Percy swims and plays with paper boats in the
nude, inviting Mary and Claire to join him), and playful (Percy and
Claire shoot spitwads at patrons and waiters in the Hotel d'Angleterre).
Byron explicitly refers to them as "brothers and sisters in exile," and
"children of the revolution," while Mary calls Polidori, frequently por-

trayed as a pouting child, her "little brother." Polidori and Claire engage in sibling rivalry for the attentions of Byron, periodically identified
as the group's capricious father, as when he teasingly leads them out to
see his new boat: "Come, poppa has surprises. Come along, children."
If Byron acts at times as the wayward and irresponsible father of the
group (including, literally) Claire's unborn child), Mary in contrast
adopts the role of wise and benevolent mother, Wendy to Byron's Peter Pan in the Never-Never Land of the Villa Diodati. When Claire,
hysterical, appears in Mary and Percy's bedroom, claiming that rats
have been crawling on her face, Mary maternally comforts and wel-
comes her into their bed. She takes Byron to task for his cruelty to
Claire and Polidori, and her love-making with both Percy and Byron
has a motherly cast; the act expresses her compassion rather than her
desire, her bare skin is scarcely glimpsed, her calm radiance beatified by
the camera. This construction of Mary projects the authority of a maternal storyteller, and that authority is exercised to generate *Frankenstein*'s cautionary tale about the dangers of the world Byron
proposes — a world without mothers.[16]

Thoroughly Modern Mary:
What Best Becomes a Myth

One final strategy employed by male filmmakers to explain Mary Shelley's ability to write a narrative of *Frankenstein*'s power depicts her as a
"modern" woman, independent-minded and forward-thinking, part of
an artistically bohemian milieu, daughter of a feminist and a political
radical. In *Haunted Summer*, Mary firmly defends women's rights
during a dinner-table conversation; she is shown as a tolerant and
amused observer, if not a participant, in nude bathing; and after several
discussions with Shelley about their shared principles of free love, she
makes love to Byron — with Percy's blessing. Similarly, in *Gothic* Mary
is shown in the midst of many forms of sexual and drug-induced li-
cense, and while not a participant in most of these excesses, neither
does she recoil or withdraw from them. In one scene she engages in sex
with Percy in the same room where Byron and Claire are similarly occupied, and the film foregrounds the fact that Mary is an unwed
mother. The narrative in *Remando al viento* begins by showing us Mary
eloping with Shelley, a married man, against the wishes of her father
(although Shelley's surprised response to this opposition tells us that in
light of Godwin's radical social and political views, he did not expect
it). Even the prologue to *The Bride of Frankenstein* originally contained

dialogue alluding to Mary and Percy living together outside of wedlock — references cut by the censors before the film's release.[17]

It is in Roger Corman's 1990 *Frankenstein Unbound* that the trope of Mary as modern woman is most thoroughly developed, despite the relative brevity of her portrait in the film. When a time anomaly of his own making causes scientist Joe Buchanan to travel backward to Switzerland in 1817,[18] the databank in the computerized car that accompanies him identifies Mary Shelley as author of the novel *Frankenstein* (of which it is said that "the subject matter is artificial intelligence") and the mistress of Lord Byron. The autonomy of this Mary is signified by her attendance, alone, at the trial of Justine Moritz and by her dismissing as "a travesty" the court's decision that the girl killed her victim with witchcraft. She is energetic in contrast to the languorous and laconic Byron and Shelley, and also more sexually liberated: "Byron and Shelley preach free love. I practice it." While Joe (and the screenwriters Roger Corman and F. X. Feeney) give Mary credit for being able to imagine and to articulate what it means to be a man of science who must live with the "madness of possibility," the narrative effectively reduces her from being the creator of an original myth to being merely a perceptive investigative reporter, for Victor Frankenstein and his creature are alive and living in nearby Sécheron. In this scenario her novel is based on her observations of only a short temporal segment of a mythic struggle that will go on through the ages — a struggle in which the protagonists — both creature and creator — are archetypically male.

The six films we have discussed divide neatly into three sub-generic pairs. The depictions of Mary Shelley in *The Bride of Frankenstein* and *Frankenstein: The True Story* serve as prologues to versions of her fiction, analogous to the introductory preface of her novel's 1831 edition. However, these two films point out the conundrum of how a female writer could have such a profound interest in, and insight into, a story in which the major emotional connections and transactions all take place between males. This suggests some intuition on the part of the writers and directors that, in attempting to conceive a horror story, little could be more terrifying to a woman than a fictional world in which women (and children — including the monster) are systematically excluded, marginalized, made monstrous, or killed.

Gothic and *Haunted Summer,* which restrict their purview to the ensemble gathered at the Villa Diodati in the summer of 1816, are both fascinated and obsessed with this catalytic or generative cultural moment. *Gothic* focuses most fixedly on the elements that produced *Frankenstein,* the gothic novel par excellence, but synthesizes and condenses all the conventions of gothic fiction — a dark and stormy night, a rambling mansion with circling staircases, dark passageways and a rat-infested cellar, vampirism, incest and other sexual aberrations, ghost stories, Fuseli's painting *The Nightmare* — into one twenty-four-hour period, observing the classical unities of time and place. Subjected to such a barrage of terrors, Mary Shelley writes *Frankenstein* to exorcize the demons raised by the film's grotesque encounter group. *Haunted Summer* foregrounds the romantic preoccupations of the Romantics. Based on a popular romance genre novel written by Anne Edwards,[19] this film presents the most stable and most self-confident Mary of these six variations. Yet the film is situated in a genre associated almost exclusively with writing and reading by women, and since its narrative is derived from a rather inept and convention-bound example of that genre, *Haunted Summer* inescapably trivializes its more serious themes and its author-heroine.

With technology and psychology as the tools for removing the boundary between *Frankenstein*'s fiction and its author's biography, the monster in *Remando al viento* and the monster, his creator, and other characters from the novel in *Frankenstein Unbound* are made just as "real" as the Mary constructs in them. Mary in *Frankenstein Unbound* is merely an observer and recorder of one facet of a tragic drama played out in three times or venues: 2010, when Joe Buchanan creates a monstrous timeslip; 1817, when Victor Frankenstein creates his monster; and some time even further in the future after civilization has been annihilated by some other techno-horror, perhaps the nuclear winter smothering the earth mirroring the arctic landscapes of the novel's denouement. *Remando al viento* also begins and ends in ice — but while internalizing the novel as Mary's psychodrama, it paradoxically manifests her creative power by incarnating the monster on screen. This produces the terrifying ontological fantasy of a fictional creature coming to life, occupying the same cinematic space inhabited by Mary and removing her circle of family and friends from existence in retribution for her presumption in bringing him into being. *Frankenstein Unbound* ultimately marginalizes Mary Shelley, distancing her as only an incidental commentator on, and Cassandra-like prophetess of, monumental male conflicts. *Remando al viento* condemns Mary to a destructive engagement with her narrative, the misfortunes of her fictional creations being transmuted by private guilts into a self-fulfilling doom of which she is sole author.

Notes

[1] Janice Hocker Rushing and Thomas S. Frentz, "The Frankenstein Myth in Contemporary Cinema," in *Critical Questions: Invention, Creativity, and the Criticism of Discourse and Media*, ed. William L. Nothstine et al. (New York: St. Martin's, 1994), 161–82 (162).

[2] Rolf Eichler, "In the Romantic Tradition: *Frankenstein* and *The Rocky Horror Picture Show*," in *Beyond the Suburbs of the Mind: Exploring English Romanticism*, ed. Michael Gassenmeier and Norbert H. Platz (Essen: verlag die blaue eule, 1987), 95–114 (95).

[3] Mary Wollstonecraft Shelley, *Frankenstein*, ed. James Rieger (New York: Pocket Books, 1976), 275, 277. All subsequent page references in the text are to this edition.

[4] Elizabeth Young, "Here Comes the Bride: Wedding Gender and Race in *Bride of Frankenstein*," *Feminist Studies* 17 (1991): 403–37 (407–08).

[5] James Curtis, *James Whale* (Metuchen, NJ: Scarecrow Press, 1982), 120.

[6] For a brief discussion of Fuseli's influence on Mary Shelley, see Anne K. Mellor, *Mary Shelley: Her Life, Her Fiction, Her Monsters* (New York: Routledge, 1989), 243n4.

[7] While such an attitude would seem somewhat anachronistic for the late 1980s, it was a common feature in 1970s commentaries on the novel, both in academic circles — e.g., Robert Kiely's observation that "like everything else" about Mary Shelley's life, *Frankenstein* "is an instance of genius observed and admired but not shared," *The Romantic Novel in England* (Cambridge· Harvard UP, 1972), 161 — and in popular circles — e.g., novelist Mario Praz, who thought that Mary Shelley's achievement was no more than "to provide a passive reflection of some of the wild fantasies which were living in the air about her," see Ellen Moers, "Female Gothic," in *The Endurance of Frankenstein: Essays on Mary Shelley's Novel*, ed. George Levine and U. C. Knoepflmacher (Berkeley and Los Angeles: California UP, 1979), 77–87 (82). Among the "complex experiences that placed young Mary Shelley, both personally and intellectually, at a point of crisis in our modern culture," George Levine identifies "the cynical diabolism of Byron" ("The Ambiguous Heritage of *Frankenstein*," in *The Endurance of Frankenstein*, 4), while Sandra Gilbert and Susan Gubar acknowledge that "critics have traditionally studied *Frankenstein* as an interesting example of Romantic myth-making, *a work ancillary to such Promethean masterpieces* as Shelley's *Prometheus Unbound* and Byron's *Manfred*" (*The Madwoman in the Attic: The Woman Writer and the Nineteenth-Century Literary Imagination* [New Haven: Yale UP, 1979], 221; our emphasis).

[8] Christopher Isherwood and Don Bachardy, *Frankenstein: The True Story* (New York: Avon Books, 1973). The made-for-television original was a three-hour production. The shortened version of *Frankenstein: The True Story*

(123 minutes) that was released theatrically (and on videocassette) "dispenses
with a lot of the wordy psychological teledrama footage" — specifically, the
first fifteen pages of the teleplay — "but the film remains trapped in its
wastefully expansive, fundamentally uncinematic television format with the
camera following the characters rather than weaving its own spells" (Tom
Milne and Paul Willeman, *The Encyclopedia of Horror Movies,* ed. Phil Hardy
[New York: Harper and Row, 1986], 276).

[9] The teleplay seems to invest Mary initially with the power of a creator, but
this — and even her *gender* — is eventually taken from her in order to allow a
final male consummation in death, as Victor triggers an avalanche to kill the
two of them together; the creature cries "(*In Henry's voice*) Well done —
Victor!" and is answered "(*Amazed, joyful*) Henry —!" (220). Upon learning
that Elizabeth/Mary is pregnant, and that he is about to be displaced in Victor's life by "a child, now. *Our* child" (216), the monster murders her while
Victor is in his ship cabin, unconscious; when Victor awakens to intense cold
and blinding light, he discovers the "*corpse of Elizabeth, weirdly beautiful, its
hair a glazed mass, its eyes open, its eyelashes and eyebrows frosted and sparkling*"
(219). The dehumanizing of Elizabeth through the use of the pronoun "it"
effectively leaves the monster as the undisputed recipient of Victor's attention.

[10] Levine, "Ambiguous Heritage of *Frankenstein,*" 4.

[11] Moers, "Female Gothic," 82–83.

[12] Curtis, *James Whale,* 120–21.

[13] For example, the film portrays her as having only one biological child, William, and delays his birth until after the generation of the monster, who is
thus her "first born." No mention is made of Percy Florence Shelley, who
survived Mary. The Mary constructed both in *Remando al viento* and in Ken
Russell's *Gothic* (1986) — which Suárez learned about while interviewing
British actors for his own film — locates a cathectic source for *Frankenstein*
and for its "creator with monstrous creation" in "the anxieties of a woman
who, as daughter, mistress and mother, was a bearer of death" (Moers, "Female Gothic," 86). *Gothic* suggests that the novel is a psychic compensation
for the loss of Mary's first baby (cf. Moers, "Female Gothic," 85), while *Remando al viento* implies the more sinister transference of the monster sup-
planting Mary's natural child, its "unnatural" birth leading inevitably to the
death of William.

[14] Mellor, *Mary Shelley,* 36–37.

[15] Mellor, *Mary Shelley,* 16.

[16] This is reinforced by the common motif of the *Frankenstein* films that such
a world can only produce monstrous offspring. It is made explicit through
satirical excess in *Andy Warhol's Frankenstein* (dir. Paul Morrissey, 1973), in
which Baron Frankenstein is married to his own sister, and their children
demonstrate the effects of this monstrous legacy during the opening credits

by applying surgical instruments with quiet, ruthless efficiency to one of their toys. However, it is equally explicit in *Mary Shelley's Frankenstein* (dir. Kenneth Branagh, 1994), as Branagh's Victor introduces the use of amniotic fluid into his motherless manufacture of life — according to the screenplay by Steph Lady and Frank Darabont, "The Creature seems as helpless as the newly born" (Kenneth Branagh, *Mary Shelley's Frankenstein: The Classic Tale of Terror Reborn on Film* [New York: Newmarket Press, 1994], 80) — and in response to his apparent failure to give his "child" life, he writes in his journal, "'Massive birth defects. Greatly enhanced physical strength, but the resulting re-animant is malfunctional and pitiful, and dead'" (Branagh, *Mary Shelley's Frankenstein*, 81).

[17] Curtis, *James Whale*, 123.

[18] The anachronistic date appears on the newspaper Victor Frankenstein is reading.

[19] Anne Edwards, *Haunted Summer* (New York: Coward, McCann and Geoghegan, 1972).

Notes on Contributors

UWE BÖKER is Professor of English at Dresden University. His research interests include the social history of English and American literature and such genres as detective fiction, science fiction, and utopian drama and poetry. He is the co-author of a *History of Old English Literature* (1971) and co-editor of *The Living Middle Ages* (1989). He has written monographs on Chaucer, Graham Greene and other writers. He has over sixty essays and articles to his credit. He has also edited two volumes of poetry in the English language from various countries of the world, *Litspeak: Voices from Dresden* (1995–96).

WERNER HUBER is Associate Professor of English Literature at the University of Paderborn, currently deputizing for the chair of English Literature at Chemnitz University of Technology. He is a founding member and former secretary-treasurer of the German Society for English Romanticism. His main research interests and publications are in the fields of Irish literature, English Romanticism (particularly Byron and the Romantic-era novel), modern drama, and the history of the book.

CHRISTOPHER INNES is Professor of English at York University in Ontario. He is Fellow of the Royal Society of Canada, Fellow of the Royal Society of Arts, as well as Killam Fellow. His books include *Modern British Drama: 1890–1990* (1992), *Avant Garde Theatre: 1892–1992* (1993), and *The Theatre of Edward Gordon Craig* (forthcoming). He has published over 70 articles on modern drama, and he is the editor of the Cambridge Directors series, the Greenwood Lives of the Theatre series, and also the editor of the *Cambridge Companion to Bernard Shaw*.

CHRISTINE KENYON JONES is pursuing doctoral studies on English Romantic-period writing at King's College, University of London. Her published work includes articles on the nineteenth-century British Parliamentary debates on animal rights (*TLS*, January 5, 1996) and on Byron, Keats, and consumption (*The Byron Journal*, 1996). Forthcoming publications include a chapter on Byron's portraits and a study of Wordsworth's ecological credentials in relation to animals.

ANNEGRET MAACK is Professor of English Literature at Wuppertal University. She has published widely in the fields of the reception of French literature in England, the English novel of the nineteenth and twentieth century, modern English drama, literature in Australia, and on postmodern fiction. Among her major publications are *Der experimentelle englische Roman der Gegenwart* (1984), *Charles Dickens* (1991), and two collections of articles on modern fiction, *Der englische Roman der Gegenwart* (1987) and *Radikalität und Mässigung: Tendenzen des zeitgenössischen englischen Romans* (1993).

SILVIA MERGENTHAL is Professor of English Literature and Literary Theory at the University of Konstanz. She has published on Scottish literature and on postwar fiction and poetry. Her latest book, *Erziehung zur Tugend* (1997), focusses on gender roles and the eighteenth-century English novel. With her current research project she has returned to contemporary literature and proposes to investigate constructions of "Englishness" in contemporary fiction. Her other research interests include Victorian literature and, increasingly, postcolonial literatures.

MARTIN MIDDEKE is Assistant Professor of English at the University of Paderborn. He has published *Stephen Poliakoff: Drama und Dramaturgie in der abstrakten Gesellschaft* (1994), a study of contemporary British drama and cultural anthropology. He is co-editor (together with Werner Huber) of *Anthropological Perspectives* (1998), a collection of essays concerned with anthropological approaches to English-language theater. Other publications include articles on Howard Brenton, Howard Barker, Timberlake Wertenbaker, and Angela Carter. Currently he is working on a study of *fin de siècle* philosophy, time-consciousness, and the aesthetics of the late-nineteenth-century English novel.

BEATE NEUMEIER is Professor of English at the University of Potsdam. She has specialized in English Renaissance drama, twentieth-century drama, the English novel, and Gender Studies. Her publications include numerous articles and two monographs, *Spiel und Politik: Aspekte der Komik bei Tom Stoppard* (1986) and *Gender and Madness in English Renaissance Drama* (forthcoming). She is the editor of *Jüdische Erfahrung in den Kulturen Großbritanniens und Nordamerikas nach 1945* (1998) and *Engendering Realism and Postmodernism: Contemporary Women Writers in Britain* (forthcoming).

ANSGAR NÜNNING is Professor of English and American Literary and Cultural Studies at the Justus Liebig University of Giessen. He is the author of books on the function of the narrator in George Eliot's novels (1989), on Virginia Woolf (1991), on historical fiction and historiographic metafiction (1995), and of an introduction to the study of literature for German students (1996). He has edited introductory volumes on literary theories, models, and methods (1995), and on the history of English literature (1996) as well as a volume entitled *Intercultural Studies: Fictions of Empire* (1996). His articles on narratology, the eighteenth- and twentieth-century British novel, the street ballad, the poetry and aesthetics of the 1890s, and literary theory have appeared in numerous scholarly journals and collections of essays.

RAMONA RALSTON received her Ph.D. from the University of Southern California, where her dissertation treated the influence of female Romantic poets on Wordsworth's sonnets. Employed as Director of Academic Services at the State University of New York at Potsdam, she continues to pursue scholarly interests in Romantic women writers and feminist film criticism.

BERNHARD REITZ is Professor of English Studies at the University of Mainz. He has taught at Humboldt University, Berlin, and he also held several guest professorships in the United States, Turkey, and Canada. He has edited and introduced numerous British and American plays as well as several collections of essays on drama, dealing with such diverse topics as "New Forms of Comedy," "Centres and Margins," "Drama and Reality," and "Right-Wing Extremism." One of his monographs, *The Stamp of Humanity* (1993), covers the development of English Drama between 1956 and the mid-nineties. Currently he is cooperating with Christopher Innes (Toronto) and Nicole Boireau (Metz) in a project on postmodernism in drama.

JILL RUBENSTEIN, Professor of English at the University of Cincinnati, has compiled two annotated bibliographies of Scott scholarship and criticism and has written extensively on early-nineteenth-century Scottish literature. She contributes the annual essay on this period to *The Year's Work in Scottish Literary and Linguistic Studies*. She edited the *Memoir of Frances Lady Douglas* by Lady Louisa Stuart as well as Hogg's *Anecdotes of Scott*, forthcoming in the Stirling-South Carolina Edition of the Works of James Hogg.

PETER PAUL SCHNIERER took his Ph.D. at Tübingen University in 1993. He has taught as a guest lecturer at the universities of Greenwich, Buckingham, Northern Arizona, and Maryland. Currently an Assistant Professor of English at Tübingen, he is about to complete a study of literary demonization from Marlowe to Rushdie. His publications include *Rekonventionalisierung im englischen Drama 1980–1990* (1994), a study of the relationship between modern English drama and literary history, *Modernes Drama und Theater seit 1945* (1997), an introduction for undergraduates, and, as editor, *Beyond the Mainstream* (1997). He is joint editor of the internet journal *Prolepsis: The Tübingen Review of English Studies*.

SID SONDERGARD is Professor of English at St. Lawrence University. His research interests range from early modern European literature to modern popular culture, and his essays have appeared in such journals as *Studies in Philology, The Journal of American Semiotics*, and *Theatre Survey*. He is co-author with Thomas Berger and William Bradford of *An Index of Characters in Early Modern English Drama: Printed Plays, 1500–1660* (rev. ed. 1998).

FRANCES WILSON teaches English Literature at Reading University. She edited Lady Caroline Lamb's biofiction *Glenarvon* (1995) and a collection of essays on the cult of Byronism, *Byromania* (forthcoming). She has published articles on Henry James and Arthur Conan Doyle, and is at present working on a book called *Literary Seductions*.

Index